THE GREAT AMERICAN WEEKEND BOOK

THE WEEK-END BOOK
(2005)

THE WEEK-END BOOK:
A SOCIABLE ANTHOLOGY
(2006)

THE WEEK-END PROBLEMS BOOK
(2006)

THE GREAT AMERICAN WEEKEND BOOK

THE OVERLOOK PRESS
NEW YORK

First published in the United States in 2009 by
The Overlook Press, Peter Mayer Publishers, Inc.
New York

NEW YORK:
141 Wooster Street
New York, NY 10012

Cataloging-in-Publication Data is available from the Library of Congress

Compiled and edited by Maura Diamond
Book design and type formatting by Bernard Schleifer
Printed in the United States of America
FIRST EDITION
1 3 5 7 9 8 6 4 2
ISBN 978-1-59020-227-2

CONTENTS

CONTENTS

> *"Twenty years from now you will be more disappointed by the things you didn't do than by the ones you did do. So throw off the bowlines. Sail away from the safe harbor. Catch the trade winds in your sails. Explore. Dream. Discover."*
>
> —MARK TWAIN

INTRODUCTION

"A day off" said Uncle Peter, settling down in his chair before the open wood-fire, with that air of complacent obstinacy which spreads over him when he is about to confess and expound his philosophy of life,—"a day off is a day that a man takes to himself."

"You mean a day of luxurious solitude," we said, "a stolen sweet of time, which he carries away into some hidden corner to enjoy alone, -a little-Jack-Horner kind of day?"

"Not at all," said Uncle Peter; "solitude is a thing which a man hardly ever enjoys by himself. He may practice it from a sense of duty. Or he may take refuge in it from other things that are less tolerable. But nine times out of ten he will find that he can't get a really good day to himself unless he shares it with some one else; if he takes it alone, it will be a heavy day, a chain-and-ball day,—anything but a day off."

"Just what do you mean, then?" we asked, knowing that nothing would please him better than the chance to discover his own meaning against a little background of apparent misunderstanding and opposition.

"I mean," said Uncle Peter, in that deliberate manner which lends a flavor of deep wisdom to the most obvious remarks, "I mean that every man owes it to himself to have some days in his life when he escapes from bondage, gets away from routine, and does something which seems to have no purpose in the world, just because he wants to do it."

"Plays truant," we interjected.

"Yes, of you like to put it in that objectionable way," he answered; "but I should rather compare it to bringing flowers into the school-room, or keeping white mice in your desk, or inventing a new game for the recess. You see we are all scholars, boarding scholars, in the House of Life, from the moment when birth matriculates us to the moment when death graduates us. We never really leave the big school, no matter what we do. But my point is this: the lessons that we learn when we do not know that we are studying are often the pleasantest, and not always the least important. There is a benefit as well as a joy in finding out that you can lay down your task for a proper while without being disloyal to your duty. Play-time is a part of school-time, not a break in it. You remember what Aristotle says: '*ascholoumetha gar hina scholazomen.*'"

"Dear uncle," said we, "there is nothing out of the common in your remarks, except of course your extraordinary habit of decorating them with a Greek quotation, like an ancient coin set as a scarf-pin and stuck carelessly into a modern neck-tie. But apart from this eccentricity, everybody admits the propriety of what you have been saying. Why, all the expensive, up-to-date schools are arranged on your principle: play-hours, exercise-hours, silent-hours, social-hours, all marked in the schedule: scholars compelled and carefully guided to amuse themselves at set times and in approved fashions: athletics, dramatics, school-politics and social ethics, all organized and co-ordinated. What you flatter yourself by putting forward as an amiable heresy has become a commonplace or orthodoxy, and your liberal theory on education and life is now one of the marks of fashionable conservatism."

Uncle Peter's face assumed the beatific expression of a man who knows that he has been completely and inexcusably misunderstood, and is therefore justified in taking as much time as he wants to make the subtlety and superiority of his ideas perfectly clear and to show how dense you have been in failing to apprehend them.

"My dears," said he, "it is very singular that you should miss my point so entirely. All these things that you have been saying about your modern schools illustrate precisely the opposite view from mine. They are signs of that idolatry of organization, of system, of the time-table and the schedule, which is making our modern life so tedious and exhausting. Those unfortunate school-boys and school-girls who have their amusements planned out for them and cultivate their social instincts according to rule, never know the joy of a real day off, unless they do as I say, and take it to themselves. The right kind of school will leave room and liberty for them to do this. It will be a miniature of what life is for all of us, - a place where law reigns and independence is rewarded, - a stream of work and duty diversified by islands of freedom and repose, - a pilgrimage in which it is permitted to follow a side-path, a mountain trail, a footway through the meadow, provided, the end of the journey is not forgotten and the day's march brings one a little nearer to that end."

"But will it do that," we asked, "unless one is careful to follow the straight line of the highway and march as fast as one can?"

"That depends," said Uncle Peter, nodding his head gravely, "upon what you consider the end of the journey. If it is something entirely outside of yourselves, a certain stint of work which you were created to perform; or if it is something altogether beyond yourselves, a certain place or office at which you are aiming to arrive; then, of course, you must stick to the highway and hurry along.

"But suppose that the real end of your journey is something of which you yourselves are a part. Suppose it is not merely to get to a certain place, but to get there in a certain condition, with the light of a sane joy in your eyes and the peace of a grateful content in your heart. Suppose it is not merely to do a certain piece of work, but to do it in a certain spirit, cheerfully and bravely and modestly, without overrating its importance or overlooking its necessity. Then, I fancy, you may find that the winding foot-path among the hills often helps you on your way as much as the high road, the day off among the islands of repose gives you a steadier hand and a braver heart to make your voyage along the stream of duty."

"You may skip the moralizing, if you please, Uncle Peter," said we, "and concentrate your mind upon giving us a reasonable account of the peculiar happiness of what you call a day off."

"Nothing could be simpler," he answered. "It is the joy of getting out of the harness that makes a horse fling up his heels, and gallop around the field, and roll over and over again in the grass, when he is turned loose in the pasture. It is the impulse of pure play that makes a little bunch of wild ducks chase one another round and round on the water, and follow their leader in circles and figures of eight; there is no possible use in it, but it gratifies their instinct of freedom and makes them feel that they are not mere animal automata, whatever the natural history men may say to the contrary. It is the sense of release that a man experiences when he unbuckles the straps of his knapsack, and lays it down under a tree, and says 'You stay there till I come back for you! I'm going to rest myself by climbing this hill, just because it is not on the road-map, and because there is nothing at the top of it except the view.'

"It is this feeling of escape," he continued, in the tone of a man who has shaken off the harness of polite conversation and let himself go for a gallop around the field of monologue, "it is just this exhilarating sense of liberation that is lacking in most of our social amusements and recreations. They are dictated by fashion and directed by routine. Men get into the so-called 'round of pleasure' and they are driven into a trot to keep up with it, just as if it were a treadmill. The only difference is that the pleasure-mill grinds no corn. Harry Bellairs was complaining to me, the other day, that after an exhausting season of cotillons in New York, he had been running his motor-car through immense fatigues in France and Italy, and he had returned barely in time to do his duty by his salmon-river in Canada, work his new boat through the annual cruise of the yacht club, finish up a round of house-parties at Bar Harbor and Lenox, and get ready for the partridge-shooting in England with his friend the Duke of Bangham, - it was a dog's life, he said, and he had no time to himself at all. I rather pitied him; he looked so frayed. It seems to me that the best way for a man or woman of pleasure to get a day off would be to do a little honest work.

"You see it is the change that makes the charm of a day off. The real joy of leisure is known only to the people who have contracted the habit of work without becoming enslaved to the vice of overwork.

"A hobby is the best thing in the world for a man with a serious vocation. It keeps him from getting muscle-bound in his own task. It helps to save him from the mistake of supposing that it is his little tick-tack that keeps the universe a-going. It leads him out, on off days, away from his own garden corner into the curious and interesting regions of this wide and various earth, of which, after all, he is a citizen.

"Do you happen to know the Reverend Doctor McHook? He is a learned preacher, a devoted churchman, a faithful minister; and in addition to this he has an extra-parochial affection for ants and spiders. He can spend a happy day in watching the busy affairs of a formicary, and to observe the progress of a bit of spider-web architecture gives him a peculiar joy. There are some severe and sour-complexioned theologians who would call this devotion to objects so far outside of his parish an illicit passion. But to me it seems a blessing conferred by heavenly wisdom upon a good man, and I doubt not he escapes from many an insoluble theological puzzle, and perhaps from many an unprofitable religious wrangle, to find refreshment and invigoration in the society of his many-legged friends."

"You are moralizing again, Uncle Peter," we objected; "or at least you are getting ready to do so. Stop it; and give us a working definition of the difference between a hobby and a fad."

"Let me give you an anecdote," said he, "instead of a definition. There was a friend of mine who went to visit a famous asylum for the insane. Among the patients who were amusing themselves in the great hall, he saw an old gentleman with a long white beard, who was sitting astride of a chair, spurring its legs with his heels, holding both ends of his handkerchief which he had knotted around the back, and crying 'Get up, get up! G'long boy, steady!' and with the utmost animation. 'You seem to be having a fine ride, sir,' said my friend. 'Capital,' said the old gentleman, 'this is a first-rate mount that I'm riding.' 'Permit me to inquire,' asked my friend, 'whether it is a fad or hobby?' 'Why, certainly!' replied the old gentleman, with a quizzical look. 'It is a hobby, you see, for I can get off whenever I have a mind to.' And with that he dismounted and walked into the garden.

"It is just this liberty of getting off that marks the superiority of a hobby to a fad. That game that you feel obliged to play every day at the same hours ceases to amuse you as soon as you realize that it is a diurnal duty. Regular exercise is good for the muscles, but there must be a bit of pure fun mixed with the sport that is to refresh your heart.

"A tour in Europe, carefully mapped out with an elaborate itinerary and a carefully connected time-table, may be full of instruction, but it often becomes a tax upon the spirit and a weariness to the flesh. Compulsory castles and mandatory museums and required ruins pall upon you, as you hurry from one to another, vaguely agitated by the fear that you may miss something that is marked with a star in the guide-book, and so be compelled to confess to your neighbor at the *table-d'hote* that you failed to see what he promptly and joyfully assures you is 'the best thing in the whole trip.' Delicate and sensitive people have been killed by taking a vacation in that way.

"I remember meeting several years ago, a party of personally conducted tourists in Venice, at the hour which their itinerary consecrated to the enjoyment of the fine arts in the gallery of the Academy. Their personal conductor led them into one of the great rooms, and they gathered close around him, with an air of determination on their tired faces, listening to the brief dry patter about the famous pictures that the room contained. He stood in the center of the room holding his watch in his hand while they dispersed themselves around the walls, looking for the paintings which they ought to see, like chickens searching for scattered grains of corn. At the expiration of five minutes he clapped his hands sharply; his flock scurried back to him; and they moved to 'do' the next room.

"I suppose that was one way of seeing Venice: but I would much rather sit at a little table on the *Riva degli Schiavoni*, with a plate of bread and cheese and a *mezzo* of Chianti before me, watching the motley crowd in the street and the many-colored sails in the harbor; or spend a lazy afternoon in a gondola, floating through the watery alley-ways that lead nowhere, and under the facades of beautiful palaces whose names I did not even care to know. Of course I should like to see a fine picture of a noble church, now and then; but only one at a time, if you please; and that one I should wish to look at as long as it said anything to me, and to revisit as often as it called me."

"That is because you have no idea of the educational uses of a vacation, Uncle Peter," said we. "You are an unsystematic person, an incorrigible idler."

"I am," he answered, without a sign of penitence, "that is precisely what I am,—in my days off. Otherwise I should not get the good of them. Even a hobby, on such days, is to be used chiefly for its lateral advantages,—the open doors of the side-shows to which it brings you, the unexpected opportunities of dismounting and tying your hobby to a tree, while you follow the trail of something strange and attractive, as Moses did when he turned aside from shepherding on Mount Horeb and climbed up among the rocks to see the burning bush.

"The value of a favorite pursuit lies not only in its calculated results but also in its by-products. You may become a collector of almost anything in the world,—orchids, postage-stamps, flint arrowheads, cook-books, varieties of the game of cat's cradle,—and if you chase your trifle in the right spirit it will lead you into pleasant surprises and bring you acquainted with delightful and amusing people. You remember when you went with Professor Rinascimento on a Della Robbia hunt among the hill towns of Italy, and how you came by accident into that deep green valley where there are more nightingales with sweeter voices than anywhere else on earth? Your best *trouvaille* on that expedition was hidden in those undreamed-of nights of moonlight and music. And it was when you were chasing first editions of Tennyson, was it not, that you discovered your little head of a marble faun, which

15

you vow is by Donatello, or one of his pupils? And what was it that that you told me about the rare friend you found when you took a couple of days off in an ancient French town, on a flying journey from Rome to London? Believe me, dears, all that we win by effort and intention is sometimes over-topped by a gift that is conferred upon us out of a secret and mysterious generosity. Wordsworth was right:

"'Think you, 'mid all this mighty sum
Of things forever speaking,
That nothing of itself will come,
But we must still be seeking?'"

"You talk," said we, "as if you thought it was a man's duty to be happy."

"I do," he answered firmly, "that is precisely and definitely what I think. It is not his chief duty, nor his only duty, nor his duty all the time. But the normal man is not intended to go through this world without learning what happiness means. If he does than he misses something that he needs to complete his nature and perfect his experience. 'Tis a poor, frail plant that can not endure the wind and the rain and the winter's cold. But is it a good plant that will not respond to the quickening touch of spring and send out its sweet odors in the embracing warmth of the summer nights? Suppose that you had made a house for a child, and given him a cor-ner of the garden to keep, and set him lessons and tasks, and provided him with teachers and masters. Would you be satis-fied with that child, however diligent and obedient, if you found that he was never happy, never enjoyed a holiday, never said to himself and to you, 'What a good place this is, and how glad I am to live here'?"

"Probably not," we answered, "but that is because we should be selfish enough to find pleasure of our own in his happiness. We should like to take a day off with him, now and then, and his gladness would increase our enjoyment. There is no morality in that. It is simply natural. We are all made that way."

"Well," said Uncle Peter, "if we are made that way we must take it into account in our philosophy of life. The fact that it is is not a sufficient reason for concluding that it is bad. There is an old and wonderful book which describes the creation of the world in poetic language; and when I read that description it makes me feel sure that something like this was purposely woven into the very web of life. After the six mystical days of making things and putting things in order, says this beautiful old book, the Person who had been doing it all took a day to Himself, in which He 'rested from all the things that He had created and made,' and looked at them, and saw how good they were. His work was not ended, of course, for it has been going on ever since, and will go on for ages of ages. But in the midst of it all it seemed right to Him to take a divine day off. And His example is commended to us for imitation because we are made in His likeness and have the same desire to enjoy as well as to create."

Uncle Peter's voice had grown very deep and gentle while he was saying these things. He sat looking far away into the rosy heart of the fire, where the bright blaze had burned itself out, and the delicate flamelets of blue and violet were playing over the glowing, crumbling logs. It seemed as if he had forgotten where we were, and gone-a-wandering into some distant region of memories and dreams.

We almost doubted whether to call him back; the silence was so full of comfortable and friendly intercourse.

"Well," said we, after a while, "you are an incorrigible moralist, but certainly a most unconventional one. The orthodox would never accept your philosophy. They would call you a hedonist, or something equally dreadful."

"Let them," he said placidly.

"But tell us:" we asked, "we have many pleasant and grateful activities and amusements, little instructions and inspirations, which seem like chapters in the volume of this doubtful idea of yours: suppose that we should write some of them down, purely in a descriptive way, without committing ourselves to any opinion as to their morality; and suppose that a few of your opinions and prejudices, briefly expressed, were interspersed in the form of chapters to be skipped: would a book like that symbolize and illustrate the true inwardness of the day off? How would it do to make such a book?"

"It would do," he answered, "provided you wanted to do it, and provided you did not try to prove anything or convince anybody."

"But would anyone read it?" we asked. "What do you think?"

"I think," said he, stretching his arms over his head as he rose and turned towards his den to plunge into a long evening's work, "I reckon, and calculate, and fancy, and guess that a few people, a very few, might browse through such a book in their days off."

WEATHER
FOLKLORE

WEATHER

Climate is what we expect, weather's what we get.

—MARK TWAIN

I T IS SAFE TO ASSUME THAT OUR FIRST PARENTS ACQUIRED weather wisdom by observing weather sequences and noting the foreshadowed effects of certain atmospheric conditions on objects animate and inanimate. We may assume further that the knowledge thus acquired was communicated to their descendants, and that it was handed down, with additions and amplifications, from generation to generation. We find in the earliest writings and in the Scriptures expressions of weather wisdom, many of which appear in collections of the popular weather sayings of today. Thus by assumption and deduction we know that man has ever employed inherited and acquired weather wisdom in the daily affairs of life. When flocks and herds have constituted his earthly possessions he has been prompted to lead his charges to places of safety when signs of impending storms appeared. As a navigator his interpretation of the signs of the air has, in innumerable instances, enabled him to adopt measures calculated to avert disaster to his frail craft. As an husbandman he has closely scanned the sky, the air, and the earth for signs that would indicate the weather of the coming day and season.

The laws that govern the distribution of the earth's atmosphere and control its phenomena necessarily produce different results on different parts of the earth's surface. The seasonal distribution of the atmosphere, as indicated by the greater, or so-called permanent, areas of high and low barometric pressure, is governed largely by the temperature of the land and water surfaces. In summer the pressure of the atmosphere is greater and its surface temperature is lower over the oceans than over the continents, and in winter the reverse of these conditions obtains. And the differences in atmospheric pressure and temperature control the seasonal directions of the winds. Similarly the smaller areas of high and low barometric pressure that appear on our daily weather maps produce the varying temperatures and winds, and, incidentally, the weather that we experience from day to day.

In the United States the centers of areas of high barometric pressure generally move in a south of east direction immediately preceded by winds that blow from points between west and north, low temperature for the season, and fair weather. Areas of low barometric pressure, or general storms, usually move in a north of east direction, and the winds in their east quadrants blow from easterly or southerly points of the compass, with high temperature for the season, and precipitation in the form of rain or snow.

Chart No. 1 shows the distribution of atmospheric pressure and temperature, the circulation of the winds, and the general character of the weather that attends the passage of well-defined areas of high and low barometric pressure over the United States.

It will be observed from the foregoing remarks and Chart No. 1 that wind directions, as influenced by areas of high and low barometric pressure, produce high and low temperatures, fair and foul weather, and the fact will be recognized that all true popular weather sayings of ancient origin have been coined from the utterances, born of experience, of men who have observed, without understanding the causes thereof, the first indications of approaching weather changes.

Chart 2 shows the winds that usually precede the beginning of rain or snow in the United States.

Weather proverbs that have been based on observations of the wind conform to a notable degree of modern meteorological knowledge. In the temperate zone of the Northern Hemisphere easterly winds are proverbially rain winds and westerly winds are invariably associated with fair or clearing weather. The reason for this is apparant when the circulation of winds about areas of high barometric pressure, and areas of low barometric pessure, or general storms is observed.

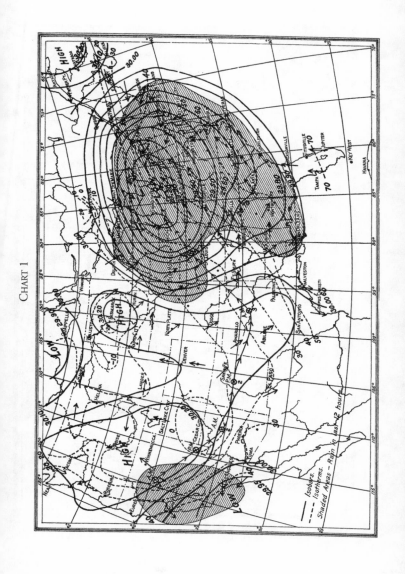

CHART 1

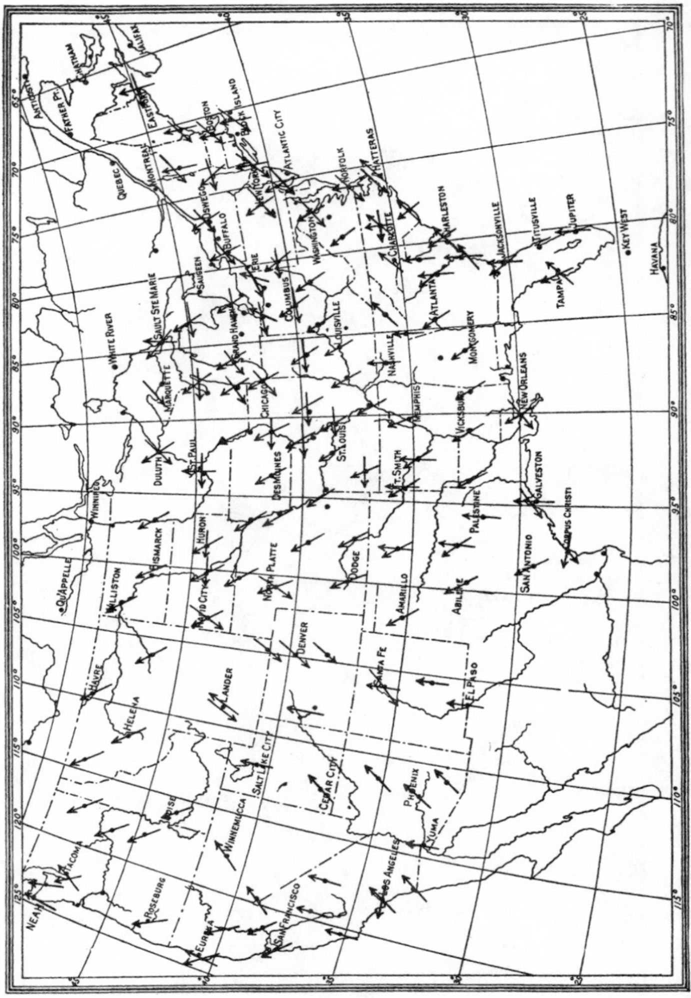

Chart 2. Rain Winds—Spring

WIND

Every wind has its weather.
—BACON

When the wind is in the north,
The skillful fisher goes not forth;
When the wind is in the east,
'Tis good for neither man nor beast;
When the wind is in the south,
It blows the flies in the fish's mouth;
When the wind is in the west,
There it is the very best.
—ISAAK WALTON

In Texas and the Southwest when the wind shifts, with strength, during a drought, expect rain.

In the West and Southwest when brisk winds from the south continue for a day or more, expect a "norther."

Over a great part of the United States a steady and strong south-to-east wind will bring rain within thirty-six hours.

Easterly winds are proverbially bringers of rain, and when they blow from the northeast quadrant in winter heavy snow is likely to be followed by severe cold.

When, during a storm, the wind shifts from the east to the west quadrants, clearing weather will soon follow.

When the wind is from points between west and north and the temperature falls to 40° or below, frost will probably occur.

•

Westerly winds (southwest to northwest) are fair-weather winds.

BAROMETER

When the glass falls low,
Prepare for a blow;
When it rises high,
Let all your kites fly.

—NAUTICAL

First rise after low,
Foretells stronger blow;
Long foretold (falling), long last;
Short notice, soon past.

—FITZROY

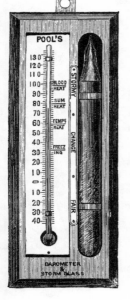

At the level of the sea the weight of the atmosphere is about 14 pounds to every square inch, or about 1 ton to every square foot of the earth's surface. The barometer is used to gauge the weight or pressure of the atmosphere. This pressure is constantly varying, and the variations are instantly and accurately indicated by standard mercurial barometers. The indications thus furnished by the barometer are the best guide we have for determining future weather conditions. As low barmeter readings generally attend stormy weather, and hight barameter readings are usually associated with clearing or fair weather, it follws that, as a rule, falling barometer indicates precipitation and wind, and rising barometer fair weather or the approach of fair weather.

In modern meteorlogical works, as conduced by the United States Weather Bureau, observations, simultaneously taken, are collected by telegraph from great areas, and it is possible to calculate for periods of one to three days in advance the local signs that will be produced by the general conditions that are presented. In other words, modern meteorological appliances, methods, and skill make possible forecasts of the conditions that produce the local signs upon which all weather proverbs are based. Furthermore, it is now practicable not only to forecast general weather changes, but also to calculate with great accuracy the intensity and durations of storms.

CLOUDS

Clouds are the storm signals of the sky.

Mackerel scales and mare's tails
Make lofty ships carry low sails.

Mackerel clouds in sky,
Expect more wet than dry.

A mackerel sky,
Not twenty-four hours dry.

Evening red and morning gray
Will set the traveler on his way;
But evening gray and morning red
Will bring down rain upon his head.

ANIMALS

Dogs making holes in the ground, eating grass in the morning, or refusing meat are said to indicate coming rain.
—*Colonel Dunwoody.*

•

All shepherds agree in saying that before a storm comes sheep become frisky, leap, and butt or "box" each *other.*
—*Folklore Journal.*

•

When horses and cattle stretch out their necks and sniff the air it will rain.

•

Horses, as well as other domestic animals, foretell the coming of rain by starting more than ordinary and appearing in other respects restless and uneasy.

•

Hogs crying and running unquietly up and down with hay or litter in their mouths foreshadow a storm to be near at hand. —*Thomas Willsford.*

•

Swine, when they assemble at one end of a field with their tails to windward, often indicate rain or wind.

•

When oxen or sheep collect together as if they were seeking shelter a storm may be expected. —*Apache Indians.*

BIRDS

If the cock goes crowing to bed,
He'll certainly rise with a watery head.

•

If the wild geese gang out to sea,
Good weather there will surely be.

•

When the peacock loudly bawls,
Soon we'll have both rain and squalls.

INSECTS

When bees to distance wing their flight,
Days are warm and skies are bright;
But when their flight ends near at home,
Stormy weather is sure to come.

STARS

Now mark where high upon the zodiac line
The stars of lustre-lacking Cancer shine.
Near to the constellation's southern bound
Phatne, a nebulous bright spot, is found.
On either side this cloud, nor distant far,
Glitters to north and south a little star.
Though not conspicuous, yet these two are famed—
The Onoi by ancient sages named.
If when the sky around be bright and clear,
Sudden from sight the Phatne disappear,
And the two Onoi north and south are seen
Ready to meet—no obstacle between—
The welkin soon will blacken with rain,
And torrents rush along the thirsty plain.
If black the Phatne, and the Onoi clear,
Sure sign again that drenching showers are near.
And if the northern star be lost to sight,
While still the southern glitters fair and bright,
Notus will blow. But if the southern fail,
And clear the northern, Boreas will prevail.
And as the skies above, the waves below
Signs of the rising wind and tempest show.

—J. LAMB'S *"Aratus"*

When the bright gems that night's black vault adorn
But faintly shine—of half their radiance shorn—
And not by cloud obscured or dimmed to sight
By the fine silvery veil of Cynthia's light,
But of themselves appear to faint away,
They warning give of a tempestuous day.

—J. LAMB'S *"Aratus"*

THE MOON

If three days old her face be bright and clear,
No rain or stormy gale the sailors fear;
But if she rise with bright and blushing cheek,
The blustering winds the bending mast will shake.
If dull her face and blunt her horns appear,
On the fourth day a breeze or rain is near.
If on the third she move with horns direct,
Not pointing downward or to heaven erect,
The western wind expect; and drenching rain,
If on the fourth her horns direct remain.
If to the earth her uppor horn she bond,
Cold Boreas from the north his blast will send;
If upward she extend it to the sky,
Loud Notus with his blustering gale is nigh.
When the fourth day around her orb is spread
A circling ring of deep and murky red,
Soon from his cave the God of Storms will rise,
Dashing with foamy waves the lowering skies.
And when fair Cynthia her full orb displays,
Or when unveiled to sight are half her rays,
Then mark the various hues that paint her face,
And thus the fickle weather's changes trace.
If smile her pearly face benign' and fair,
Calm and serene will breathe the balmy air;
If with deep blush her maiden cheek be red,
Then boisterous wind the cautious sailors dread;
If sullen blackness hang upon her brow,
From clouds as black will rainy torrents flow.
Not through the month their power these signs extend,
But all their influence with the quarter end.

—J. LAMB'S *"Aratus"*

WEATHER PATTERNS OF
TEN GREAT AMERICAN CITIES

NEW YORK, NEW YORK

IN SPRING, AUTUMN, AND WINTER PRECIPITATION IS PRECEDED twelve to twenty-four hours by south to southeast winds, and in summer twentyfour to forty-eight hours by southerly winds. In spring and autumn the barometer usually falls to 29.90 or below and in winter to 30 or below before precipitation begins, in summer showers generally begin about the turn of the barometer from falling to rising. In the case of storms that come from the south or southwest, however, precipitation is preceded by east to northeast winds, and rain or snow begins closely following the shift of wind to these quarters and the turn in the barometer from rising to falling.

As a rule there is an increase in relative humidity twelve to twenty-four hours before precipitation, and in spring, autumn, and winter rain or snow may be expected when the atmosphere is becoming highly charged with moisture.

Generally speaking, the formation of cirrus and cirro-stratus clouds indicates the coming of rain or snow. No definite interval has been observed between the appearance of these clouds and the beginning of precipitation, but it probably varies from eighteen to thirty-six hours. In the spring and winter cirrus and cirro-stratus clouds come from the west, in summer from the southwest, and in autumn from the west and southwest. Precipitation is indicated in spring by the formation of low clouds, without a very pronounced movement, but usually from easterly quadrants, in summer by the rapid formation of thunder clouds, with shifting and increasing winds, in autumn by low cloud formations moving from easterly quadrants, and in winter by high cloud formation, followed by heavy low clouds and easterly winds.

In all seasons the highest winds generally come from the northwest, with rising barometer.

During periods of abnormally high temperature the wind is from the south in spring and winter, and from the southwest in summer and autumn. During periods of abnormally low temperature the wind is from the northwest in spring, autumn, and winter, and from northwest, north, or northeast in summer.

Frost is likely to damage fruit or other crops in this section from April 1 to May 20. Heavy frost is preceded by high and nearly stationary barometer, temperature below 44°, relative humidity about normal, gentle, or light winds, and an absence of clouds, or, when existing, cirrus clouds.

PHILADELPHIA, PENNSYLVANIA

Precipitation is generally preceded twelve to twenty-four hours by south to east winds and falling barometer, and the barometer usually falls to 30 or below before precipitation begins. In the case of storms that advance from the south and southwest, however, precipitation begins closely following the shift of the wind to east or northeast, and often when the barometer is on the turn from rising to falling; this is more particularly true with regard to south and southwest storms of the colder months.

In spring, autumn, and winter there is an increase in relative humidity to 80 per cent or, over six to twelve hours before precipitation begins, and in summer there-is an increase to 70 per cent or over one to six hours before rain.

Cirrus and cirro-stratus clouds moving from the west are frequently observed twelve to twenty-four hours before precipitation. First comes the cirrus then cirro-stratus, followed by haze or stratus, and sometimes cirro-cumulus.

High northwest winds occur with rising barometer in spring, autumn, and winter, and high northeast winds with falling barometer. In summer high winds usually come from the south and southwest about the time of the turn in the barometer from falling to rising.

The warmer winds of all seasons come from the southwest. During the warmer months the cool winds come from the northeast, and during the colder months the cold winds come from the northwest.

Frost is likely to damage fruit and other crops from April 10 to May 10, and before October 15.

The conditions that favor the occurrence of heavy frost are high and increasing barometric pressure, temperature 40° and falling, relative humidity normal or below, cumulus clouds followed by clearing, and light northerly or westerly winds.

COLUMBUS, OHIO

In spring and autumn precipitation is most frequently preceded by southeast winds and falling barometer, and the barometer generally falls to about 30 inches before rain begins; in summer southerly winds and falling barometer precede rain, and rain usually begins just after or "on the turn" from falling to rising barometer; in winter southwest winds and falling barometer usually precede precipitation, and the barometer falls on an average to about 29.85 inches before rain begins.

The relative humidity seems to change very little until nearly the time of the beginning of rain; sometimes it is lower than usual, and, in some instances, a slight increase is shown several hours before rain begins. Increases in relative humidity that have been noted are invariably at the beginning or early in the rain period. There seems to be a decidedly high humidity at the beginning of rain, which becomes less as rain continues. If the humidity is high and the temperature fall promises to be decided, the rainfall is usually heavy.

While cirrus clouds are nearly always observed before rain, and cirro-stratus clouds have been marked before a heavy rainfall, the cirrus clouds are so frequently noted when no rain follows that they are not considered of much value in forecasting. Strato-cumulus clouds are usually followed by rain in ten to eighteen hours; cirrus and cirro-stratus clouds have been observed forty-eight hours before rain, and again rain has occurred within twelve hours after their appearance. The average interval is estimated at thirty-six hours. Cirro-stratus clouds are observed moving from the west in spring and autumn, from west to southwest in summer, and from west to northwest in winter. The following special character-istics of cloud formations often presage rain: Upper clouds of the cirrus type are followed by haze and very delicately fibered cirro-cumulus. All classes of cirrus clouds are noted, and their movements are usually rapid; altostratus follow, and their direction is most favorable for rain when they are from south to southwest. The varied movements and marked char-acter of each type of clouds in the order observed presage rain.

In summer high winds usually occur with falling barome-ter or barometer "on the turn " from falling to rising, and are easterly when the barometer is falling and westerly. when it is rising. The high winds of summer, autumn, and winter are southwest to northwest with rising barometer.

During periods of abnormally high temperature the wind is from the southeast to south in spring, from southwest in summer, from south in autumn, and from south to southeast in winter. During periods of abnormally low temperature the wind is from north to northwest in spring and autumn, from northeast to northwest in summer, and from southwest to northwest in winter.

Frost is likely to damage fruit after April 15, and after about May 15 it will injure garden crops and field corn. In the fall late garden crops and field corn are injured as late as September 25 to October 1, and injury is sometimes caused to late potatoes as late as October 15.

The conditions favorable to frost are high and nearly sta-tionary barometer, low temperature, no clouds, very light winds, and low humidity. In several instances, however, heavy frost, with temperature at freezing or below, did very little damage to fruit in blossom, and this fact was attributed by local farmers to the dryness of the air.

DETROIT, MICHIGAN

Precipitation is usually preceded ten to twelve hours by southeast to southwest winds. In summer the barometer generally falls to 29.80 before rain begins, in spring and autumn to 29.85, and in winter to 29.90. In spring rain begins with falling barometer, just after the turn from rising to falling; in summer with stationary or falling barometer; and in autumn and winter with falling barometer. Snow flurries or light showers sometimes occur twelve to twenty-four hours after the barometer begins to rise during clearing weather. A rapid fall in the barometer with east to south winds immediately precedes precipitation. When the barometer rises slowly precipitation usually continues until the barometer reaches 29.95; in winter, however, the weather will clear shortly after the barometer begins to rise, especially if the pressure has been quite low.

During the summer months the relative humidity has been observed to be abnormally low ten to fourteen hours before thunderstorms, especially in the afternoon when thunderstorms occur the following in morning. In all other seasons no connection has been noted between atmospheric moisture and approaching precipitation.

The only special rain indication noted in connection with clouds is a peculiar formation of cirro-cumulus clouds during spring, autumn, and winter, when clouds of this class that present a creamy appearance indicate rain or snow within about twelve hours. In spring, autumn, and winter cirro-cumulus clouds at night in long lines, frequently with halos, indicate rain or snow. The movement of these clouds is usually moderately rapid. Cirrus and cirro-stratus clouds move from the west, but the interval between their appearance and the beginning of precipitation has not been observed.

The high winds of spring are from northeast with falling barometer, and from southwest to west with low and rapidly rising barometer; of summer from southwest with rising barometer; of autumn from southwest to west with rapidly rising barometer; and of winter from northeast to east with rapidly falling barometer, and from southwest to west with rapidly rising barometer.

During periods of abnormally high temperature the winds are usually from south to southwest. In spring the cold winds are from northwest to northeast, in summer from northeast to east, in autumn from west to northwest, and in winter from southwest to west, and on rare occasions, from the northeast.

Frost is likely to damage fruit or other crops from April 15 to May 15, and from September 1 to 20. Frost is usually preceded by barometer above 30 and rising, an indicated temperature fall to between 300 and 35°, relative humidity 70 to 75 per cent; in spring northwest to northeast winds, cumulo-stratus moving rapidly in the afternoon, and evening clear; in autumn light westerly winds and no clouds.

CORPUS CHRISTI, TEXAS

In spring rain is usually preceded about twenty-four hours by backing east and northeast winds and barometer "on the turn" from falling to rising, and rising. In this season a steady fall in barometer with wind from the southeast means clearing weather. In summer easterly winds backing from southerly precede rain twenty-four to thirty-six hours, and rain usually begins after the barometer has fallen to 29.90 or 30 inches and begins to rise. After periods of low barometer in summer, showers follow on the rise if the winds are backing; if the barometer is 29.80 and falling no rain occurs until the rise begins; when the barometer is above 30 and fluctuating thunderstorms and heavy rains are likely to occur. In autumn rain is generally preceded about twenty-four hours by east to northeast winds and rising barometer, except in November, when rain follows falling barometer and winds north and veering. In winter northeast winds usually precede rain twelve to twenty-four hours with barometer falling; rain also occurs with rising barometer and backing southerly winds. In all seasons the barometer falls to a height of 29.90 to 30 inches before rain begins.

In spring and summer there is a notable decrease in relative humidity thirty-six to forty-eight hours before precipitation begins, but nearly all rainfall occurs with relative humidity between 80 and 90 per cent. In autumn and winter the humidity increases twelve to twenty-four hours before precipitation to about 90 per cent in autumn and to 80 per cent or above in winter.

Cirrus or cirro-stratus clouds do not to any extent indicate precipitation when moving from the northwest, west, or southwest, but rain follows in thirty-six hours when these clouds are observed moving from the north. In summer cirrus and cirro-stratis clouds from the south and southeast are sometimes followed within thirty-six to forty-eight hours by rain. In autumn and winter, cirrus or cirrostratus clouds from the south are almost invariably followed by rain within thirty-six hours. In summer lower cumulus, changing shape and color, with rising barometer, presage rain.

In spring the highest winds usually occur from the southeast, with falling barometer; in summer from the northeast with falling, and from north to west with rising barometer; in autumn from north and northwest with rising barometer, except in September, when they come from east to northeast with falling barometer; in winter from the north and northwest with rising barometer.

During periods of abnormally high temperature the winds are usually from the southeast in spring, except sometimes from the west in May; in summer the winds are westerly; in autumn the warm winds are westerly in September and October and southeasterly in November; the warm winds of winter are from the southeast. During periods of abnormally low temperature the winds are from north to northeast in spring and autumn, from easterly in summer, and from northeast to northwest in winter.

Frost is most likely to damage fruit or other crops from November 15 to March 20. Vegetables are raised during all the winter months when there is *sufficient rainfall;* after the 15th of January is the most critical time, however. Shipping to northern markets begins in February and continues to about the last of April.

The general conditions most favorable to frost in spring and autumn are high barometer, temperature 38° and below, humidity 70 per cent and under, clear weather, brisk north to westerly winds, subsiding at sunset; in winter high barometer, temperature 45° and below, relative humidity 70 per cent and under, and clear weather. Frost is not a frequent occurrence at any season; it generally follows after the low barometer area has crossed the meridian twenty-four to thirty-six hours, and the center of the high barometer area is west and south of the Missouri River. A gathering of cirro-stratus or alto-stratus clouds in the west is an indication of a rapidly diminishing high barometer area, and frost is not likely to occur at such times.

MEMPHIS, TENNESSEE

In spring, autumn, and winter precipitation is preceded by south to southeast winds, and in summer by southwest winds. Preceding storms that advance from the southwest the winds come from the east or northeast. In all seasons, except in winter, precipitation that is preceded by south to southeast winds begins about the time the barometer is on the turn from falling to rising. When the wind is from the east and northeast rain begins with the barometer falling. In winter rain comes with falling, and snow with rising, barometer. Precipitation begins in spring with the barometer about '29.90, or below; in summer and autumn, with the barometer 30, or below; and in winter, with the barometer about 30.10, or below.

An increase in relative humidity is observed twenty-four hours or more before precipitation begins, except that a decrease in humidity is frequently noted at the morning observation on the day preceding rain.

In the spring cirrus clouds moving from the west or southwest and cirro-stratus from the. southwest precede rain six to twelve hours. In summer cirrus or cirro-stratus clouds moving from the southwest are followed by rain in from twelve to twenty hours. In autumn and winter cirrus or cirro-stratus clouds from the west or southwest (especially from the southwest) are followed by rain within twenty-four hours, and this cloud movement is a sure sign of rain when the surface wind is from south or southeast.

During periods of abnormally high temperature the prevailing winds are from the southeast in spring, from the southwest in summer, and from south to southwest in autumn and winter. In all seasons the cold winds come from the northwest and incline more toward northerly in the autumn. During winter, early spring, and late autumn periods of unusual cold are usually followed by rain within thirty-six to forty-eight hours. The high winds of all seasons come from west to northwest with rising barometer, except in the case of summer thunderstorms, when they are from southwest to west.

Frost is most likely to damage fruit or other crops in March, April, May, September, and October. The greatest damage to fruit can occur during the latter part of March and the early part of April. Frosts late in October injure the "top crop" in cotton. The general conditions that favor heavy frost are rising barometer for twenty-four hours, wind shifting to fresh northwest, and decreasing, low relative humidity, and clearing or clear sky.

PHOENIX, ARIZONA

In spring and winter southeast to southwest winds and falling barometer precede precipitation for periods that average about twenty-four hours, and the barometer falls to about 29.90 or below before precipitation begins. From late in the spring until the beginning of winter the prevailing winds are from the easterly, and preceding rain the wind shifts to northerly or northwesterly, with falling barometer.

While there is usually an increase in relative humidity preceding rain, rain sometimes occurs when the surface air shows a decreasing amount of moisture.

Cirrus and cirro-stratus clouds move from the west and are forerunners of rain only to a limited extent.

High winds occur with a falling barometer from the south-west in spring, from east and southeast in summer, from southeast in autumn, and from the west in winter.

The cold winds of spring, autumn, and winter come from the west and northwest.

Frost is likely to do damage in December, when citrus fruits are still on the trees, and in February and March, when citrus trees and almond trees are budding and blooming.

The conditions favorable for frost are low followed by rising barometer, temperature falling to or below 40°, few if any clouds, and southwest or west veering to light northwest or north winds.

DENVER, COLORADO

In all seasons precipitation is generally preceded several hours by northeast winds, and begins with rising barometer. The usual height of the barometer observed at the beginning of precipitation is 29.90 in spring, 29.95 in summer and autumn, and about 30.15 inches in winter.

The moisture of the air is not an indicator of approaching precipitation, and an increase or decrease in relative humidity is observed occasionally only an hour or two in advance of precipitation.

During the colder half of the year cirrus clouds from the west are generally a reliable indication of a low barometer area in the northwest and rising temperature. A long and narrow bank of stratus clouds above the mountains in the west at about 30° altitude is indicative of chinook conditions within twenty-four hours. In summer cumulus clouds on the mountains early in the morning rapidly develop thunderstorm conditions if pressure distribution is favorable to northeast winds.

The highest winds of spring and autumn tire from north-west, with rising and from southwest with falling barometer; and of winter from northwest with rising barometer.

Westerly winds prevail during periods of abnormally high temperature. During periods of abnormally low temperature the winds are northeasterly during the day and southerly at night.

Frost is most likely to damage fruit or other crops between April 10 and September 30.

The conditions which usually precede frost are high barometer, temperature below 44°, humidity above normal, light precipitation, light winds, and clearing weather, with no clouds when frost occurs.

LOS ANGELES, CALIFORNIA

In spring and winter, including October and November, easterly winds set in twelve and twenty-four hours before pre-cipitation. Normal, followed by falling barometer, generally precedes rain winds. Rain is more likely to begin with the barometer about 29.90 or below in spring and about 29.80 or below in winter.

No increase or decrease in relative humidity is noted pre-ceding rain. Excessive humidity occurs with fog which is rarely an accompaniment of rain, and more than the average humidity follows west to southwest winds from the ocean which are not rain-bearing winds.

Cirro-stratus clouds moving from the west generally fore-run storms by periods that vary in length from one to three days, depending upon the movement of the storm-center; when these clouds are not followed by rain the weather usu-ally becomes threatening. Detached masses of clouds, more nearly resembling stratus, are generally observed about mid-way up the slopes of the Sierra Madre Mountains to the northeast of the station preceding general storms. These clouds are considered a good local sign of rain.

During periods of abnormally high temperature the prevailing winds are from the northeast to northwest in spring, from north to northwest in summer, from east to northwest in autumn, and from northeast to north in winter. The cold winds of all seasons are northerly winds.

Frost is most likely to damage fruit or other crops from December to March. The conditions that generally precede frost are: barometric pressure above the normal but relatively low as compared with pressures to the northward, temperatures at or below normal, low relative humidity, light winds, and a cloudless sky.

PORTLAND, OREGON

In all seasons precipitation in preceded by southeast winds and falling barometer. In spring the rain winds set in about fourteen hours, in summer about twelve hours, and in autumn and winter about twenty hours before precipitation begins. In spring, summer, and autumn the barometer usually falls to 29.95 or below and in winter to 30 or below before precipitation begins. Wind shifting from rain at any season of the year. Wind shifting to northwest is a sign of clearing weather.

The relative humidity usually increases fifteen to twenty-four hours before precipitation begins. An increase of 25 to 50 percent in relative humidity is a fair indication of rain in spring, summer, and fall.

Cirrus and cirro-stratus clouds are generally followed by rain in spring, autumn, and winter, but are not a good indication of rain in summer. Cirro-cumulus clouds are an almost sure sign of rain in autumn, spring, and winter, but are only a fair indication in summer. Cirro-stratus and cirrus clouds move from the west in spring, summer, and winter, and from the northwest in autumn, and appear thirty to thirty-six hours before rain begins.

The high wind velocities occur with southerly winds and falling barometer.

The warm winds of spring, summer, and autumn come

from the northwest, and of winter from the south. The cold winds of spring and summer come from southeast, south, and southwest, and of autumn and winter from southeast to northeast.

Frost is most likely to damage fruit during the month of April, when prunes, peaches, cherries, and pears are in bloom.

Frost is generally preceded by a rather high or rising barometer, temperature slightly higher than usual, relative humidity 60 to 70 per cent, light to brisk northwest or northeast winds, or light winds if from east or southeast and clear weather.

OUTDOOR PURSUITS

TENNIS

Attire, How to Play, and How to Make a Tennis Net

LET US SEE; IT WAS THAT OLD MEDICAL GENTLEMAN, GALEN the Greek, who first wrote upon tennis, speaking of the sport as healthy exercise, was it not? Well it really does not matter much to us whether he was the first to write it up and the Greeks the first to play it, or whether the game originated in France in the fifteenth century, as some claim. What we want to know is, can we all learn to play tennis? Does it cost much? What kind of garments and shoes must we wear? And is it an enjoyable game?

There is no doubt, we think, of its being a right royal pastime, as it has been called both the "king of games" and the "game of kings;" the latter because it was enjoyed by princes and nobles—so much enjoyed, that in both England and France edicts were published forbidding the common people to play it.

Do you wonder if they always had the choice of courts, and so never took part in the fun of spinning the racket in the air while the adversary called out "rough" or "smooth;" or whether they played as we do, taking their defeats pleasantly and wearing their honors gracefully, while always doing their very best?

They must have played well, for it is said that Louis XI, Henry II, and Charles IX, were experts, and that Henry VIII of England was extremely fond of the sport.

We can easily learn to play this most popular and exhilarating of games. But we must be suitably clothed in order to thoroughly enjoy it and receive all the benefit the recreation brings to both mind and body.

Flannel seems to be the best material for a tennis suit—it is so soft and yielding, and so well adapted for a defence against either cold or heat. Then, make your tennis attire of flannel.

Sew the skirt of your gown on a sleeveless waist, made of lining or muslin. The Jersey will fit nicely over this, and you can play better and feel far more comfortable than when the weight is allowed to drag on the hips. For it is nonsense to attempt to take part in any athletic game unless you can have perfect freedom of action; in short, you should be so dressed as to be utterly unconscious of your clothing.

Either crochet a Tam O' Shanter hat or make one of the dress material, as these are not so apt to fall off while running as a straw hat. "Last, but not least," come the shoes. Of course, rubber-soled shoes are the best. But if these are not to be had, remove the heels from an old pair of ordinary shoes, and they will do very well; heels roughen and cut the courts.

How to Make a Lawn-Tennis Net

The actual cost of a lawn-tennis set need only be the price of the rackets and balls, and rope and cord necessary when you learn which is not difficult.

First procure two pieces of cotton rope, three-sixteenths of an inch in size, each thirty-four feet long, costing about twenty-five cents apiece. Then one and a half pound of hammock twine or macrimé cord, No. 24, which will not cost more than fifty cents. Next, two lengths of cotton rope for guy-ropes, each five feet, price, both included, ten cents; making the total amount $1.10 for a strong, firm, tennis net which will prove serviceable and last many a season.

The other materials necessary are all home-made. These consist of two stakes, each five feet long (FIG. 1). Any kind of a strong pole, when sharpened at one end and a notch cut at the other, will answer the purpose. Four pegs, each one foot long (FIG. 2). These may be easily made of old broomsticks. Four runners (FIG. 3), each five inches long, one and a quarter wide, and about half an inch thick, with holes bored near each end large enough to allow the guy-rope (FIG. 4) to pass through. A fid or mesh-stick of any kind of wood (FIG. 5),

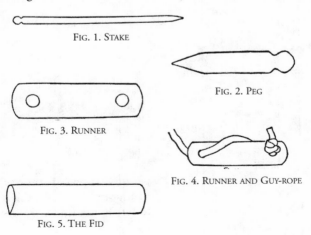

FIG. 1. STAKE

FIG. 2. PEG

FIG. 3. RUNNER

FIG. 4. RUNNER AND GUY-ROPE

FIG. 5. THE FID

about a foot or ten inches long, with circumference measuring three inches. A hammock-needle (FIG. 6), nine or ten inches long and one wide, which may be bought for ten cents, or whittled out of a piece of ash or hickory. Tassels are not necessary, though it is much better to have them, as they make the top line of the net more distinct and add to its appearance. Make about forty bright-colored tassels of worsted, or bits of flannel cut in very narrow strips, three inches long, allowing ten or twelve strips to each tassel. Commence your tennis net by first threading the needle; take it in the left hand, and use the thumb to hold the end of the cord in place while looping it over the tongue (see FIG. 7); pass the cord down under the needle to the opposite side, and catch it over the tongue. Repeat this until the needle is full.

Next, take a piece of rope thirty-four feet long, and make a long loop in one end, tying the knot so that it can readily be untied again. Throw the loop over some convenient hook or door-knob (FIG. 8) with the knot at the knob or hook. Tie the cord on the needle to the loop, place the fid or mesh-stick under the cord close to the loop (FIG. 9), with the thumb on the cord to hold it in place (FIG: 14), while you pass the needle

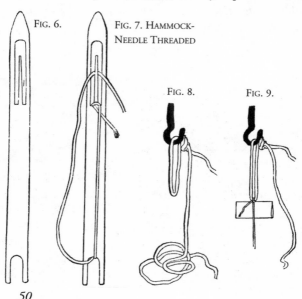

FIG. 6.

FIG. 7. HAMMOCK-NEEDLE THREADED

FIG. 8.

FIG. 9.

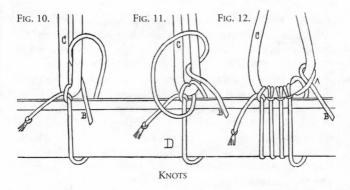

FIG. 10.   FIG. 11.   FIG. 12.

KNOTS

around the mesh-stick, and, with its point toward you, pass it through the loop from the top, bringing it over the mesh-stick. This will make the first half of the knot (FIG. 10). Pull this tight, holding it in place with the thumb while you throw the cord over your hand, which forms the loop as seen in FIG. 11. Then pass the needle from under through the loop, pulling it tight to fasten the knot. Hold it in place with the thumb, and repeat these movements for the next knot. FIG. 12 shows a number of these knots finished. A in FIG. 12 is a knot before it is drawn tight; B in FIGS. 10, 11, 12 is the string that runs to the needle, C is the rope, and D is the mesh-stick. About two hundred and sixty-four of these knots or meshes will make the net the regular length, thirty-three feet.

In knitting across, the meshes will accumulate on the lid; shove them off to the left, a few at a time, to make space for others. When the desired number of meshes are finished to form the first row, shove them all off the lid, as shown in FIG. 13.

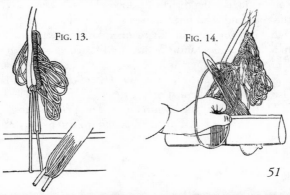

FIG. 13.   FIG. 14.

Begin the next row by again placing the fid under the cord (FIG. 13). Take up the first mesh, drawing it close to the mesh-stick, hold it in place with the thumb while throwing the cord over your hand, pass the needle on the left-hand side of the mesh from under through the loop (FIG. 14); pull this tight, and you will have tied the common knitting-knot. Repeat this with all the loops until the row is finished.

When it becomes necessary to thread or fill the needle, tie the ends of the cord with the knot shown in FIG. 15, which, when properly tightened, cannot slip. Wrap each end of the cord from the knot securely to the main cord with strong thread, to give the net a neat appearance.

FIG. 15.

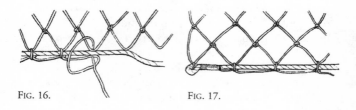

FIG. 16.   FIG. 17.

Continue netting until the net is three feet wide. Then untie the rope, and spread the net by sliding the knots apart, and fasten the second rope to the bottom of the net by tying the rope securely to the first mesh with the cord on the needle; then carry the rope and cord to the next mesh, hold the rope, cord, and mesh firmly in place, and throw the cord over your hand, passing the needle down through the mesh under the rope and cord out through the loop (FIG. 16). Pull this tight, and continue in like manner, knitting each successive mesh to the rope until the net is all fastened on. Turn back the end of the rope and wrap it down neatly with strong string (FIG. 17). In the same way secure the other end, and also the ends of the first or top rope.

This completes the lawn-tennis net proper. The bright tassels can now be tied at intervals along the top of the net, and four pieces of twine fastened on each end of the net at equal distances apart. These are for tying the net to the poles (FIG. 18).

To erect the lawn-tennis net, plant the two poles firmly in the ground a little over thirty-three feet apart, tie the net to the poles, then drive in the pegs, two to each pole, about five feet from the pole (FIG. 19); slide a runner on each end of the two guy-ropes by first threading the rope through one of the holes in the runner, then pass the rope over the side down

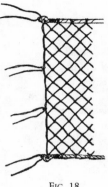

FIG. 18.

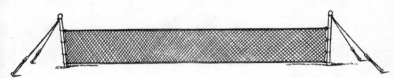

FIG. 19.

through the other hole and fasten it with a knot (Fig. 4). Next tie around the notch in the top of the poles the guy-ropes, with runners attached, and slip each loop made by the runner over each peg (FIG. 20), allowing the rope to fall in the groove A near the top of the peg; tighten the rope by pushing up the runners. The stakes are thus held in position by ropes running out to the pegs in the ground (FIG. 19).

Now we understand how to make and erect a lawn-tennis net; but what shall we do about the court? Of

FIG. 20.

course, that must be all ready before we can set up the net. We must now learn how to lay out a . . .

Lawn-Tennis Court

The best ground for this is turf, though it may be of asphalt, or earth mixed with fine gravel; sometimes wood is used.

The diagram on the facing page (FIG. 21) shows the construction of a lawn-tennis court for two, three, or four-handed games.

Lay out the court with a hundred-foot measuring-tape, by marking the lines with whitewash, chalk, paint, or plaster-of-Paris.

First the side line, seventy-eight feet, AB. This gives you one side of your court. Then the base line, thirty-six feet, AC, which, with their parallel lines CD and DB, form the boundaries of a court for fourhanded games. Now lay off the side lines of the single court, EG and FH, which are parallel to the others and four and a half feet inside of them. Divide the court across the centre by the net, fastened to the poles O and P. The lines EF and GH are called base lines. Twenty-one feet from the net, mark the service lines, MN and TV. Then make the central longitudinal line, IJ, and the court is complete.

Now everything is prepared for the game. Hold your racket firmly, and try to keep the ball flying over the net, back and forth, as often as possible.

For the guidance of those who have had no opportunity of learning to play lawn-tennis the following rules are given, as adopted by the United States National Lawn-Tennis Association.

First, however, we would say that it is not necessary always to have an umpire or a referee, as spoken of in the rules for lawn-tennis.

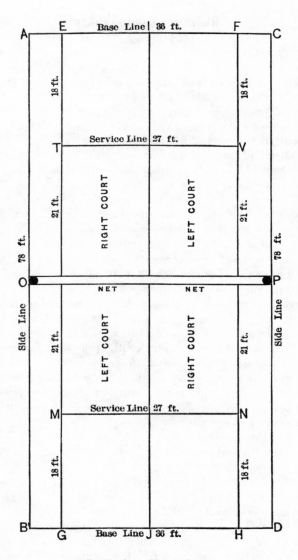

Fig. 21. LAWN-TENNIS COURT

Rules for Lawn-Tennis

THE GAME

1. The choice of sides, and the right to serve in the first game, shall be decided by toss; provided that, if the winner of the toss choose the right to serve, the other player shall have choice of sides, and *vice versa*. If one player chooses the court, the other may elect not to serve.

2. The players shall stand on opposite sides of the net; the player who first delivers the ball shall be called the *server*, and the other the *striker-out*.

3. At the end of the first game the striker-out shall become server, and the server shall become striker-out; and so on, alternately, in all the subsequent games of the set, or series of sets.

4. The server shall serve with one foot on the base line, and with the other foot behind that line, but not necessarily upon the ground. He shall deliver the service from the right to the left courts alternately, beginning from the right.

5. The ball served must drop between the service line, half-court line, and side line of the court, diagonally opposite to that from which it was served.

6. It is a *fault* if the server fails to strike the ball, or if the ball served drop in the net, or beyond the service line, or out of court, or in the wrong court; or if the server does not stand as directed by law 4.

7. A ball falling on a line is regarded as falling in the court bounded by that line.

8. A fault cannot be taken.

9. After a fault the server shall serve again from the same court from which he served that fault, unless it was a fault because he served from the wrong court.

10. A fault cannot be claimed after the next service is delivered.

11. The server shall not serve till the striker-out is ready. If

the latter attempt to return the service he shall be deemed ready.

12. A service or fault, delivered when the striker-out is not ready counts for nothing.

13. The service shall not be *volleyed, i.e.,* taken, before it has touched the ground.

14. A ball is in play on leaving the server's racket, except as provided for in law 6.

15. It is a good return, although the ball touch the net; but a service, otherwise good, which touches the net, shall count for nothing.

16. The server wins a stroke if the striker-out volley the service, or if he fails to return the service or the ball in play; or if he returns the service or the ball in play so that it drops outside of his opponent's court; or if he otherwise loses a stroke, as provided by law 18.

17. The striker-out wins a stroke if the server serves two consecutive faults; or if he fails to return the ball in play; or if he returns the ball in play so that it drops outside of his opponent's court; or if he otherwise loses a stroke as provided by law 18.

18. Either player loses a stroke if he returns the service or the ball in play so that it touches a post of the net; or if the ball touches him or anything that he wears or carries, except his racket in the act of striking; or if he touches the ball with his racket more than once; or if he touches the net or any of its supports while the ball is in play; or if he volleys the ball before it has passed the net.

19. In case any player is obstructed by any accident, the ball shall be considered a *let*.

20. On either player winning his first stroke,, the score is called 15 for that player; on either player winning his second stroke, the score is called 30 for that player; on either player winning his third stroke, the score is called 40 for that player; and the fourth stroke won by either player is scored game for that player, except as below: If both players have won three strokes, the score is called *deuce*; and the next stroke won by either player is scored *advantage* for that player. If the same

player wins the next stroke, he wins the game; if he loses the next stroke the score returns to deuce; and so on, until one player wins the two strokes immediately following the score of deuce, when game is scored for that player.

21. The player who first wins six games wins the set; except as follows: If both players win five games, the score is called *games all*; and the next game won by either player is scored *advantage game* for that player. If the same player wins the next game, he wins the set; if he loses the next game, the score returns to games all; and so on, until either player wins the two games immediately following the score of games all, when he wins the set. But individual clubs, at their own tournaments, may modify this rule at their discretion.

22. The players shall change sides at the end of every set; but the umpire, on appeal from either player, before the toss for choice, may direct the players to change sides at the end of every game of each set, if, in his opinion, either side have a distinct advantage, owing to the sun, wind, or any other accidental cause; but if the appeal be made after the toss for choice, the umpire can only direct the players to change sides at the end of every game of the odd or deciding set.

23. When a series of sets is played, the player who served in the last game of one set shall be striker-out in the first game of the next.

24. The referee shall call the game after an interval of five minutes between sets, if either player so order.

25. The above laws shall apply to the three-handed and four-handed games, except as below:

26. In the three-handed game, the single player shall serve in every alternate game.

27. In the four-handed game, the pair who have the right to serve in the first game shall decide which partner shall do so and the opposing pair shall decide in like manner for the second game. The partner of the player who served in the first game shall serve in the third, and the partner of the player who served in the second game shall serve in the fourth; and the same order shall be maintained in all the subsequent games of the set.

28. At the beginning of the next set, either partner of the pair which struck out in the last game of the last set may serve, and the same privilege is given to their opponents in the second game of the new set.

29. The players shall take the service alternately throughout the game; a player cannot receive a service delivered to his partner; and the order of service and striking out once established shall not be altered, nor shall the striker-out change courts to receive the service, till the end of the set.

30. It is a fault if the ball served does not drop between the service line, half-court line, and service side line of the court, diagonally opposite to that from which it was served.

31. In matches, the decision of the umpire shall be final. Should there be two umpires, they shall divide the court between them, and the decision of each shall be final in his share of the court.

ODDS

A *bisque* is one point which can be taken by the receiver of the odds at any time in the set except as follows

> *(a)* A bisque cannot be taken after a service is delivered.
> *(b)* The server may not take a bisque after a fault, but the striker-out may do so.

One or more bisques may be given to increase or diminish other odds.

Half fifteen is one stroke given at the beginning of the second, fourth, and every subsequent alternate game of a set.

Fifteen is one stroke given at the beginning of every game of a set.

Half thirty is one stroke given at the beginning of the first game, two strokes given at the beginning of the second game; and so on, alternately, in all the subsequent games of the set.

Thirty is two strokes given at the beginning of every game of a set.

Half forty is two strokes given at the beginning of the first game, three strokes given at the beginning of the second game; and so on, alternately, in all the subsequent games of the set.

Forty is three strokes given at the beginning of every game of a set.

Half court: The players may agree into which half court, right or left, the giver of the odds shall play; and the latter loses a stroke if the ball returned by him drop outside any of the lines which bound that half court.

The Balls

The balls shall measure not less than $2\frac{15}{32}$ inches, nor more than $2\frac{1}{2}$ inches in diameter; and shall weigh not less than $1\frac{15}{16}$ oz., nor more than 2 oz.

SAILING
How to Rig and Sail Small Boats

To have the tiller in one's own hands and feel competent, under all ordinary circumstances, to bring a boat safely into port, gives the same zest and excitement to a sail (only in a far greater degree) that the handling of the whip and reins over a lively trotter does to a drive.

Knowing and feeling this, it was our intention to devote a couple of pages to telling how to sail a boat; but through the kind courtesy of the editor of The *American Canoeist,* We are able to do much better by giving our readers a talk on this subject by one whose theoretical knowledge and practical experience renders him pre-eminently fit to give reliable advice and counsel. The following is what Mr. Charles Ledyard Norton, editor of the above-mentioned journal, says:

Very many persons seem to ignore the fact that a boy who knows how to manage a gun is, upon the whole, less likely to be shot than one who is a bungler through ignorance, or that a good swimmer is less likely to be drowned than a poor one. Such, however, is the truth beyond question. If a skilled sportsman is now and then shot, or an expert swimmer drowned, the fault is not apt to be his own, and if the one who is really to blame had received proper training, it is not likely that the accident would have occurred at all. The same argument holds good with regard to the management of boats, and the author is confident that he merits thanks, whether he receives them or not, for giving a few hints as to practical rigging and sailing.

In general, there are three ways of learning how to sail boats. First, from the light of nature, which is a poor way; second, from books, which is better; and third, from another who knows how, which is best of all. We will try to make this article as much like the other fellow and as little bookish as possible.

Of course, what shall be said in these few paragraphs will be of small use to those who live within reach of the sea or some big lake, and have always been used to boats; but there are thousands and thousands men who never saw the sea, nor even set eyes on a sail, and who have not the least idea how to make the wind take them where they want to go. We once knew some young men from the interior who went down to the sea-side and hired a boat, with the idea that they had nothing to do but hoist the sail and be blown wherever they liked. The result was that they performed a remarkable set of manœuvres within sight of the boat-house, and at last went helplessly out to sea and had to be sent after and brought back, when they were well laughed at for their performances, and had reason to consider themselves lucky for having gotten off so cheaply.

The general principles of sailing are as simple as the national game of "one ole cat." That is to say, if the wind always blew moderately and steadily, it would be as easy and as safe to sail boat as it is to drive a steady old family horse of good and regular habits. The fact, however, is that winds and currents are variable in their moods, and as capable of unexpected freaks as the most fiery of unbroken colts; but when properly watched and humored they are tractable and fascinating playmates and servants.

Now, let us come right down to first principles. Take a bit of pine board, sharpen it at one end, set up a mast about a quarter of the length of the whole piece from the bow, fit on a square piece of stiff paper or card for a sail, and you are ready for action. Put this in the water, with the sail set squarely across (A, FIG. 22), and she will run off before the wind—which is supposed to be blowing as indicated by the arrow—at a good rate of speed. If she does not steer herself, put a small weight near the stern, or square end; or, if you like, arrange a thin bit of wood for a rudder.

Probably the first primeval man who was born with nautical instincts discovered this fact, and, using a bush for a sail, greatly astonished his fellow primevals by winning some prehistoric regatta. But that was all he could do. He was as help-

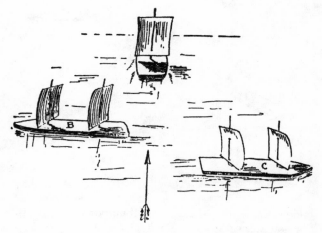

Fig. 22.

less as a balloonist is in mid-air. He could go, but he could not get back, and we may be sure that ages passed away before the possibility of sailing to windward was discovered.

Now, put up, or "step,"another mast and sail like the first, about as far from the stern as the first is from the bow. Turn the two sails at an angle of forty-five degrees across the boat (B or C, Fig. 22), and set her adrift. She will make considerable progress across the course of the wind, although she will at the same time drift with it. If she wholly refuses to go in the right direction, place a light weight on her bow, so that she will be a little "down by the head," or move the after-most mast and sail a little nearer to the stern.

The little rude affair thus used for experiment will not actually make any progress to windward, because she is so light that she moves sidewise almost as easily as she does forward. With a larger, deeper boat, and with sails which can be set at any angle, the effect will be different. So long as the wind presses against the after side of the sail, the boat will move through the water in the direction of the least resistance, which is forward. A square sail, having the mast in the

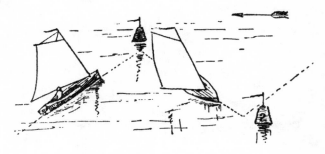

FIG. 23.

middle, was easiest to begin with for purposes of explanation; but now we will change to a "fore-and-aft" rig-that is, one with the mast at the forward edge or 'luff' of the sail, as in FIG. 23. Suppose the sail to be set at the angle shown, and the wind blowing as the arrow points. The boat cannot readily move sidewise, because of the broadside resistance; she does not move backward, because the wind is pressing on the aftermost side of the sail. So she very naturally moves forward. When she nears buoy No. 1, the helmsman moves the "tiller," or handle of the rudder, toward the sail. This causes the boat to turn her head toward buoy No. 2, the sail swings across to the other side of the boat and fills on that side, which now in turn becomes the aftermost, and she moves toward buoy No. 2 nearly at right angles to her former course. Thus, through a series of zig-zags, the wind is made to work against itself. This operation is called "tacking," or "working to windward," and the act of turning, as at the buoys No. 1 and No. 2, is called "going about."

It will be seen, then, that the science of sailing lies in being able to manage a boat with her head pointing at any possible angle to or from the wind. Nothing but experience can teach one all the niceties of the art, but a little aptitude and address will do to start with, keeping near shore and carrying little sail.

Simplest Rig Possible

We will suppose that the reader has the use of a broad, flat-bottomed boat without any rudder. (See FIG. 24) She cannot be made to work like a racing yacht under canvas, but lots of fun can be had out of her.

Do not go to any considerable expense at the outset. Procure an old sheet, or an old hay-cover, six or eight feet square, and experiment with that before spending your money on new material. If it is a sheet, and somewhat weakly in its texture, turn all the edges in and sew them, so that it shall not give way at the hems. At each corner sew on a few inches of strong twine, forming loops at the angles. Sew on, also, eyelets or small loops along the edge which is intended for the luff of the sail, so that it can be laced to the mast.

You are now ready for your spars, namely, a mast and a "sprit," the former a couple of feet longer than the luff of the sail, and the latter to be cut off when you find how long you want it. Let these spars be of pine, or spruce, or bamboo—as light as possible, especially the sprit. An inch and a half diameter will do for the mast, and an inch and a quarter for the

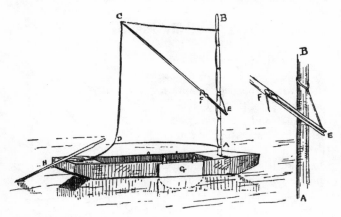

FIG. 24.

sprit, tapering to an inch at the top. To "step" the mast, bore a hole through one of the thwarts (seats) near the bow, and make a socket or step on the bottom of the boat, just under the aforesaid hole—or if anything a trifle farther forward—to receive the foot of the mast. This will hold the mast upright, or with a slight "rake" aft.

Lace the luff of the sail to the mast so that its lower edge will swing clear by a foot or so of the boat's sides. Make fast to the loop at D a stout line, ten or twelve feet long. This is called the "sheet," and gives control of the sail. The upper end of the sprit, C, E, is trimmed so that the loop at C will fit over it but not slip down. The lower end is simply notched to receive a short line called a "snotter," as shown in the detailed drawing at the right of the cut (FIG. 24). It will be readily understood that, when the sprit is pushed upward in the direction of C, the sail will stand spread out. The line is placed in the notch at E and pulled up until the sail sets properly, when it is made fast to a cleat or to a cross piece at F. This device is in common use and has its advantages, but a simple loop for the foot of the sprit to rest in is more easily made and will do nearly as well. H is an oar for steering. Having thus described the simplest rig possible, we may turn our attention to more elegant and elaborate but not always preferable outfits.

Leg-of-Mutton Rig

One of the prettiest and most convenient rigs for a small boat is known as the "leg-of-mutton sharpie rig" (FIG. 25). The sail is triangular, and the sprit, instead of reaching to its upper corner, stands nearly at right angles to the mast. It is held in position at the mast by the devices already described. This rig has the advantage of keeping the whole sail flatter than any other, for the

FIG. 25.

Fig. 26.

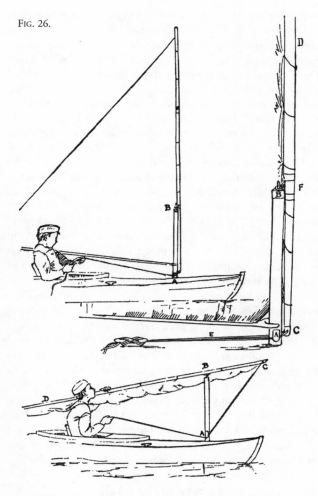

end of the sprit cannot 'kick up,' as the phrase goes, and so the sail holds all the wind it receives.

Fig. 26 shows a device, published for the first time in the *St. Nicholas Magazine* for September, 1880, which enables the sailor to step and unstep his mast, and hoist or lower his sail without leaving his seat—a matter of great importance when the boat is light and tottlish, as in the case of that most beautiful of small craft, the modern canoe, where the navigator sits habitually amidships. The lower mast (A, B, Fig. 26) stands about two and a half feet above the deck. It is fitted at the head with a metal ferrule and pin, and just above the deck with two half-cleats or other similar devices (A). The topmast (C, D) is fitted at F with a stout ring, and has double halyards (E) rove through or around its foot. The lower mast being in position (see lower part of Fig. 24), the canoeist desiring to make sail brings the boat's head to the wind, takes the top-mast with the sail loosely furled in one hand, and the halyards in the other. It is easy for him by raising this mast, without leaving his seat, to pass the halyards one on each side of the lower mast and let them fall into place close to the deck under the half- cleats at A. Then, holding the halyards taut enough to keep them in position, he will hook the topmast ring over the pin in the lower mast-head and haul away (see top part of Fig. 26). The mast will rise into place, where it is made fast. A collar of leather, or a knob of some kind, placed on the topmast just below the ring, will act as a fulcrum when the halyards are hauled taut, and keep the mast from working to and fro.

The advantages of the rig are obvious. The mast can be raised without standing up, and in case of necessity the halyards can be let go and the mast and sail unshipped and stowed below with the greatest ease and expedition, leaving only the short lower mast standing. A leg-of-mutton sail with a common boom along the foot is shown in the cut as the most easily illustrated application of the device, but there is no reason why it may not be applied to a sail of different shape, with a sprit instead of a boom, and a square instead of a pointed head.

How to Make a Sail

For the sails of such boats as are considered in these pages, there is no better material than unbleached twilled cotton sheeting. It is to be had two and a half or even three yards wide. In cutting out your sail, let the selvedge be at the "leech," or aftermost edge. This, of course, makes it necessary to cut the luff and foot 'bias,' and they are very likely to stretch in the making, so that the sail will assume a different shape from what was intended. To avoid this, baste the hem carefully before sewing, and "hold in" a little to prevent fulling. It is a good plan to tack the material on the floor before cutting, and mark the outline of the sail with pencil. Stout tape stitched along the bias edges will make a sure thing of it, and the material can be cut, making due allowance for the hem. Better take feminine advice on this process. The hems should be half an inch deep all around, selvedge and all, and it will do no harm to reinforce them with cord if you wish to make a thoroughly good piece of work.

For running-rigging, nothing is better than laid or braided cotton cord, such as is used for awnings and sash-cords. If this is not easily procured, any stout twine will answer. It can be doubled and twisted as often as necessary. The smallest manila rope is rather stiff and unmanageable for such light sails as ours.

In fitting out a boat of any kind, iron, unless galvanized, is to be avoided as much as possible, on account of its liability to rust. Use brass or copper instead.

Hints to Beginners

Nothing has been said about reefing thus far, because small boats under the management of beginners should not be afloat in a "reefing breeze." Reefing is the operation of reducing the spread of sail when the wind becomes too fresh. If you will look at Fig. 27 you will see rows of short marks on the sail above the boom. These are "reef-points"—bits of line about a foot long passing through holes in the sail, and knotted so that they will not slip. In reefing, the sail is lowered and that portion of it between the boom and the reef-points is gathered together, and the points are tied around both it and the boom. When the lower row of points is used it is a single reef. Both rows together are a double reef.

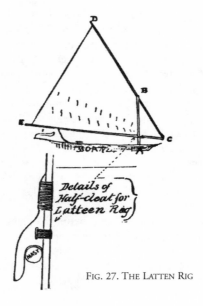

FIG. 27. THE LATTEN RIG

Make your first practical experiment with a small sail and with the wind blowing toward the shore. Row out a little way, and then sail in any direction in which you can make the boat go, straight back to shore if you can, with the sail out nearly at right angles with the boat. Then try running along shore with the sheet hauled in a little, and the sail on the side nearest the shore. You will soon learn what your craft can do, and will probably find that she will make very little, if any, headway to windward. This is partly because she slides sidewise over the water. To prevent it you may use a "leeboard" —namely, a broad board hung over the side of the boat (G, FIG. 24). This must be held by stout lines, as the strain upon it is very heavy. It should be placed a little forward of the middle of the boat. It must be on the side away from the wind—the lee side—and must be shifted when you go about. Keels and centre-boards are permanent contrivances for the same purpose, but a leeboard answers very well as a makeshift, and is even used habitually by some canoeists and other boatmen.

In small boats it is sometimes desirable to sit amidships, because sitting in the stern raises the bow too high out of water; steering may be done with an oar over the lee side, or with "yoke-lines" attached to a cross piece on the rudder-head, or even to the tiller. In this last case, the lines must be rove through rings or pulleys at the sides of the boat opposite the end of the tiller. When the handle of the oar (H, Fig. 24)—or the tiller (F, Fig. 27) if a rudder is used—is pushed to the right, the boat will turn to the left, and *vice versa*. The science of steering consists in knowing when to push and how much to push-very simple, you see, in the statement, but not always so easy in practice.

"The sail should be so adjusted in relation to the rest of the boat that, when the sheet is hauled close in and made fast, the boat, if left to herself, will point her head to the wind like a weather-cock, and drift slowly astern. If it is found that the sail is so far forward that she will not do this, the fault may be remedied by stepping the mast further aft, or by rigging a small sail near the stern. This is called a "dandy," or "steering-sail," and is especially convenient in a boat whose size or arrangement necessitates sitting amidships. It may be rigged like the mainsail, and when its sheet is once made fast will ordinarily take care of itself in tacking.

Remember that, if the wind freshens or a squall strikes you, the position of safety is with the boat's head to the wind. When in doubt what to do, push the helm down (toward the sail) and haul in the slack of the sheet as the boat comes up into the wind. If she is moving astern, or will not mind her helm—and of course she will not if she is not moving—pull her head around to the wind with an oar, and experiment cautiously until you find which way you can make her go.

In making a landing, always calculate to have the boat's head as near the wind as possible when she ceases to move. Do this whether you lower your sail or not.

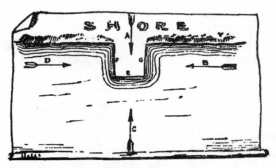

FIG. 28. MAKING A LANDING

"Thus, if the wind is off shore, as shown at A, FIG. 28, land at F or G, with the bow toward the shore. If the wind is from the direction of B, land at E with the bow toward B, or at F; if at the latter, the boom will swing away from the wharf and permit you to lie alongside. If the wind is from D, reverse these positions. lithe wind comes from the direction of C, land either at F or G, with the bow pointing off shore.

If you have no one to tell you what to do, you will have to feel your way slowly and learn by experience; but if you have nautical instincts you will soon make your boat do what you wish her to do as far as she is able. *But first learn to swim before you try to sail a boat.*

Volumes have been written on the subject treated in these few pages, and it is not yet exhausted. The hints here given are safe ones to follow, and will, it is hoped, be of service to many a young sailor in many a corner of the world.

FISHING

"Jugging for Cats"

EARLY ONE MORNING, WHILE SAUNTERING ALONG THE LEVEE of a small town upon the Mississippi, the authors met an old friend, Uncle Eanes, famous in these parts for his unusual method of catching fish. Uncle Eanes invited us to go "jugging for cats." Intrigued, the authors accepted, and the were initiated into the mysteries of "jugging for cats," which we found to combine exercise, excitement, and fun in a much greater degree than the usual method of angling with rod and reel.

The tackle necessary in this sport is very simple; it consists of five or six empty jugs tightly corked with corn cobs, as many stout lines, each about five feet long with a sinker and large hook at the end. One of these lines is tied to the handle of each jug. Fresh liver, angle worms, and balls made of corn meal and cotton, are used for bait; but a bit of cheese, tied up in a piece of mosquito netting to prevent its washing away, appears to be considered the most tempting morsel.

When all the hooks are baited, and the fisherman has inspected his lines and found everything ready, he puts the jugs into a boat and rows out upon the river, dropping the earthenware floats about ten feet apart in a line across the middle of the stream. The jugs will, of course, be carried down with the current, and will have to be followed and watched. When one of them begins to behave in a strange manner, turning upside down, bobbing about, darting up stream and down, the fisherman knows that a large fish is hooked, and an exciting chase ensues. It sometimes requires hard rowing to catch the jug, for often when the fisherman feels sure of his prize and stretches forth his hand to grasp the runaway, it darts off anew, frequently disappearing from view beneath the water, and coming to the surface again, yards and yards away from where it had left the disappointed sportsman.

One would think that the pursuit of just one jug, which a fish is piloting around, might prove exciting enough. But imagine the sport of seeing four or five of them start off on their antics at about the same moment. It is at such a time that the skill of a fisherman is tested, for a novice, in his hurry, is apt to lose his head, thereby losing his fish also. Instead of hauling in his line carefully and steadily, he generally pulls it up in such a hasty manner that the fish is able, by a vigorous flop, to tear himself away from the hook. To be a successful "jugger," one must be as careful and deliberate in taking out his fish as though he had only that one jug to attend to, no matter how many others may be claiming his attention by their frantic signals. FIG. 29 shows how the line is rigged.

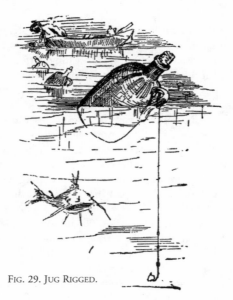

FIG. 29. JUG RIGGED.

The Dancing Fisherman

Another method of catching fish, in principle similar to jugging, by means of a jumping-jack, or small, jointed man whose limbs are moved by jerking a string attached to them is the "dancing fisherman." This little figure is fastened to a stick, which is secured in an upright position on a float made of a piece of board. Through a hole in the float a string is passed, attached to the figure, and tied securely to this are the hook and line. After the hook is baited, the float is placed on the surface of the water, and the little man, standing upright, is left to wait in patience.

Presently a fish, attracted by the bait, comes nearer the surface, seizes the hook quickly, and darts downward, pulling the string, and making the little figure throw up its arms and legs as though dancing for joy at having performed its task so well. The capering of Jack is the signal to his master that a

Fig. 30.

fish has been caught and is struggling to free itself from the hook. This manner of fishing is necessarily confined to quiet bodies of water, such as small lakes or ponds; for in rough water poor little Jack would be upset. FIG. 30 shows how to rig the "dancing fisherman."

Home-made Fishing Tackle

THE ROD

It not unfrequently happens that an amateur is unable to take advantage of most excellent fishing, for the want of proper or necessary tackle.

It may be that he is accidentally in the neighborhood of a pickerel pond or trout stream, or that his fishing tackle is lost or delayed in transit. Under such circumstances a little practical ingenuity is invaluable. If within reach of any human habitation you can, in all probability, succeed in finding sufficient material with which to manufacture not only a rod which will answer your purpose, but a very serviceable reel. To rig up a home-made trout rod, you need a straight, slender, elastic pole, such as can be found in any wood or thicket, some pins, and a small piece of wire. File off the head of several pins, sharpen the blunt ends, and bend them into the form of the letter U. At a point about two feet from the butt end of the rod drive the first pin, leaving enough of the loop above the wood to allow the fish line to pass freely through; drive the other pins upon the same side of the rod and at regular intervals. Make the tip of a piece of wire by bending a neat circular loop in the centre, and then knitting or binding the wire on the end of the pole (FIG. 31). Should you have enough wire, it will answer much better for the other loops than the pins. If at a farm-house look in the attic for an old bonnet frame, or some similar object likely to be at hand, and

FIG. 31.

it will furnish you with plenty of material. Cut the wire in pieces about two and a half inches long, make a simple loop in the centre of each piece, and with a "waxed end" or strong thread bind the ends of the wire lengthwise on the rod, then give each loop a turn, twisting it in proper position (FIG. 32). With a large wooden spool, an old tin can, and a piece of thick wire, a first-rate reel may be manufactured.

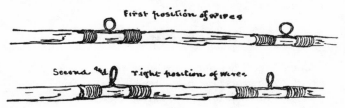

FIG. 32.

Put the wire through the spool, allowing about one inch to protrude at one end and about three inches at the opposite end. Wedge the wire in firmly by driving soft pine sticks around it, and trim off the protruding ends of the sticks. Cut a piece of tin in the shape shown by the diagram (FIG. 33),

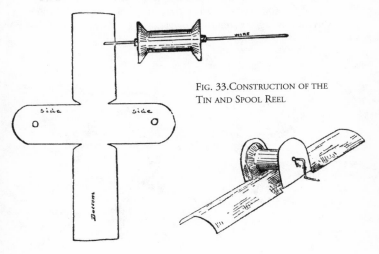

FIG. 33. CONSTRUCTION OF THE TIN AND SPOOL REEL

punch a hole in each side piece for the wire to pass through, leaving plenty of room for the spool to revolve freely. Turn the side-pieces up upon each side of the spool, and bend the long end of the wire in the form of a crank. Hammer the bottom piece of tin over the rod until it takes the curved form, and fits tightly, then with strong wax string bind it firmly to the rod. If it should happen that a piece of tin could not be procured, a reel can be made of a forked stick and a spool.

The Forked-Stick Reel

Cut a forked stick and shave off the inside fiat, as in FIG. 34, cut two notches near the bottom, one upon each side; this will allow the fork to bend readily at these points. Make a small groove for a string at the top of each prong. Put the spool between the prongs, allowing the wire to protrude through holes bored for that purpose. Bend the long end of the wire in the form of a crank. Tie a string across from end to end of the prongs to hold them in proper position, and you have a rustic but serviceable reel (FIG. 35). It may be attached to the pole in either manner shown by FIGS. 36 AND 37. Those who find pleasure in outdoor sports should always be ready with expedients for any emergency. A fish hook is rather a difficult thing to manufacture, though I have seen them

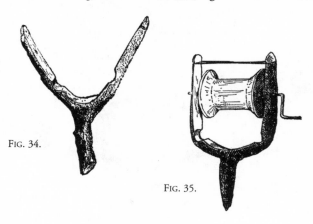

FIG. 34.

FIG. 35.

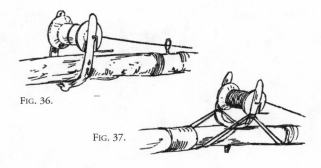

FIG. 36.

FIG. 37.

made of a bird's claw bound to a piece of shell by vegetable fibre. I would not advise my readers to attempt to make one. A better plan is to always carry a supply about your person, inside the lining of your hat being a good place to deposit small hooks. For black bass, pickerel, and many other fish, live minnows are the best bait. To catch them you need a net.

Home-Made fishing Nets

A simple way to make a minnow net is to stretch a piece of mosquito netting between two stout sticks. If deemed necessary, floats may be fastened at the top and sinkers at the bottom edge of the net (FIG. 38). Coarse bagging may be used if mosquito netting is not obtainable. But with a forked stick and a ball of string for material, a jack-knife, and your fingers for tools, a splendid scoop-net can be made that will not only

FIG. 38.

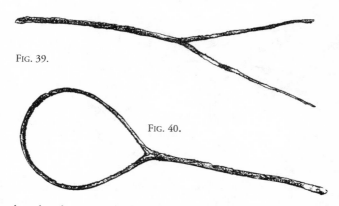

FIG. 39.

FIG. 40.

last, but be as good, if not better, than any you could purchase. Cut a good stout sapling that has two branches
(FIG. 39). Trim off all other appendages, and bend the two
branches until the ends over-lap each other for some distance,
bind the ends firmly and neatly together with waxed twine, if
it can be had—if not, with what string you have (FIG. 40).

Fasten the pole in a convenient position so that the hoop
is about level with your face. If you want the net two feet
deep, cut a number of pieces of twine seven or eight feet long,
double them, and slip them on the hoop in the manner
shown by the first string (FIG. 41).

Beginning at the most convenient point, take a string from
each adjoining pair and make a simple knot of them, as
shown by the diagram. Continue all the way around the
hoop knotting the strings together in this manner. Then
commence on the next lower row and so on until you reach
a point where, in your judgment the net ought to commence
to narrow or taper down. This can be accomplished by knotting the strings a little closer together, and cutting off one
string of a pair at four equidistant points in the same row.
Knot as before until you come to a clipped line; here you
must take a string from each side of the single one and knot
them, being careful to make it come even with others in the
same row. Before tightening the double knot pass the single
string through, and after tying a knot close to the double one

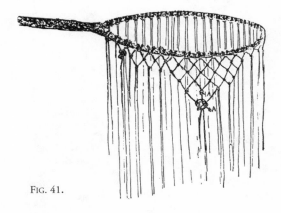

FIG. 41.

cut the string off close. (See FIG. 41A.)

Continue as before until the row is finished; only deviating from the original plan when a single string is reached. Proceed in a like manner with the next and the next rows, increasing the number of strings eliminated until the remaining ones meet at the bottom, being careful not to let one drop mesh come directly under another of the same kind.

A scoop-net can be made of a piece of mosquito netting by sewing it in the form of a bag, and fastening it to a pole and hoop made of a forked stick like the one just described.

Minnows must be kept alive, and tin buckets, with the top half perforated with holes, are made for that purpose. These buckets, when in use, are secured by a string and hung in the water, the holes in the sides allowing a constant supply of fresh breathing material to the little fish within.

SHOOTING

Selecting a Revolver and Ammunition

Fig. 42. Webley Fosbury Automatic Revolver.

YOU MUST FIRST DECIDE FOR WHAT PURPOSE YOU WANT the revolver; a "general utility" one is about as much use as a hunter who goes in harness—not much good for either purpose. If you want a hunter, buy an English hunter; if a harness horse, buy an American trotter. In the same way, for whatever purpose you want a revolver, buy one, if by any means you can do so, especially for that purpose. Anyhow, it is useless to compete with a short-barrelled pocket revolver against target revolvers. This class of revolver is intended only for self defence at short range, and has no pretensions to accuracy.

Six and a half inches in the barrel, exclusive of cylinder, is about the most practical length; of course, a longer barrel theoretically gives greater accuracy, especially at long range, owing to there being more length to burn the powder in, and to the sights being farther apart, which minimises error in aiming; but practically this advantage is more than counter-balanced by making the revolver heavy at the muzzle, so that it therefore balances badly. The balance ought to be as near the trigger as possible. For a pocket revolver, a short barrel may be absolutely necessary for portability. Some men use very long barrels, seven-and-a-half-inch barrels are not unusual in their revolvers.

See that the trigger-pull is "sweet," and has no "drag." Also, have your trigger-pull not over four and a half pounds. The pull is often left very heavy, so as to be alterable to suit customers, and the shopman may forget to have this altered. Have the thumb-piece of the hammer slightly roughed to prevent slipping. For rapid cocking, a rather long thumb-piece is an advantage.

For a man whose hands are apt to get moist, roughing the trigger may prevent slipping; but it may also make the finger sore if roughed too sharp.

Get a revolver which, when you grip the stock properly, has the barrel and your arm as nearly in a horizontal line as possible. Many makes of revolvers and automatic pistols have the stock much below the level of the barrel, which, consequently, is above the hand. This makes shooting more difficult; you are apt to cant the weapon to one side, and the recoil is more severe on your wrist. A man who holds a revolver properly does not need a big stock, even if he has a big hand.

FIG. 43 shows of three makes of revolvers: Smith & Wesson ("Winans's Model"), "Bisley" Colt, and "Target" Webley.

FIG. 43 TOP TO BOTTOM: SMITH & WESSON ("WINANS'S MODEL"), "BISLEY" COLT, AND "TARGET" WEBLEY.

Revolver ammunition (Fig. 44) is usually made in the following calibres: .32, .38, .41, .44, .45, .455. Most of these can be had loaded with various smokeless powders, as King's semi-smokeless, Riflite, Cordite, Walsrode, etc.

.32-.44 is a special target cartridge, containing 11 grs. of powder and 83 grs. of lead. Bullet seated even with mouth of shell. Penetration 5⅞-in. pine boards. Gallery charge, 6 grs. of powder and 50 gr. Round ball loaded in same shell.

.38-.44 is also a special target cartridge, containing 20 grs. of powder and 146 of lead, either self-lubricating or grooved bullet. Bullet is seated even with mouth of shell. Penetration, 6⅞-in. pine boards. gallery charge, 6 grs. of powder and 70 gr. Round ball loaded in same shell.

.38 Winchester rifle cartridge, containing 40 grs. of powder and 180 grs. of lead. Penetration, 7⅞-in. pine boards.

.44 Russian Model is a cartridge for long-range target work. It contains 23 grs. of powder and 256 grs. of lead. Bullets are either self-lubricating or the regular grooved. Penetration 7½ ⅞-in. pine boards. Gallery charge, 7 grs. of powder and 110 grs. round ball loaded in same shell.

.44 Winchester is the regular model 73 Winchester rifle cartridge, and contains 40 grs. of powder and 217 grains of lead. Penetration 6½ ⅞-in.. pine boards.

.450 cartridge contains 13 grs. of powder and 226 grs. of lead. English or American cartridges can be used.

Fig. 44. Revolver Ammunition

Be sure to use only low-pressure powder, if you use smokeless, as high-pressure powders are dangerous in a revolver.

Many people do not understand this difference in powder pressure, and injure their revolvers by experimenting with what become practically "blasting" instead of propelling charges.

Never use any ammunition different from that recommended by the makers of the particular revolver you are using, without consulting them.

There have been several narrow escapes (in one case having a bullet stop half-way in the barrel) when experimenting with various powders suitable for rifles, but not for revolvers.

The Smith & Wesson cartridge with "Self-Lubricating bullet was specially designed to fouling and so do away with the necessity of constantly cleaning a revolver while shooting. (See FIGS. 45-46.)

FIG. 45. COMPLETE SELF-LUBRICATING CARTRIDGE

FIG. 46. CUT AWAY SHOWING DETAILS OF CONSTRUCTION

A. LUBRICANT; B. PLUNGER; C. DUCTS; D. METAL LINING

EXPLANATION—At the moment of explosion, the lead plunger (B), being driven forward, forces the lubricant contained in the cavity (A) out through the ducts (C) in front of the bullet, and at a point where most effective.

The ducts being completely closed by the plunger, all escape of gas and loss of force is consequently prevented.

Cleaning and Care of Weapons

Always clean your revolver the moment you have finished shooting. If you leave it over till the next day, you may as well throw the revolver away.

Clean from the breech, not the muzzle end; the last fraction of an inch at the muzzle is where the rifling, if damaged, spoils the shooting most. For the same reason, it is as well to have the rifling "reamed off" at the mouth of the muzzle, so that the edge of it is protected. If you use nitro-powders, examine the interior of your barrel at frequent intervals after cleaning, to see if there is any damage going on.

Use the cleaning fluids recommended for the particular powder you are using, as what may be good for one powder is of no use for another.

The great thing is to clean very thoroughly. Use cotton-wool of the best quality rather than tow, and do not use boiling water unless in very exceptional cases, for fear of overlooking a spot in drying, and getting rust in consequence. If necessary to use water to remove fouling, let it be as hot as possible.

Do not try to oil the lock, or put it right; send it occasionally to the maker to be seen to. It is also well to have a cleaning kit with wooden, not metal (except for calibres of .32 or less), cleaning rods, cotton-wool, cleaning fluids, screwdrivers, etc., all in proper compartments, and to *put them*

FIG. 47. EXTENSION STOCK AS APPLIED TO
.44 SINGLE-ACTION REVOLVER

back when used. See that the cotton-wool is absolutely dry and clean before using it. Throw away such pieces as are used. Do not use too big a piece on your rod, such as would get the latter jammed in the barrel, as you may ruin the shooting qualities of the barrel by using force to remove it. Have the cleaning rods long enough, or you may bark your knuckles.

Sights

SIGHTS are made in many forms. Some suit one man best; others another. You cannot decide which suits your individual case without trying each sort for yourself.

When you find one form which suits you, it is a pity to risk spoiling your shooting by changing to others; a beginner should never do so, as he will get into an uncertain way of taking his sights, instead of always the same, which is the only way to make reliable, consistent, shooting.

The main point is to have a front sight at once easily seen, and of which you see each time the *same amount,* not sometimes more and at other times less, else you cannot keep your elevation.

Fig. 48.

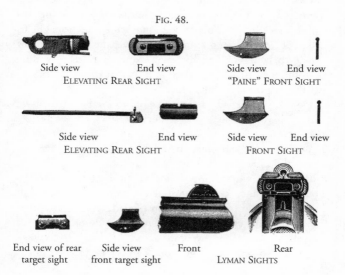

Side view	End view
Elevating Rear Sight	

Side view	End view
"Paine" Front Sight	

Side view	End view
Elevating Rear Sight	

Side view	End view
Front Sight	

End view of rear target sight	Side view front target sight	Front	Rear
		Lyman Sights	

Also the "U" in the back sight should have bevelled edges, so as to give a sharp edge, else it looks "woolly."

Again, if you are not able to see daylight each side of the front sight when it is in the "U," you cannot be aware that you are not covering part of the front sight on one side or the other, and, therefore, whether your aim is in horizontal axis with your barrel.

The reason we prefer a "U"- to a "V"-shaped notch in the hind sight is because in the "V" you do not see this daylight so well.

As soon as you can shoot well enough to know whether bad shots are the fault of the sighting of the revolver or of your own holding, you can sight the revolver properly for yourself; and in this way you can do the sighting much more accurately, and with greater nicety, than by taking it to a gun-maker and saying: "Alter the sights to shoot three inches higher and two to the left at twenty yards, and open the 'U' a little," etc. To do this, have front and hind sights made of horn, put in temporarily, without any "U" in the hind sight, and both hind and front sights a little higher than you think necessary. Then go to the range with your revolver and several files of various sizes, including some that are round. Make a slight "U" in the *measured* centre of the top edge of the back sight. Shoot a few shots at the range you want to sight for (taking care that you do not go clean over the top of the butt, owing to being sighted too high), and then keep working with the files, first at one sight and then at the other, till you get them approximately right.

Do not get the "U" down too close to the barrel, as it will thus give you a blurry aim, especially when the barrel gets hot. If you find you shoot too high, unless you cut this "U" down take out the front sight and. put in another higher one, rather than file the "U" unduly low.

Remember when filing: Filing at the bottom of the "U" makes you shoot *lower*, filing at the top of the front sight makes you shoot *higher*; filing on the side of the "U" or the front sight makes you shoot *towards* the side on which you have filed. Therefore, by filing a very little at a time where necessary, you can at last get your sighting perfect. Be sure to file a very little at a time, or you will overdo it. As in sculpture, you can easily take off, but cannot replace. If you have taken off too much anywhere, you may be able to correct this by filing so as to alter the direction. For instance, if you have been shooting too much to the right, you can correct this by filing on the left of the front sight or the left of the "U," whichever makes the more symmetrical job; but if, by doing so, you make the front sight too small or too narrow or make the "U" too wide, there is nothing to do but to put in a new front or hind sight and begin shooting and filing again.

When you have got the sighting perfect, work carefully with your file (taking great care not to spoil the edge of the "U" nearest to the eye when aiming), and give a chamfered or bevelled edge to the other side of the "U" so that it has a knife-edge. This is to make the "U" look clear and yet allow the back sight to be strong. On this principle, you can let the hind sight be strong and over a quarter of an inch thick, and yet have a nice, clear 'U." Do not have the "U" deeper than a semicircle. If this "U" is too deep, it hampers your view of the object aimed at. In fact, it should not be quite a real "U," but a semicircle. You can also file all round the front sight, giving it a taper toward the muzzle, but keeping unaltered the silhouette that you see when aiming, so that the outline shall then stand clear to the eye.

A gunmaker's vise (padded, so as not to bruise the revolver) is a useful thing, as it leaves both your hands free to use the files.

When you have finished, and have had a final shoot to see if this finishing has not spoilt your elevation, etc., you can send your revolver to the maker, and ask him to make your sights precisely like your model ones, and to fix them permanently on the revolver. When you get the revolver with these sights, if the work has been properly done, a very little more filing will put the matter right.

Carry a miniature folding gilt screw-driver and sight-case on your watch-chain, as we do, arid you will then be able to shoot in any light, at any range, or in any style of shooting, by merely giving a slight turn to the adjusting screws to alter your elevation or direction; or take out a sight from your little case of sights, if a sight breaks or you want a different size or shape. Public opinion has not yet been educated to the point of considering this "a practical military sight," but this will come—in time.

Learning to Use the Revolver

It is assumed that you have procured an accurate revolver, properly sighted.

First, open the revolver, and make sure that it is unloaded. *Always* do this before handling a revolver.

Take a bottle of sight-black and paint both sights over with the liquid. We have seen men try to compete, with their sights in a shiny state, which made it impossible for them to make good shooting on a white target with black "bull."

For game shooting, or for military purposes, of course, a "dead" white (ivory for choice) tip to the front sight is preferable, or military front sight, which answers the purposes both of a light on dark, or dark on light, sight.

With a revolver, the first thing to consider is safety. It is, owing to its shortness, one of the most dangerous of firearms to handle. Even an expert must exercise great care; and in the hands of a beginner or a careless person it may be fearfully dangerous. There have been many very narrow escapes in teaching men how to shoot; it is not even safe to be behind them; they will turn round with the revolver at full-cock, pointing it at you, and say: "I cannot understand why it will not go off; see! I am pulling as hard as I can at the trigger."

It is indispensable to have a safe background. Some people think that if the target is fastened to the trunk of a tree it is all safe, since the bullet will not go through the tree. This may be so if the tree is hit, but the bullet will, most likely, go past the tree when the beginner fires; or, what is just as dangerous, graze the tree and go off at an angle. Also, in shooting with round bullets, and light gallery ammunition, the bullets may rebound from a hard tree and come back on the shooter.

A good background is a high sandy bank, a thick pile of fagots, or, if not closer than fifty yards, a high brick or stone wall. The target may be stood some fifteen yards away from the wall to prevent danger of a bullet coming back on the shooter, and then the shooter can be far enough from the wall, if the wall is a background. If a lot of shooting is done, it is not very good for the wall, and if many shots hit the same spot they may gradually make a hole. Iron butts are expensive, especially for the large surface required by a beginner; at twenty yards, a beginner could not safely shoot at a background less than twelve feet high and some ten in width. Even then there should not be any one beyond it within half a mile, lest he should happen to let off by accident. Shooting out to sea is safe, if one keeps a good lookout for boats; but the glare from the water is bad. A sand- or chalk-pit is a good place to shoot in, or one can shoot against a high chalk cliff. It is dangerous to shoot anywhere where people cross unexpectedly, as from round the corner of a building.

The great thing is that *the revolver should never point in any direction where it would matter if it went off by accident.* This rule should be observed even with an empty revolver, because so many "I-did-not-know-it-was-loaded" accidents occur.

Having got a butt, the learner should take a firm, narrow wooden table and place it some ten yards from the target.

Place your empty revolver on the table, the weapon lying on its left side with the muzzle towards the target. The table is preferably a narrow one, so that, during the process of loading, the muzzle points to the ground beyond the table and not to the table itself, an accidental discharge being thus immaterial; a foot wide is about right; the length does not matter, so long as it will hold your telescope, cleaning things, and cartridges.

Stand facing the target; the right foot pointing straight for the target, or perhaps a shade to the left (if the ground is slippery, this gives you a firmer foothold); the left heel distant from six to nine inches to the left of the right foot, according to your height, and about an inch farther back; the feet turned out about as much as is natural to you when standing.

Stand perfectly upright, not craning your head forward; the left arm should hang down straight and close to the side in the position of "Attention." Some people bend the left arm and rest the hand on the hip; this looks affected, and it is not as workmanlike as if the arm hangs straight down.

If you are trying to "hold" an especially important shot, and find yourself wobbling off your aim, it is a great help to grip your thigh hard with your left hand; this especially applies in a gusty wind.

Now lift the revolver with your right hand (the weapon is empty, remember) and cock it. There are two ways of cocking: one using both hands and one using only the shooting hand.

This single-handed cocking (Fig. 49) is done by putting the thumb on the hammer and by the action of the thumb muscles alone bring it to full-cock. Take particular care that the first finger is clear of the trigger, or else you will either break or injure the sear notch, or have an accidental "let-off."

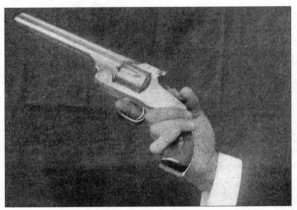

Fig. 49. How to Cock a Revolver

With practice, this way of cocking becomes very easy, and can be done with great rapidity.

By practice, the thumb and forefinger muscles (*abductor pollicis* and *adductor indicis*) develop enormously, and you need not mind if at first it seems difficult; but stop at first as soon as they feel tired, or you may strain them. Revolver-shooting is good also for the flexors of the forearm and for the dorsal muscles. A small hammer with short "fall" is easiest to cock, as well as to make good shooting with, for such a hammer takes less time in falling, and the aim is, in consequence, less likely to be disturbed.

The beginner will find that it assists the cocking to give the revolver a slight tilt to the right and upwards, taking great care to bring it back with the hind sights *horizontal* afterwards, as holding the sight stilted is one of the chief causes of bad shooting.

For double-handed cocking, assist the right hand by taking the revolver behind the chambers with the left hand, so as not to get burnt if it should go off by accident; keep the barrel horizontal and pointed at the target, not towards your left-hand neighbor, as is often done; and, while it is thus steadied, cock the revolver gently, not with a jerk, bringing the hammer well beyond full. cock, so that it sinks back into the bent with a well-defined click, keeping the first finger clear of the trigger.

Now, stand with the revolver in your right hand, just clear of the table; right arm full stretch; thumb stretched out along the revolver (see FIG. 50), but the first finger must be outside the trigger-guard (not touching the trigger) during this stage.

FIG. 50. THE CORRECT WAY TO HOLD A REVOLVER

Some men shoot with the second finger on the trigger and the first along the revolver; but this is a clumsy way, and the first finger is apt to be burnt with the escape of gas from the cylinder. The habit was acquired from shooting the Martini rifle, the clumsy "grip" of which made this manner of holding necessary.

The great thing is to have your grip *as high as you can* on the stock, in line with the axis of the barrel, or as near this as is practicable.

Some American revolvers often have specially long, big handles, or stocks, because of the habit of holding the stock low down with the little finger beneath. Now this sort of position makes the recoil come at an angle to the wrist, throws the barrel up at the recoil, spoiling the accuracy, and puts more strain on the wrist than is necessary.

FIG. 51. THE CORRECT POSITION OF THE THUMB

The revolver barrel, hand, and arm should all be nearly in one line, the thumb along the left side, so as to prevent jerking to the left in pressing the trigger (in the same way as the left arm is fully extended in shooting with the shotgun), and not crooked, as all beginners insist on holding it.

You must be constantly on the watch that you do not crook your thumb, until the extended position becomes second nature to you (FIG. 51). Some makes of revolvers have the extractor lever in a position which renders this grip with extended thumb impossible.

First take a deep breath, and fill your lungs. Now slowly bring your right arm to the horizontal, keeping your eyes fixed on the bottom edge,-at "six o'clock" of the "bull"; whilst you are doing this, put your forefinger inside the trigger-guard, and gradually begin to feel the trigger and steadily increase the pressure on it *straight back, not sideways*. Whilst you are doing all this, also gradually stiffen all your muscles so that you are braced up, especially about the right shoulder, as though you were walking along the pavement and saw a man coming towards you whom you meant to shoulder out of your path.

You may breathe naturally until the revolver is levelled, then hold your breath; if you cannot get your aim satisfactorily before you feel you want to take a fresh breath, lower the pistol, take a deep breath, and try again. If you have followed these directions carefully, you will find, when the hind sight comes to the level of your eyes (closing your left eye or not, as you find best, without any movement of the head), the front sight will be seen through the middle of the "U" pointed at the bottom of the bull's-eye, the top of the front sight just touching it at "six o'clock." If everything has been done perfectly, at the moment this occurs the pressure on the trigger will have been increased sufficiently to cause the hammer to fall, and, after it has fallen, you will see the top of the front sight *still* just touching the bulls-eye at its bottom edge.

If the revolver had been loaded (assuming, of course, that it was an accurate-shooting one and properly sighted), you would have had a central bull's-eye for your shot. Most likely, however, you will find that the revolver came up all of a tremble, and that, as the hammer fell, the front sight was jerked very wide of the 'bull' and perhaps even hidden by the hind sight.

The action of "letting off" should be like squeezing an orange-a squeeze of the *whole hand*. Start with a light grip when your hand is down, and gradually squeeze as you come up, the trigger-finger squeezing *back;* and the hammer will fall without the least tremor or without the sights moving off the point they covered during the fall of the hammer. The main thing of all in revolver-shooting is to *squeeze straight back.* Whenever you find yourself shooting badly see if you are not *"pulling off to one side";* and in nine cases out of ten you will discover that this was the cause of your bad shooting.

Some men can never squeeze the trigger straight back, and have to allow for this by getting the hind sight "set over" to one side to correct it; but this is a slovenly way of shooting, and, as the pull to one side may vary according to the "Jumpiness" of the shooter, it prevents his being a really first-class shot.

Keep the hind sight perfectly horizontal; beginners are prone to cant it on one side, which puts the bullet to the side towards which you cant.

After a little practice, you will be able to "call" your shots, that is to say, you will be able, the moment the cartridge explodes, to say where the shot has struck the target, as you know where the sights were pointed at the "squeeze-off."

After six shots, make a pencil-cross over each bullet-hole, so as to know where your former shots hit. After twelve hits it is best to take a fresh target. At the end of the day's shooting, you can cover the holes by pasting black patches on the bull's-eye holes and white on the rest, and use the target again.

We remember once a man telling us (he professed to be an expert with the revolver) that we were wrong in keeping our revolvers pointed in front of us toward the target when preparing to shoot. "You ought to hold it like this," he said, letting his right arm hang close to his side and keeping the revolver pointing downwards; "then it is quite safe." At that moment it went off and blew a big hole in the ground within an inch of his foot!

By our system of having a table in front of the shooter,

close to which he stands, and from which he lifts the revolver, he cannot shoot down into his feet. But he must never turn round or leave the table without first unloading the revolver and placing it on the table; nor, on any account, must he let any one go up to the target or be in front or even get level with him whilst the revolver is in his hand.

Now, as to the trick of lifting the revolver above one's head before firing: We cannot understand why people want to do this. It only frightens spectators; besides, the shooter is running the risk of shooting himself through the head; and in competitions or in self-defence time is too valuable to waste in such antics.

When you are pretty confident that you can keep your sights properly aligned at the bottom edge of the "bull" while the hammer is falling, you can try a few shots with a loaded revolver. It is best to load only some of the chambers, irregularly spin the cylinder round, after the revolver is closed and at half-cock, so as not to know which chambers are loaded, and every time you find you jerk off with a shot, return to the snapping-empty-cartridge practice. This latter is good practice, even when you become a skilled shot.

Place the box of cartridges beside, and to the right of, the revolver. Use only a very small charge (gallery ammunition for choice) at first, as nothing puts a beginner off so much as the fear of recoil. Stand behind the table, the revolver being between you and the target, and take the revolver by its stock in the right hand. Do not turn the muzzle to the left, but straight out towards the target. Put it in your left hand and load it. This procedure varies with different makes; with the Smith & Wesson, Russian, and Winans models, you lift the catch with your left thumb and press the barrel down with the same hand till it (the barrel) is perpendicular, pointing to the ground. But whatever the mechanism, when the revolver is open for loading, the barrel should be pointing downwards, yet in line for the target.

If a cartridge projects too much, remove it, as it is dangerous and may explode prematurely from friction against the breech of the revolver. In loading; of course have the revolver at half-, not fullcock. Close the revolver by elevating the breech with the right hand, not by raising the barrel with the left, as in the latter case the cartridges may drop out. This rule applies also to the hand ejecting revolvers. See that the snap, or other fastening, is properly closed. If your shot goes wide of the bull, be sure, before you alter your aim for the next shot, whether it is not your "squeeze-off" which is wrong.

A practiced shot can correct the shooting of his revolver by "aiming off" enough to rectify any error in sights. But the beginner had better not attempt this: he will find enough to do in trying to hold straight under the bull.

It is best to have your cleaning appliances on the table, or otherwise handy, when shooting, and every now and again to have a look through the barrel and a wipe-out; you might otherwise be inclined to attribute to bad shooting what may be caused by leading or hard fouling in the barrel. We have a little cupboard under our table with a lock and key, in which we keep my cleaning apparatus, cartridges, etc. (but *not* the revolver to save the trouble of carrying them to the range.

Always clean a revolver as soon after shooting as possible, and clean very thoroughly.

A revolver first shows signs of wear at the breech end of the barrel; it looks there as though rats had been gnawing it. At first, we have a fancy that this makes the revolver shoot "sweeter," but when this gets too bad, it affects its accuracy for target work. For real work, we prefer a revolver when it is half worn out, as everything then works smoothly and there is less danger of jambing. Rust in the rifling may entirely spoil accuracy, as, if you work it off, the bore gets enlarged and the bullets "strip." All revolvers have their peculiarities, and it is necessary to get used to one, to "break it in," before trusting it to obey one's slightest hint.

It is sometimes useful to be able to shoot with the left

hand; as, for instance, if the right hand is disabled, the right arm held, etc., and for an officer with a sword in his right hand. If the novice has resolution enough to divide his practising, *from the beginning,* between both hands, he will be able to shoot nearly as well with his "left" hand as with his right. We have put quotation marks round "left" as We mean by this the hand not usually employed; a left-handed man's right hand being in this sense his "left."

We have also noticed that a left-handed man can shoot more evenly with both hands; that is to say, he is not much better or worse with either hand, not being so helpless with his right hand as a normally handed man is with his left. In all the directions for shooting, for left-handed work merely change "right leg" to "left leg"; "right arm" to "left arm," etc.

KITE FLYING

I T IS A PLEASANT SENSATION TO SIT IN THE FIRST spring sunshine and feel the steady pull of a good kite upon the string, and watch its graceful movements as it sways from side to side, ever mounting higher and higher, as if impatient to free itself and soar away amid the clouds. The pleasure is, however, greatly enhanced by the knowledge that the object skimming so bird-like and beautifully through the air is a kite of your own manufacture.

Man Kite

To make this kite you will require four sticks, some rattan and some paper. In regard to his size, we would suggest that the larger the man is, the better he will fly. Now let us suppose you are going to make this fellow four feet high. First, cut two straight sticks three feet nine inches long; these are to serve for the legs and body; cut another straight stick two and one-half feet in length for the spine, and a fourth stick, three feet five inches long, for the arms. For the head select a light piece of split rattan—any light, tough wood that will bend readily will do—bend this in a circle eight inches in diameter, fasten it securely to one end of the spine by binding it with strong thread, being careful that the spine runs exactly through the centre of the circle (FIG. 52). Next find the exact centre of the arm stick, and with a pin or small tack fasten it at this point to the spine, a few inches below the chin (FIG. 53). After wrapping the joint tightly with strong thread, lay the part of the skeleton which is finished flat upon the floor, mark two points upon the arm. sticks for the shoulder-joints, each seven inches from the intersection of the spine and arm-stick, which will place them fourteen inches apart. At these points fasten with a pin the two long sticks that are to serve for the body and legs (FIG. 54). Now cross these sticks as shown in diagram, being careful that the terminations of the lower limbs are at least three feet apart; the waist-joint ought then to be about ten inches below the arm-stick. After taking the greatest pains to see that the arm-stick is perfectly at right angles with the spine, fasten all the joints securely. Upon the arms bind oblong loops of rattan, or of the same material as the head-frame. These hand-loops ought to be about three inches broad at their widest parts, and exact counterparts of each other. The loops for the feet must approach as nearly as possible the shape of feet, and these, too, must be exactly alike, or the kite will be "lopsided," or unequally balanced. Now cut two sticks three inches long for the ends of sleeves, and two others four inches long for bottoms of trousers (FIG. 55); fasten the two former near the ends of the arm-stick, and the two latter near the ends of the leg-sticks, as in the illustration. The strings of the frame must next be put on, as shown by the dotted lines (FIG. 56). Commence with the neck, at equal distances from the spine, and about seven inches apart; tie two strings to the arm-sticks; extend these strings slantingly to the head, and fasten them to the hoop, one on each side of the spine, and about five inch-

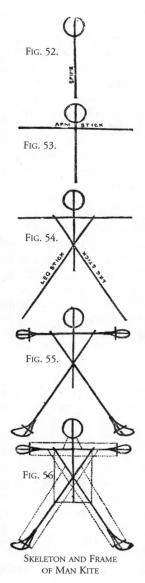

FIG. 52.

SPINE

FIG. 53.

ARM STICK

FIG. 54.

LEG STICK   LEG STICK

FIG. 55.

FIG. 56.

SKELETON AND FRAME
OF MAN KITE

es apart. Take another thread and fasten to the top of cross-stick of right arm, pass it over and take a wrap around the spine, continue it to top of cross-stick upon left arm, and there tie it. Fasten another string to bottom of cross-stick on right arm, draw it tight and wrap it on spine four inches below intersection of arm-stick, pass it on to the bottom of cross stick on left arm, draw taut and fasten it. Tie the body-string at the right shoulder-joint, drop the thread down to a point exactly opposite the termination of spine upon the right leg, take a wrap, and draw the line across to point upon left leg exactly opposite, bind it there, then bring it up to left shoulder-joint and tie it. For the trousers fasten a string at a point on right arm-stick, eleven inches from the intersection of spine, extend it down in a straight line to inside end of cross-stick of left limb and fasten it there. Tie another string at a point one inch and a half to the left of spine upon right arm-stick, extend it down in a straight line to outside end of cross-stick of left limb. Go through the same process for right leg of trousers, and the frame-work will be complete.

For the covering of a kite of this size we have always used tissue paper; it is pretty in color and very light in weight. Paste some sheets of tissue paper together, red for the trousers, hands and face, blue for the coat, and black, or some dark color, for the feet. Use paste made of flour and water boiled to the consistency of starch. Put the paste on with a small bristle brush, make the seams or over-laps hardly more than one-fourth of an inch wide, and press them together with a soft rag or towel; measure the paper so that the coat will join the trousers at the proper place. When you are satisfied that this is all right, lay the paper smoothly on the floor and place the frame of the kite upon it, using heavy books or paper-weights to hold it in place. Then with a pair of scissors cut the paper around the frame, leaving a clear edge of one-half inch, and making a slit in this margin or edge every six or seven inches and at each angle; around the head these slits must be made about two or three inches apart to prevent the paper from wrinkling when you commence to paste. With your brush cover the margin with paste one section at a time, turn them over, and with the towel or rag press them down. After the kite is all pasted and dry, take a large paint-brush, and with black marking-paint, india ink, or common writing fluid, put in the buttons and binding on coat with a good broad touch. The face and hair must be painted with broad lines, so that they may be seen clearly at a great height. Follow this rule wherever you have to use paint upon any kind of kite.

The breast-band, or "belly-band," of the man kite should be arranged in the same manner as it is upon the common hexagonal or coffin-shaped kite with which all Americans are familiar; but for fear some of our readers may not quite understand we will try and tell them exactly how to do it. First, punch small holes through the paper, one upon each side of the leg-sticks just above the bottom of the pants, and one upon each side of the arm-stick at the shoulders. Run one end of the breast-band through the holes at the bottom of the left limb and tie it fast to the leg-stick; tie the other end at the right shoulder. Take another string of the same length as the first and fasten one end in the same manner at the bottom of the right leg, pass the string up, crossing the first band, and tie the end at the left shoulder. Attach your kite-string to the breast-band where the two strings intersect in such a manner that you can slide the kite-string up or down until it is properly adjusted. For the tail-band, tie a string (to the leg - sticks) at the bottom of the breast-band and let hang slack from one leg to the other.

Attach the tail to the centre of this string.

The Woman Kite

The Woman Kite, though differing in form, is made after the same method as the man kite, and with the aid of the diagram any one can build one if he is careful to keep the proper proportions. Remember that the dotted lines in each of these diagrams represent the strings or thread of the framework (FIG. 57). Use small, smooth twine on large kites, and good strong thread on the small-

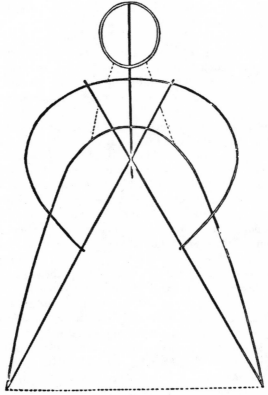

FIG. 57. FRAME OF WOMAN KITE

er ones. A very comical effect can be had by making the feet of the woman kite of stiff paste-board, and fastening them on to the line which forms the bottom of the skirt with a string after the manner here illustrated (FIG. 58), allowing them to dangle loosely from below, to be moved and swayed by each motion of the kite, looking as if it was indeed a live woman or girl of the Kate Greenaway style, dancing and kicking in the clouds. FIG. 59 shows a girl kite with feet attached.

The costume given in the illustration may be varied

according to fancy, with the same framework. A Dolly Varden or a Martha Washington costume can be made. A blue overskirt and waist covered with stars, and a red and white striped skirt, give us Columbia or a Goddess of Liberty. Attach the breast-band in the same manner as upon the man kite. Let the tail-band hang loosely below the skirt.

FIG. 58. FOOT OF THE GIRL

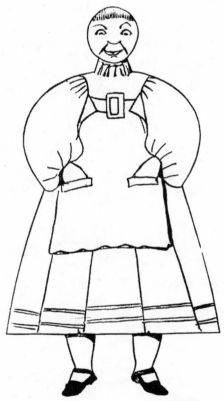

FIG. 59. COMIC GIRL KITE

A Boy Kite

By a slight modification of the frame of the man kite you can produce a boy kite. This will create an unlimited amount of fun whenever he makeshift appearance in his aesthetic Kate Greenaway suit. By carefully following the construcion according to the diagram (FIG. 60) you will find little difficulty in building a twin brother to the kite in FIG. 61.

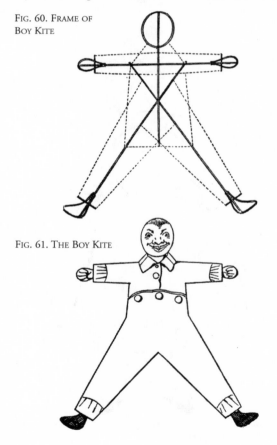

FIG. 60. FRAME OF BOY KITE

FIG. 61. THE BOY KITE

Frog Kite

It is not worth while to build one less than two feet high. Let us suppose that the particular batrachian we are now about to make is to be just that height; in this case the leg-sticks must be each two feet long, and as you will want to bend them at the knees, these points should be made considerably thinner than the other parts of the sticks. The spine must be about one foot seven inches long, or a little over three-quarters of the length of the leg-sticks. Place the two latter ones above the other, lay the spine on top of them, and see that the tops of all three are flush, or perfectly even. Then at a point eight inches from the top, drive a pin through all three sticks, carefully clamping it upon the

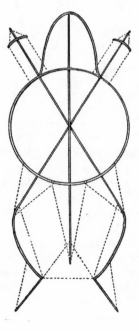

FIG. 62. FRAME OF FROG KITE

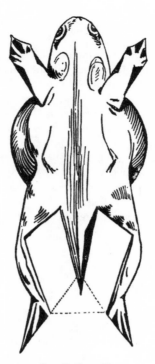

FIG. 63. FROG KITE

other side where the point protrudes. For the body, take a piece of thin rattan two feet five or six inches in length, bend it into the form of a circle, allowing the ends to over- lap an inch or two that they may be firmly bound together with thread by winding it around the joint. The circle will be about eight inches in diameter. Take the three sticks you pinned together and lay them on the floor, spreading them apart in the form of an irregular star, in such a manner that the top of the spine will be just half-way between the tops of the leg-sticks and about five inches from each; when you have proceeded thus far place the rattan circle over the other sticks; the intersection of the sticks should be the centre of the circle; with pins and thread fasten the frame together in this position. The lower limbs will be spread wide apart; they must be carefully drawn closer together and held in position by a string tied near the termination of each leg-stick. Cross sticks for hands and feet may now be added, and the strings put on as shown in FIG. 62. This kite should be covered with green tissue paper. A few marks of the paint-brush will give it the appearance of FIG. 63. The breast and tail-band can be put on as described in the man kite.

The Butterfly Kite

Make a thin straight stick of a piece of elastic wood, or split rattan; to the top end of this attach a piece of thread or string; bend the stick as you would a bow until it forms an arc or part of a circle; then holding the stick in this position tie the other end of the string to point on the stock, about one-quarter the distance from the top, tie another string, draw it taut, and fasten it to the bottom end of the bow. Take another stock of exactly the same length and thickness as first, and go through the same process, making a frame that must be a duplicate of of the other. Then fasten the two frames together, as shown

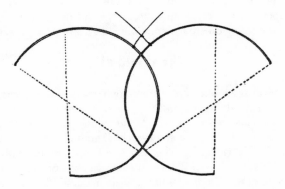

FIG. 64. FRAME OF THE BUTTERFLY KITE

FIG. 65. BUTTERFLY KITE

by FIG. 64, allowing the arcs to overlap several inches, and bind the joints securely with thread.

The head of the insect is made by attaching two broom straws to the top part of the wings where they join, the straws must be crossed, the projecting ends serving for antennae or, as boys call them, the "smellers" of the butterfly. Now select a piece of yellow or blue tissue paper, place your frame over it, cut and paste as directed in in the description of the Man Kite (page 94). When the kite is dry, with black paint make some marking upon the wings similar to those shown in FIG. 65; or better still, cut out some pieces of dark colored paper in the form of these markings and paste them on, of course taking care to have one wing like the other, as in nature.

The Shield Kite

Make the frame of four sticks, two straight cross-sticks and two bent side-sticks (FIG. 66); cover it with red, white, and blue tissue paper. Paste red and white paper together in stripes for the bottom, and use a blue ground with white stars for the top (FIG. 67). The next kite is not original with the authors, but is well known in some sections of the country. We have made a diagram of it at the request of a number of boys who did not know how to make one.

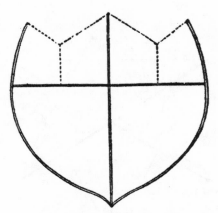

FIG. 66. FRAME OF THE SHIELD KITE

FIG. 67. SHIELD KITE

A Star Kite

Build it according to the diagrams (FIGS. 68 AND 69), making the sticks all of equal length, and cover the kite with any colored paper that may suit your fancy.

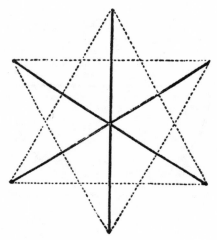

FIG. 68. FRAME OF STAR KITE

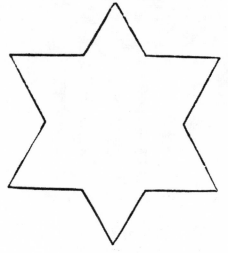

FIG. 69. STAR KITE

CAMPING
How to Camp Out Without a Tent

THE NEXT BEST THING TO REALLY LIVING IN THE WOODS IS talking over such an experience. A thousand little incidents, scarcely thought of at the time, crowd upon the mind, and bring back with them the feeling of freedom and adventure so dear to the heart of every American. Shall we ever enjoy any flavor earth can afford as we did our coffee's aroma? The flapjacks—how good and appetizing! the fish—how delicate and sweet! And the wonderful cottage of boughs, thatched with the tassels of the pine—was there ever a cottage out of a fairy tale that could compare with it?

In fancy we can see it now. There stands the little cot, flooded with the light of the setting sun; those who built it and use it for a habitation are off exploring, hunting, fishing, and foraging for their evening meal, and the small, shy creatures of the wood take the opportunity to satisfy the curiosity with which they have, from a safe distance, viewed the erection of so large and singular a nest.

The outdoors men will soon return, each with his contribution to the larder—a fish, a squirrel, a bird, or a rabbit, which will be cooked and eaten with better appetite and enjoyment than the most elaborate viands that home could afford. And although such joys are denied to us now, we can, at least, in remembering them, give others an opportunity to possess similar pleasures. It shall be our object to describe how these houses may be built and these dinners cooked, and that, too, where there are neither planks, nor nails, nor stoves. To those well informed in woodcraft, only a few hints need be given; but for the benefit of amateurs we will go more into detail.

Four persons make a good camping-party. Before arriving at their destination these persons should choose one of their number as captain.

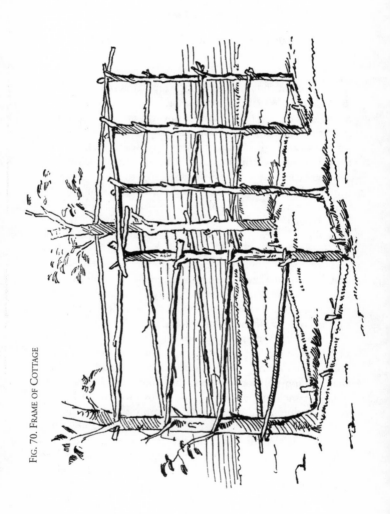

FIG. 70. FRAME OF COTTAGE

The captain gives directions and superintends the pitching of the tent or the building of the rustic cottage. The site for the camp should be upon a knoll, mound, or rising ground, so as to afford a good drainage. If the forest abounds in pine trees, the young cottage-builder's task is an easy one. It often happens that two or three trees already standing can be made to serve for the corners of the proposed edifice, though trees for corners are not absolutely necessary.

Fig. 70 represents part of the framework of one of the simplest forms of rustic cottage. In this case, two trees serve for the two posts of the rear wall. The front posts are young trees that have been cut down and firmly planted at about four or five paces in front of the trees, as shown in the illustration. Enough of the branches have been left adhering to the trunks of the upright posts to serve as rests for the cross bars. To prevent complication in the diagram, the roof is not shown. To make this, fasten on an additional cross bar or two to the rear wall, then put a pole at each side, slanting down from the rear to the front, and cover these poles with cross sticks. When the framework is finished, the security and durability of the structure will be improved by fastening all the loose joints, tying them together with withes of willow, grass, or reeds. The next step is to cover the frame. This is done after the method shown in Fig. 71. From among some boughs, saved for this purpose, take one and hang it upon the third cross

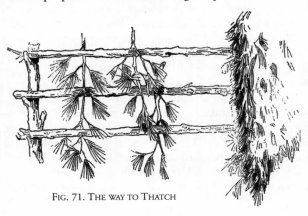

Fig. 71. The way to Thatch

115

bar, counting from the ground up; bring the bough down, passing it inside the second bar and resting the end on the ground outside the first bar; repeat this with other boughs until the row is finished. Then begin at the fourth bar, passing the boughs down inside the third and outside the second bar, so that they will overlap the first row. Continue in this manner until the four walls are closed in, leaving spaces open where windows or doors are wanted. The roof is thatched after the same method, beginning at the front and working upward and backward to the rear wall, each row overlapping the preceding row of thatch. The more closely and compactly you thatch the roof and walls, the better protection will they afford from any passing shower. This completed, the house is finished, and you will be astonished to see what a lovely little green cot you have built.

A cottage may be built differing from the one we have just described by having the roof extended so as to form a sort of verandah, or porch, in front; the floor of the porch may be covered with a layer of pine-needles. Should you find your house too small to accommodate your party, you can, by erecting a duplicate cottage four or five paces at one side, and roofing over the intervening space, have a house of two rooms with an open hall-way between.

Before going to housekeeping, some furniture will be necessary; and for this we propose to do our shopping right in the neighborhood of our cottage. Here is our cabinet and upholstery shop, in the wholesome fragrance of the pines.

After the labor of building, your thoughts will naturally turn to a place for sleeping. Cut four forked sticks, sharpen the ends, and drive them firmly into the ground at the spot where you wish the bed to stand in your room. Two strong poles, long enough to reach lengthwise from fork to fork, will serve for side boards; a number of short sticks will answer for slats; after these are fastened in place you have the rustic bedstead shown in FIG. 72. A good spring mattress is very desirable, and not difficult to obtain. Gather a lot of small green branches, or brush, and cover your bed, stead with a layer of it about one foot thick; this you will find a capital substitute

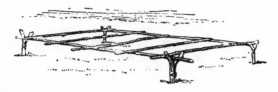

Fig. 72. Bedstead

Fig. 73. Bed Made Up

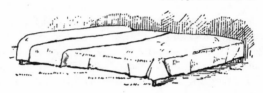

for springs. For your mattress proper, go to your upholstery shop under the pine tree and gather several armfuls of the dry pine-needles cover the elastic brush springs with a thick layer of these needles; over this spread your India-rubber blanket, with the rubber side under, so that any moisture or dampness there may be in your mattress may be prevented from coming through. You may now make up your bed with what wraps or blankets you have with you, and you have (FIG. 73) as complete and comfortable a bed as any forester need wish for. In the place of pine-needles, hay or grass may be used. It is possible to sleep very comfortably upon a brush mattress covered with iron-weed.*

We would suggest to any one who means to try this rustic cabinet-making, to select carefully for the bed-posts sticks strong enough to support the weight he intends them to bear, otherwise his slumbers may be interrupted in an abrupt and disagreeable manner. Our first experiment in this line proved disastrous. We spent the greater part of one day in building and neatly finishing a bed like the one described. After it was made up, with an army blanket for a coverlid, it looked so

*Iron-weed, flat-top (Vernonia noveboracensis), a common Kentucky weed, with beautiful purple blossoms.

soft, comfortable, and inviting that we scarcely could wait for bedtime to try it.

When the evening meal was over and the last story told around the blazing camp-fire, we took off hats, coats, and boots and snuggled down in the new and original couch, curiously watched by our companions, who lay, rolled in their blankets, upon the hard ground. It does not take a man long to fall asleep, particularly after a hard day's work in the open air, but it takes longer, after being aroused from a sound nap, for him to get his wits together—especially when suddenly dumped upon the ground with a crash, amid a heap of broken sticks and dry brush, as we happened to be on that eventful night. Loud and long were the shouts of laughter of our companions when they discovered our misfortune. Theoretically, the bed was well planned, but practically it was a failure, because it had rotten sticks for bed-posts.

How to Cook without a Kitchen

Having provided bed and shelter, it is high time to look after the inner man; and while the foragers are off in search of provisions, it will be the cook's duty to provide some method of cooking the food that will be brought in.

FIG. 74. BARREL IN BANK

FIG. 75. HEATING THE OVEN

One of the simplest and most practical forms of bake-oven can be made of clay and an old barrel. Remove one head of the barrel, scoop out a space in the nearest bank, and fit the barrel in (FIG. 74). If the mud or clay is not damp enough, moisten it and plaster it over the barrel to the depth of a foot or more, leaving a place for a chimney at the back end, where part of a stave has been cut away; around this place build a chimney of sticks arranged log-cabin fashion and plastered with mud (FIG. 75). After this, make a good, rousing fire in the barrel, and keep adding fuel until all the staves are burned out and the surrounding clay is baked hard. This makes an oven that will bake as well, if not better, than any new patented stove or range at home. To use it, build a fire inside and let it burn until the oven is thoroughly heated, then rake out all the coal and embers, put your dinner in and close up the front with the head of the barrel preserved for this purpose. The clay will remain hot for several hours and keep the inside of the oven hot enough to roast meat or bake bread.

If there be no bank convenient, or if you have no barrel with which to build this style of oven, there are other methods that will answer for all the cooking necessary to a party

FIG. 76. A STONE STOVE

camping out. Many rare fish have we eaten in our time. The delicious pompano at New Orleans, the brook-trout and grayling, fresh from the cold water of Northern Michigan, but never has fish tasted better than did a certain large cat-fish that we once caught on a set-line in Kentucky. We built a fire-place of flat stones, a picture of which you have in FIG. 76, covered it with a thin piece of slate, cleaned the fish and with its skin still on, placed it upon the slate. When it was brown upon one side we turned it over until it was thoroughly cooked. With green sticks we lifted off the fish and placed it upon a piece of clean bark; the skin adhered to the stone, and the meat came off in smoking, snowy pieces, which we ate with the aid of our pocket-knives and rustic forks made of small green twigs with the forked ends sharpened.

If stones cannot be had to answer for this stove, there still remains the old, primitive camp-fire and pot-hook. The very sight of this iron pot swinging over a blazing fire suggests

FIG. 77. A BUTTER-KNIFE

Fig. 78. Frame of Rustic Chair

Fig. 79. Frame of Rustic Chair

soup, to eat which with any comfort spoons are necessary. These are quickly and easily made by thrusting clam or mussel shells into splits made in the ends of sticks. A splendid butter-knife can be made from the shell of a razor-oyster with a little care in a similar manner (see Fig. 77).

If you stay any time in your forest home you can, by a little ingenuity, add many comforts and conveniences. Drawn are some diagrams, as hints, in this direction. For instance, Fig. 78 shows the manner of making an excellent rustic chair of two stout poles and two cross poles, to which are fastened the ends of a piece of canvas, carpet or leather (Fig. 79) which, swinging loose, fits itself exactly to your form, making a most comfortable easy-chair in which to rest or take a nap after a hard day's tramp. It often happens that the peculiar formation of some stump of branch suggests new styles of seats. A table can be very readily made by driving four forked sticks into the ground for legs, and covering the cross sticks upon the top with pieces of birch or other smooth bark. Fig. 80 shows a table made in

FIG. 80. A CAMP TABLE

this manner, with one piece of bark removed to reveal its construction.

As a general rule, what is taught in books, though correct in theory, when tried proves impracticable. This brings to mind an incident that happened to a party of young hunters camping out in Ohio. Early one morning one of the campers procured from a distant farm-house a dozen pretty little white bantam eggs. Having no game, and only one small fish in the way of fresh meat, the party congratulated themselves upon the elegant breakfast they would make of fresh eggs, toasted crackers, and coffee. How to cook the eggs was the question. One of the party proposed his plan.

"I have just read a book," said he, "which tells how some travellers cooked fowls and fish by rolling them up in clay and tossing them into the fire. Shall we try that plan with the eggs?"

The rest of the party assented, and soon all were busy rolling rather large balls of blue clay, in the centre of each of which was an egg. A dozen were placed in the midst of the hottest embers, and the boys seated themselves around the fire, impatiently waiting for the eggs to cook. They did cook-with a vengeance! Zip, bang! went one, then another and another, until, in less time than it takes to tell it, not an egg remained unexploded; and the hot embers and bits of clay that stuck to the boys' hair and clothes were all that was left to remind them of those nice, fresh bantam eggs. It was all very funny, but ever after the boys of that party showed the greatest caution in trying new schemes, no matter how well they might seem to be endorsed.

Hints to Amateur Campers

From time immemorial it has been the custom of the city fellows to laugh at their country cousins, and to poke all manner of fun at them on account of their verdancy in regard to city manners and customs. This is hardly fair, for if a real city fellow be placed on a farm, or in the woods, his ignorance is just as laughable and absurd. It was only the other day I saw a young New York artist refuse to drink from a spring because something *was bubbling up at the bottom.* Experience is a great teacher. Even the artist just mentioned, after making himself sick upon stagnant water, would, no doubt, learn to select bubbling springs in the future. A few timely hints may, however, prevent many mishaps and unpleasant accidents.

Provisions

It is always desirable to take as large a stock of provisions as can be conveniently transported. In these days of canned meats, soups, vegetables, and fruits, a large amount of provisions may be stored in a small space. Do not fail to take a plentiful supply of salt, pepper, and sugar; also bacon, flour, meal, grits, or hominy, tea, coffee, and condensed milk. If you have any sort of luck with your rod, gun, or traps, the forest and stream ought to supply fresh meat, and with the appetite only enjoyed by people who live out doors you can "live like a king."

Shelter

Because we have described but one sort of shelter our readers must not suppose that it is absolutely necessary to build a cottage like the one described. On the contrary, there are a thousand different plans that will suggest themselves to fellows who are accustomed to camping out. The huts, or sheds, built of "slabs" by some of the Adirondack hunters are very convenient, but unless the open ends are protected, in time of a storm, the rain is apt to drive in and soak the inmates. The two sheds face each other, and in the middle of the space between the camp-fire blazes, throwing a ruddy light at night into both compartments.

By taking advantage of a rock, a fallen or uprooted tree, the work of building a hut is ofttimes materially lessened.

Tents, of course, are very handy and comfortable, and if obtainable should by all means be used. At least one or two good sharp hatchets should form a part of the equipment of every camp; it is astonishing, with their aid and a little practice, what a comfortable house may be built in a very short time.

Choosing Companions

Never join a camping party that has among its members a single peevish, irritable, or selfish person, or a "shirk." Although the company of such a person may be only slightly annoying at school or upon the play-ground, in camp the companionship of a fellow of this description becomes unbearable. Even if the game fill the woods and the waters are alive with fish, an irritable or selfish companion will spoil all the fun and take the sunshine out of the brightest day. The whole party should be composed of fellows who are willing to take things as they come and make the best of everything. With such companions there is no such thing as "bad luck;" rain or shine everything is always jolly, and when you return from the woods, strengthened in mind and body, you will always remember with pleasure your camping experience.

DOGS

What They are Good For
and How to Train Them

IT IS TRUE THAT ONE *CAN* DO WITHOUT A CANINE companion and live to enjoy life, but he is almost incomplete; he lacks something; he has lost a gratification, a harmless, pleasant experience, and the loss leaves an empty space in his life that nothing can ever quite fill up. A man without a dog is like an unfinished story. What your left hand is to your right, a man's dog is to the man. More particularly is all this true of he who lives either in the country or within walking distance of forest and stream.

To be of any value either as a hunting dog, a watch dog or even a companion in one's rambles, it is absolutely necessary that the dog should be educated, and where there is a possibility of doing so, it is desirable to secure a young puppy. No matter what your choice in breed may be, whether it is a Newfoundland, bull, skye, greyhound, pointer, setter, or toy terrier, get the pup and *train it yourself.*

FIG. 81

How to Choose a Dog

"Blood will tell," whether it flows in the veins of a horse, man, or dog. The reader can readily understand that it would be not only absurd but absolutely cruel to keep a Newfoundland, deer-hound, water spaniel, pointer, setter, or any other similar breed of dog confined within the narrow limits of that small bit of ground attached to the city house and dignified by the name of a yard. It would be equally as absurd and almost as cruel for a farmer to try and keep one of those expensive, diminutive, delicate, nervous, city dogs known under the general title of a "toy dog" or "fancy breed." The agile, bright-eyed "black-and-tan," and the delicate and graceful Italian greyhound, are full of fun, but as unreliable as beautiful. Thoughtless, rollicking, exquisites! Such dogs are scarcely the kind either city or country folk would choose for playmates or companions. What most people want is a dog that combines the qualities of a boon companion and a good watch dog. By the latter is meant a dog whose intelligence is sufficient for it to discriminate between friend and foe, and whose courage will prompt it to attack the latter without hesitancy. It must also be a dog that may be taught to "fetch" and carry, to hunt for rat, squirrel, or rabbit, as well as to obey and trust in its master. It should be so cleanly in his habits as to be unobjectionable in-doors, and should possess judgment enough to know when its company is not agreeable, and at such times keep out of the way.

The poodle is perhaps the best trick dog, but is disliked by many on account of its thick woolly coat being so difficult to keep clean. The wirey-haired Scotch terrier is a comical, intelligent animal, and a first-rate comrade. The Newfoundland is faithful, companionable, and powerful enough to protect children, to whom, if there be any around the house, it will become very much attached and a self-constituted guardian. The spaniel is pretty, affectionate, and docile.

Almost all the sporting dogs make first-class watch-dogs, but are restless and troublesome if confined, and, as a rule,

Fig. 82

they are too large for the house. The shepherd is remarkably intelligent, and, when well trained, makes a trusty dog for general purposes.

The bull, although not necessarily as fierce and vicious as one would suppose from its looks and reputation, still is hardly the dog for a pet or companion, being of a dull and heavy nature, and not lively enough to suit the taste of a man of the period. A little of the bull mixed in the blood of another more lively breed makes a good dog, of which a thoroughbred bull-terrier is an example. The Rev. J. G. Wood, in speaking of the latter, says:

"The skilful dog-fancier contrives a judicious mixture of the two breeds, and engrafts the tenacity, endurance, and dauntless courage of the bull-dog upon the more agile and frivolous terrier. Thus he obtains a dog that can do almost anything, and though, perhaps, it may not surpass, it certainly rivals almost every other variety of dog in its accomplishments. In the capacity for learning tricks it scarcely yields, if it does yield at all, to the poodle. It can retrieve as well as the dog which is especially bred for that purpose. It can hunt the fox with the regular hounds, it can swim and dive as well as the Newfoundland dog. In the house it is one of the wariest and most intelligent of dogs, permitting no unaccustomed footstep to enter the domains without giving warning.'" Although some may think the Rev. J. G. Wood to be a little too enthusiastic in his description of the bull-terrier's good qualities, still if they have ever owned a properly trained animal of this breed, they will undoubtedly agree with the great naturalist so far as to acknowledge this particular dog to be about the best. With an ardor not excelled by his master, the bull-terrier will chase any sort of game, and will attack and fight any foe at its master's bidding. Indeed the great fault of this kind of dog is that it is inclined to be too quarrelsome among other dogs, and careful attention should be paid to correcting this fault, which may be entirely eradicated by kind and firm treatment; but should any canine bully attack your pet, woe be unto him, for, unless he comes from good fighting stock, he will rue the day he ever picked that quarrel.

How to Train Dogs

First of all teach your dog that you mean *exactly what you say*, and that he *must* obey you. To do this you should never give a foolish command; but if a thoughtless order be once given, even though you repent it as soon as it has escaped from your lips, do not hesitate, but insist upon your pupil instantly obeying—that is, if the dog, in your judgment, understands the order. Never, under any circumstances, allow him to shirk, and even a naturally stupid pup will learn to look upon your word as law and not think of disobeying.

Strict obedience to your word, whistle or slightest gesture once obtained, it is an easy task to finish the dog's education. Bear in mind that there is about as great a difference in the character and natural intelligence of dogs as there is in boys. Not only does this exist between the distinct varieties of dogs, but also between the different individuals of the same variety. All Newfoundlands possess similar characteristics, but each individual varies considerably in intelligence, amiability, and all those little traits that go to make tip a dog's character. I mention this fact that you may not be disappointed, or make your poor dog suffer because it cannot learn as fast or as much as some one you may know of. And here let me say, and impress upon your mind, that to make your dog obey, or to teach it the most difficult trick or feat, it is seldom necessary to use the whip. If the dog, as he sometimes will do, knowingly and willfully disobeys, the whip may be used sparingly; one sharp blow is generally sufficient; it should be accompanied with a reprimand in words. Never lose your patience and beat an animal in anger. To successfully train a dog it is necessary to place the greatest restraint upon your own feelings, for if you once give way to anger the dog will know it, and one-half your influence is gone. To be sure the special line of education depends upon the kind of a dog you have, and what you want him to do.

The pointer or setter you may commence to teach to "stand," at a very early age, using first a piece of meat, praising and petting him, when he does well, and reprimanding when required. Do not tire your pup out, but if he does well once let him play and sleep before trying again. As he grows older, replace the meat with a dead bird. The best sportsmen of today do not allow their bird dogs to retrieve, saying that the "mouthing" of the dead and bloody birds affects the fineness of their noses. To bring in birds, the sportsman has following at his heels a cocker spaniel, large poodle, or almost any kind of dog, who is taught to follow patiently and obediently until game is killed and he receives the order to "fetch."

Fig. 83

To Teach a Dog to Retrieve

Commence with the young pup. Almost any dog will chase a ball and very soon learn to bring it to his master. When you have taught your dog to "fetch," he may be tried with game. It is very probable that the first bird he brings will be badly "mouthed;" that is, bitten and mangled; to break him of this, prepare a ball of yarn so wound over pins that the slightest pressure will cause the points to protrude and prick any object pressed against the ball. After the dog has pricked his mouth once or twice with this ball he will learn to pick it up and carry it in the most delicate manner; he may then be tried again with a bird. This time he will probably bring it to you without so much as ruffling a feather; but if notwithstanding his experience with a ball of pins your dog still "mouths" the game, you must skin a bird and arrange the ball and pins inside the bird skin so as to prick sharply upon a light pressure; make the dog "fetch" the bird skin until he is completely broken of his bad habit of biting or "mouthing" game.

Pointers and Setters

At first you will have to give your commands by word of mouth, but if you accompany each command by an appropriate gesture, the pup will soon learn to understand and obey the slightest motion of the hand or head. The less noise there is the greater is the chance of killing game. Nothing is more unsportsmanlike than shouting in a loud voice to your dog while in the field.

After teaching a dog to "heel," "down charge," and to "hi on" at command, you may show him game and teach him to "quarter" his ground by moving yourself in the direction you wish the dog to go. The dog will not be long in understanding and obeying.

When your pointer comes to a point teach him to be steady by repeating softly, "steady, boy, steady," at the same time holding up your hand, In course of time the words may be omitted; the hand raised as a caution will keep the dog steady; but should he break point and flush the game, as a young dog is more than liable to do, you may give him the whip and at the same time use some appropriate words that the dog will remember; the next time the word without the whip will correct him. After your dog has been taught to obey, it is well to put him in the field with an old, well-trained dog.

As every sportsman has a peculiar system of his own for breaking a dog, it is scarcely necessary to give more than these few hints; only let us again caution you against using the whip too often. Spare the lash and keep a good stock of patience on hand; otherwise in breaking the dog you will also break his spirit and have a mean, treacherous animal that will slink and cringe at your slightest look, but seldom obey you when he thinks he is out of reach of the dreaded whip.

Pet Dogs

All dogs, whether intended for the field, for pets, or for companions, should be taught to follow at their master's heels at the command of "heel," to run ahead at the command of "hi on," and to drop at the command of "charge" or "down charge." When your dog learns to obey these simple commands, it will be found an easy matter to extricate and keep your canine friend out of scrapes. Suppose you have a

FIG. 84

small but pugnacious dog and in your walk you meet a large, ugly-tempered brute much too powerful for your own dog to master in the fight that is certain to ensue unless by some command you can prevent it. The strange dog will not obey you, but if you give the order to "heel" to your own dog he will follow with his nose at your heels, and the enemy will seldom if ever attack a dog while so near his master.

Study the characteristics of your dog, and by taking advantage of its peculiarities it may be taught many amusing tricks. There is a little dog called Monad, and whether his master walks, drives, sails or rows Monad always accompanies him, even sitting in front of the sliding seat of a single shell boat for hours at a time, perfectly happy and apparently conscious of the attention he attracts from all people on the shore or in the passing boats; the latter he generally salutes with a bark. Monad will, when requested to do so, close a door, sneeze, bark, or sit upon his haunches and rub his nose, besides numerous other amusing tricks.

One day Monad smelled a lighted cigar; the smoke inhaled caused him to sneeze; this gave us an idea; lighting a match we held it toward him, at the same time repeating, "sneeze! sneeze, sir!" The smoke made him sneeze, and after repeating the operation several times we held out an unlighted match and commanded him to sneeze; the dog sneezed at once. It was then an easy step to make him sneeze at the word without the match. Monad is now very proud of this accomplishment, and when desirous of "showing off" always commences by sneezing.

MONAD

In much the same manner he was taught to rub his nose by blowing in his face and repeating the words, "rub your nose." The breath coming in contact with that sensitive organ apparently tickled it and he would rub it with his paws. After one or two trials he learned to rub

his little black nose in a very comical manner whenever commanded to do so. By patting your leg with your hand and at
the same time calling your dog, it will learn to come to you
and place his fore paws against your leg. If you take advantage of this and pat the door the next time with your hand,
the dog will stand on its hind legs and rest its fore: paws
against the door. Reward him with a bit of meat or a caress,
and then opening the door a few inches go through with the
same performance, giving the command to close the door; by
degrees, as the dog learns, open the door wider, and without
moving from your chair or position in the room give the
command, "close the door, sir." The dog will by this time
understand your meaning, and resting his fore paws against
the panels, follow the door until it closes with a bang.
Perhaps there is no simple trick that excites more surprise
than this. A friend comes in and leaves the door open; you
rise, greet your friend, ask him to be seated; then, as if for the
first time noticing the fact of the door being open, speak to
your dog; the latter closes the door and lies down again by
the fireside in a most methodical manner. The friend is thoroughly convinced that that particular dog has more sense
than any other canine in the world, and ever after, when dogs
are the topic of conversation, he will tell the story of the dog
that shut the door.

In the same manner innumerable odd, amusing, or useful
tricks may be taught, among the simplest of which are the
ones which excite the most applause from spectators. If your
dog is fond of carrying a stick in his mouth, it will be an easy
matter to make him carry a basket. Take advantage of every
peculiarity of your pet's character, encouraging and develop-
ing the good points, but keeping the bad traits subdued, and
you will soon have an amusing and reasoning canine companion.

Never throw a dog into the water; it frightens him and
makes the poor animal dread a bath. Let the dog wade at
first; then by throwing sticks or other objects a little further
out each time, and commanding him to fetch, the dog will
not only learn to swim after the object, but also learn to thor-

FIG. 85

oughly enjoy the bath, and can even be taught to dive and jump off of high places. There are dogs that will jump from an elevation twelve feet above the water. Always be firm but kind; teach your dog to have confidence in you, and you may place implicit trust in your canine friend, and be sure whatever misfortune befalls you, you will have a friend who, though he be a four-footed one, will never forsake you, but live and be for the master it has learned to love and trust.

Indoor Pursuits

INDOOR PURSUITS

THERE WILL FREQUENTLY OCCUR GAPS, IN THE LONG WINTER evenings, that are hard to fill up satisfactorily, hours when, tired of reading or study, one does not know what to do. Again, occasionally through the winter one's companions and friends are likely to drop in and spend an evening. The most accomplished host is at times at a loss to know how to entertain his company, after the old, worn, threadbare games have been repeated until they have become monotonous and tiresome.

To the filling of these gaps, and for the relief of the worried host, we propose to devote a limited space in explaining and suggesting some novelties in the way of in-door amusements.

GATHERING WILD FLOWERS

WILD FLOWERS AND THEIR PRESERVATION

LONG BEFORE THE FIRST GREEN LEAVES MAKE THEIR appearance, while the snows of winter still linger in the shaded nooks, and the branches are still bare, though blushing with the full, flowing sap that tinges their tips pink, yellow, and red—when the air is filled with a sweet freshness and delicate fragrance—it is charming in our rambles to find scattered here and there upon the hill-side, down among the roots of the great trees, or under the hedges delicate little wild flowers waving on their fragile stalks with the faintest passing breeze. They are so exquisitely beautiful with their tender hues and graceful shapes, that a longing comes to possess them.

And why not keep them fresh at home? Plants live in the earth and require light, air, and moisture. All of these requirements can be and are fulfilled in thousands of homes where plants are kept, all over the world. But these are *wild flowers*. True, and they may need something to be found only in the wild woods. What, then, is it? Let us see. Earth, light, and air abound everywhere. Still, upon inspection we discover that the soil around our timid wild flowers is somewhat different from that to be found in our door-yards. But what is simpler than to take the earth up with the plant?

Transplanting Wild Flowers

Be careful to dig well all around and under the roots, so that the earth surrounding and clinging to the plant may be taken up at the same time (FIG. 86). After covering the root and soil adhering to it with a layer of clay, mud, or damp earth (FIG. 87) set the root in a large leaf, and tie it up with string or a wisp of grass (FIG 88), in order to make sure the soil does not fall off the plant. Thus secured the specimens will keep nicely until you reach home; then plant them in a shady place and keep the ground moist. Beautiful little woodland gardens are made in this way, where within a few steps of the door a glimpse may be had of the fair forest flowers.

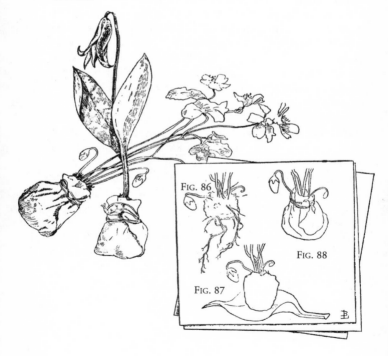

FIG. 86

FIG. 88

FIG. 87

Cut Wild Flowers

For these it is best to use a tin box of convenient size and form shutting closely. The flowers must be fresh and not at all damp; in such a box they can be kept for days bright and unfading. They may also safely be sent to friends at a distance.

Sending Flowers by Mail

If you wish to send a quantity, to pack them in a strong pasteboard or wooden box. First lay down a piece of oiled paper of the proper size; spread a thin layer of damp paper on this; next a layer of flowers, then one of thin wet paper; and so on until the box is full. Over the last layer place a dry paper, and cover this with oiled paper or tin-foil; put the lid on the box and tie it down securely.

By this method a larger number of flowers can be sent in a given space than when simply inclosed in a tin box.

In this way, daisies can be sent from New York to Cincinnati where they will arrive as fresh as when first gathered.

For the benefit of those who wish directions for sending flowers by mail, we give the following on authority of the *American Agriculturist.*

> The law passed some years since by Congress, allowing packages of plants to be sent by mail, if not over four pounds in weight, was a capital arrangement for those who lived at a distance from railroad and express offices, but it is so hampered with the various constructions given by the Post Office Department, that it is difficult to know what is required by the officials. The law now is, we believe, as follows: A package, weighing four pounds or less, can be sent at the rate of two cents per four ounces, but the writing of the words "roots" or "plants" makes a letter of it, and is charged letter postage. Nothing should be written except the address, and the package must not be sealed, or contain

any writing, and it must be so fastened that the postmaster can examine the contents if he wishes. The plants may, however, be numbered, and their names sent by letter.

Now let us think of some way in which these lovely blossoms can be preserved.

In Germany they excel in making decorations for rooms, dinner-tables, etc., of

Preserved Flowers

Bright-colored flowers are best adapted to this method. White flowers are apt to turn yellow. Jack-in-the-pulpits, clover, roses, and daisies came out beautifully when we dried them, and why should not many other kinds do just as well? Try and see.

Procure three or four quarts of fine sand; white scouring-sand is the best; wash it perfectly clean. This can be tested by pouring the water off until it looks quite clear; then dry the sand, by placing it in a clean tin in the oven. When it is dry—fully dry and cool—pour enough in a box to enable the flowers to stand by themselves, their stems embedded in the sand, which should be a mass of fine particles of uniform size.

If the flowers are cut so that they all measure nearly the same length from the tip of the blossom to the end of the stem, they can more readily be covered with sand. The flowers must be fresh and entirely free from moisture. Place them stem downward in the sandy layer, and very gently and slowly pour in the sand a little at a time, until each leaf and petal is firmly held in place (FIG. 89); then fill the box with sand nearly two inches above the level of the flowers.

It is very essential that every particle of the flower rest in the sand, and that in filling up, the smallest petal has not been bent or crumpled.

Take care not to shake the box lest the flowers inside be injured. Set it in a warm, dry place, and let it stand at least two weeks.

FIG. 89. PRESERVED FLOWERS

This manner of preserving flowers retains the color, while the shape of the leaves and petals remains unaltered. The flowers will keep for years.

There are other ways also of preserving flowers.

Pressed Flowers and Leaves

Although these are perfectly flat, they seldom fade and are very pretty and useful. Have ready a large book or a quantity of old newspapers and several weights. Use the newspapers for leaves and ferns—blotting-paper is best for the flowers. Both the flowers and leaves should be fresh and without moisture. Place them as nearly in their natural positions as possible in the book or papers, and press, allowing several thicknesses of paper between each layer. Remove the specimens to dry papers each day until perfectly dry.

Some flowers must be immersed—all but the flower head—in boiling water for a few minutes, before pressing, to prevent them from turning black. Orchids are of this nature.

If possible, it is well to obtain all parts of a plant, the roots as well as the seeds, for a more interesting collection can thus be made than from the flower and leaf alone.

It is advisable to be provided with a blank book or, what is still better, pieces of stiff white paper of uniform size on which to mount the flowers or leaves when dried; also with a small bottle of mucilage and a brush for fastening them, and some narrow strips of court-plaster or gummed paper for the stems and thicker parts of the plants. The sooner they can be mounted the better. Place them carefully on the paper, writing beneath the locality and date of finding. Flowers and leaves thus prepared make beautiful herbariums.

Leaves and Ferns for Decoration

Should you desire leaves and ferns for decoration, first press them nicely; then give them a coat of wax, by ironing them on both sides with a hot iron over which a piece of beeswax has first been rubbed. Cover the specimens completely with wax, as this renders them quite pliable, and they are no longer brittle nor easily broken. Sprays of small leaves can be pressed entire.

To heighten the effect, use dry colors, rubbing them in, and selecting those corresponding with the color of the leaves when first gathered.

The colors must be put on before tile coating of wax. Ferns should be gathered when nearly full grown, and, after they are pressed, painted light green with oil-colors; in that case the beeswax is not used. The oil in the paint, like the wax, makes the specimens more substantial, and they look quite fresh and fair.

Sometimes the late autumn frosts will bleach the ferns perfectly white; then are they even more delicate than before Nature changed their color. We have seen the Color of Flowers Changed and it is a very pretty experiment, very simple, too. Immerse the flowers in ammonia, and you will be surprised to see white lilies change to a delicate yellow, pink roses turn a lovely light green, while dark-red sweet-peas assume blue and rich purple tints; and the change is so rapid it is almost like magic.

Natural Wax Flowers

Another interesting experiment is making natural was xflowers by dipping the fresh buds and blossoms in paraffine just sufficiently hot to liquefy it; first the stems of the flowers; when these have cooled and hardened, then the flowers or sprays, holding them by the stalks and moving them gently. When they are completely covered the flowers are removed and lightly shaken, in order to throw off the superfluous wax. The flowers are then suspended until perfectly dry, when they are found hermetically sealed in a film of paraffine, while they still keep their beautiful coloring and natural forms, and for a while even their perfume.

Freshening Cut Flowers

When the heat has made them wilt, clip the stems and set the flowers in cold water; in a few hours they will regain their freshness and beauty.

Some flowers, however, must be differently treated, such as heliotrope and mignonette; these keep if placed upon damp moss or cotton and set in a cold place at night.

Rosebuds will retain their freshness for hours when not placed in water, if the ends of the stems are snipped off, and immediately tipped with melted sealing-wax; this excludes the air, and so keeps the flowers from drooping.

If roses are wilted before they can be placed in water, cut

off the ends of the stalks and immerse in very hot water for a minute or two, and they will regain their pristine freshness.

Another way to keep flowers fresh is to put a pinch of nitrate of soda into the glass each time you change the water. Nitrate of potash or saltpetre in a powder has nearly the same effect, or a drop of hartshorn. If plants are chilled by frost, shower them with cold water, and leave in a cool room; or set the pot in cold water and keep in a moderately cool place.

Crystallized Flowers

These delicate wonders sparkle and look so beautiful. They must first be dried in sand, then crystallized in the same way as dried grasses—the rougher the surface the better will it crystallize. Dissolve as much alum in boiling water as it will hold; when this is determined, pour it off and boil the solution down to one-half.

Suspend the flowers by a net-work of string tied across the top of a pail into which they must hang; then pour into the pail the boiling alum water, which must completely cover the flowers, and leave it undisturbed twelve hours, or all night.

The flowers should not touch each other or the sides of the bucket. Be careful in removing them the next morning, as the crystals are easily broken off.

Flowers or sprays of grass may be beautifully frosted by dipping them in a solution of gum-arabic and sprinkling them with powdered isinglass.

Perfume of Flowers

Flowers are not only very beautiful, but many of them possess a fragrance so sweet that we ought to learn how to keep the perfume of flowers. Rose-leaves are the most simply prepared. Take a covered jar, fill it with sweet-scented rose-leaves, and scatter through them some salt. Keep the jar closed tight, and when the petals have dried the "scent of the roses will cling to them still," so that every time the jar is opened a delicious fragrance will fill the air. Or you can cover the rose-leaves with melted lard, and leave them for a day or two in some place at a temperature of about 140° F.; then cool it and knead the lard in alcohol. Pour off the alcohol in fancy glass bottles and use as handkerchief perfume.

For varieties we find this method:

The delicate odor of pinks and other flowers may be obtained as follows Get a glass funnel, with the narrow end drawn to a point; in this place lumps of ice with salt, by which a very low temperature is produced. The funnel should be supported on an ordinary retort-stand and placed near the flowering plants, when water and the ethereal odor of the blossom will be deposited on the exterior of the glass funnel, and will trickle down to the point, from which it drops at intervals into a glass vessel below. The scent thus obtained is very perfect, but is apt to become sour in a few days unless some pure alcohol is added. By this process many odors may be procured for comparison and study. To obtain the odor in perfection the blossom must be in its prime.

Dry some sweet clover, and the fragrance will be sweet and pleasant. Fill a fancy bag of some thin sheer material with the clover, and you will find that you have imprisoned the fresh breath of summer.

Old-time lavender can be prepared in the same way.

Spring Flowers in Winter

Our thoughts so far have been for the flowers in their season. But did it ever occur to you that it is possible to have flowers in winter? If you search in the woods during December you may find, tucked away in sheltered spots, little woodland plants which, when taken up and carefully transplanted in a flower-pot and set in a sunny window, will soon begin to grow, sending up tender stems, and in about three weeks will blossom. The little fairy-like flowers seem even more beautiful coming in the cold wintry weather.

Fruit-tree twigs and sprays from flowering shrubs will blossom when the ground is white with snow, if cut from trees about the first of February, placed in well-heated water in a warm room, and the water changed every day for some that is almost but not quite hot.

The twigs being kept warm will blossom in a few weeks.

It is quite a pretty idea to take up and plant in a little flower-pot of Four-leaved Clovers. Very frequently you may find a tuft bearing only the mystic number, and should it happen to have a five- or six-leaved clover in with the others, they will add to the luck.

If you possess one of these charmed plants, it is said "good luck" will always be near at hand.

Some Old-fashioned Methods of Preserving Flowers

Besides the foregoing directions for the preservation of flowers, plants, etc., there are numerous other methods, which, although not experimentally verified by us, are no doubt as worthy of a place here as any of the former.

The following recipes have been culled from various old papers, books, etc.

The first of these ways is more properly intended for botanical collections, and is often resorted to by collectors of rare blossoms. It consists in placing flowers in alcohol, and possesses the great advantage of preserving the flowers for years, and keeping their most delicate fibers uninjured. They make invaluable specimens to sketch from, and though their beauty may be somewhat impaired by loss of color, their outlines remain perfect.

Place the flowers in a wide-mouthed bottle, fill it to the top with alcohol, cork it tightly, and cover the cork with plaster-of-Paris or melted beeswax, thus hermetically sealing it. Do not use sealing-wax, as experience has taught us that the fumes of the alcohol soften the wax, and not only spoil the neat appearance of the bottle, but allow the spirits to evaporate.

Another way is to bottle flowers. Carefully seal the ends of the stems with sealing-wax, place them in an empty bottle—both flowers and bottle must be perfectly dry—cork the bottle, and hermetically seal it with either sealing-wax or beeswax.

The next method has greater possibilities of beauty, and consequently the reader will be more interested in learning how to preserve a vaseful of flowers for a year. Take home your basket of wild flowers, "nodding violets," cowslips, bright-eyed anemones, and all the lovely offerings of the woods, and before arranging them in the vase, carefully seal the stem of each flower. Place a glass shade over the vase; be careful that flowers, vase, and shade are perfectly dry; then fill up the groove in the wood, in which the shade stands, with melted wax. By covering the wax with chenille it can be perfectly hidden.

Flowers kept in this way will last for a twelvemonth.

The flowers preserved in an empty bottle may be taken out, the wax cut from the stems, and, if arranged in a bouquet, will last as long as perfectly fresh flowers.

Those in the alcohol lose their color after being immersed for a time, and will not last when removed from the alcohol.

In following any of these directions be careful not to tie the flowers. No string must be used. The flower stems must be loose and separate from each other.

A florist of much experience in preserving bouquets for an indefinite period gives this recipe for keeping bouquets fresh for a long time.

When you receive a bouquet sprinkle it lightly with fresh water, then put it into a vessel containing some soapsuds; this will take the place of the roots and keep the flowers bright as new. Take the bouquet out of the suds every morning, and lay it sideways, the stems entering first, in clean water; keep it there a minute or two, then take it out, and sprinkle the flowers lightly by the hand with water; replace it in the soapsuds, and it will bloom as fresh as when first gathered.

The soapsuds need changing every three or four days. By observing these rules a bouquet can be kept bright and beautiful for at least a month, and will last longer in a very passable state.

To keep flowers or fruit perfectly fresh for a whole year, mix one pound of nitre with two pounds of sal ammoniac and three pounds of clean common sand. Then in dry weather take fruit of any sort which is not fully ripe, allowing the stalks to remain, and put them one by one into an open glass until it is quite full; cover the glass with oiled cloth, closely tied down. Put the glass three or four inches down in the earth in a dry cellar, and surround it on all sides to the depth of three or four inches with the above mixture. The fruit will thus be preserved quite fresh all the year round.

Rose-water

"When the bushes of roses are full,
As most of them are about June,
'Tis high time to gather, or pull
The leaves of the flowers. As soon
As you've picked all you need for the time,
To each *quart of water* unite
A *peck of the leaves,* which, if prime—
And they will be, if pulled off aright—
May be *placed in a still* near at hand,
On a *very slow fire.* When done,
Bottle off, and permit it to *stand*
For three days ere you cork down each one."

KNOTS, BENDS, AND HITCHES

THE ART OF TYING KNOTS IS AN ALMOST NECESSARY ADJUNCT to not a few recreations.

Any one who has been aboard a yacht or a sail-boat, must have realized that the safety of the vessel and all aboard may be imperilled by ignorance or negligence in the tying of a knot or fastening of a rope.

With some, the knack of tying a good, strong knot in a heavy rope, or light cord, seems to be a natural gift; it is certainly a very convenient accomplishment, and one that with practice and a little perseverance may be acquired even by those who at first make the most awkward and bungling attempts.

A bulky, cumbersome knot is not only ungainly, but is generally insecure.

As a rule, the strength of a knot is in direct proportion to its neat and handsome appearance.

To our minds, it is as necessary that the archer should know how to make the proper loops at the end of his bow-string, as it is that a hunter should understand how to load his gun.

Every fisherman should be able to join two lines neatly and securely, and should know the best and most expeditious method of attaching an extra hook or fly; and any boy who rigs up a hammock or swing with a "granny," or other insecure knot, deserves the ugly tumble and sore bones that are more than liable to result from his ignorance.

A knot, nautically speaking, is a "bend" that is more permanent than a "hitch." A knot properly tied never slips, nor does it jam so that it cannot be readily untied. A "hitch" might be termed a temporary bend, as it is seldom relied upon for permanent service. The "hitch" is so made that it can be cast off, or unfastened, more quickly than a knot.

It is impossible for the brightest to learn to make "knots, bends, and hitches" by simply reading over a description of the methods; for, although he may understand them at the time, five minutes after reading the article the process will have escaped his memory; but if he take a piece of cord or rope, and sit down with the diagrams in front of him, he will find little difficulty in managing the most complicated knots; and he will not only acquire an accomplishment from which he can derive infinite amusement for himself and a means of entertainment for others, but the knowledge gained may, in case of accident by fire or flood, be the means of saving both life and property.

The accompanying diagrams show a number of useful and important bends, splices, etc. To simplify matters, let us commence with FIG. 90, and go through the diagrams in the order in which they come:

The "English," or "common single fisherman's knot" (FIG. 90, I), is neat and strong enough for any ordinary strain. The diagram shows the knots before being tightened and drawn together.

When exceptional strength is required it can be obtained by joining the lines in the ordinary single fisherman's knot (FIG. 90, I.), and pulling each of the half knots as tight as possible, then drawing them within an eighth of an inch of each other and wrapping between with fine gut that has been previously softened in water, or with light-colored silk.

An additional line, or a sinker may be attached by tying a knot in the end of the extra line, and inserting it between the parts of the single fisherman's knot before they are drawn together and tightened.

The "fisherman's double half knot," FIG. 90 (II and III). After the gut has been passed around the main line and through itself, it is passed around the line once more and through the same loop again, and drawn close.

FIG. 90 (IV, V and IX). Here are three methods of joining

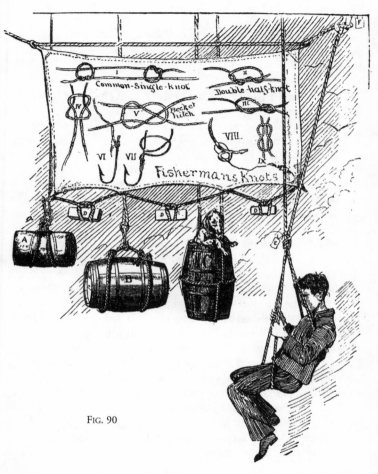

FIG. 90

the ends of two lines together; the diagrams explain them much better than words can. Take a piece of string, try each one, and test their relative strength.

FIG. 90 (VI). It often happens, while fishing, that a hook is caught in a snag, or by some other means lost. The diagram shows the most expeditious manner of attaching another hook by what is known as the "sinker hitch," described further on (FIG. 90, D, D, D, and FIG. 91, XIV, XV, and XVI).

FIG. 90, VII is another and more secure method of attaching a hook by knitting the line on with a succession of hitches.

How To Make a Horse-Hair Watch-Guard

The same hitches are used in the manufacture of horse-hair watch-guards, much in vogue with the boys in some sections of the country. As regularly as "kite-time," "top-time," or "ball-time," comes "horse-hair watch-guard time."

About once a year the rage for making watch-guards used to seize the boys of our school, and by some means or other almost every boy would have a supply of horse-hair on hand. With the first tap of the bell for recess, some fifty hands would dive into the mysterious depths of about fifty pockets, and before the bell had stopped ringing about fifty watch-guards, in a more or less incomplete state, would be produced.

Whenever a teamster's unlucky stars caused him to stop near the school-house, a chorus of voices greeted him with "Mister, please let us have some hair from your horses' tails."

The request was at first seldom refused, possibly because its nature was not at the time properly understood; but lucky was the boy considered who succeeded in pulling a supply of hair from the horses' tails without being interrupted by the heels of the animals or by the teamster, who, when he saw the swarm of boys tugging at his horses' tails, generally repented his first good-natured assent, and with a gruff" Get out, you young rascals!" sent the lads scampering to the school-yard fence.

Select a lot of long hair of the color desired; make it into a switch about the eighth of an inch thick by tying one end in a simple knot. Pick out a good, long hair and tie it around the switch close to the knotted end; then take the free end of the single hair in your right hand and pass it under the switch on one side, thus forming a loop through which the end of the hair must pass after it is brought up and over from the other side of the switch. Draw the knot tight by pulling the free end of the hair as shown by Fig. 90, VII. Every time this operation is repeated a wrap and a knot is produced. The knots follow each other in a spiral around the switch, giving it a very pretty, ornamented appearance. When one hair is used up select another, and commence knitting with it as you did with the first, being careful to cover and conceal the short end of the first hair, and to make the knots on the second commence where the former stop. A guard made of white horse-hair looks as if it might be composed of spun glass, and produces a very odd and pretty effect. A black one is very genteel in appearance.

Further Knots and Hitches

FIG. 90, VIII. shows a simple and expeditious manner of attaching a trolling hook to a fish-line.

FIG. 90, F is a hitch used on shipboard, or wherever lines and cables are used. It is called the Blackwall hitch.

FIG. 90, E is a fire-escape made of a double bowline knot, useful as a sling for hoisting persons up or letting them down from any high place; the window of a burning building, for instance. Fig. 91, XVIII, XIX and XX show how this knot is made. It is described on the following page.

FIG. 90, A is a "bale hitch," made of a loop of rope. To make it, take a piece of rope that has its two ends joined; lay the rope down and place the bale on it; bring the loop opposite you up, on that side of the bale, and the loop in front up, on the side of the bale next to you; thrust the latter loop under and through the first and attach the hoisting rope. The heavier the object to be lifted, the tighter the hitch becomes. An excellent substitute for a shawl-strap can be made of a cord by using the bale hitch, the loop at the top being a first-rate handle.

FIG. 90, B is called a cask sling, and C is called a butt sling. The manner of making these last two and their uses may be seen by referring to the illustration. It will be noticed that a line is attached to the bale hitch in a peculiar manner (FIG. 90, A). This is called the "anchor bend." If while aboard a

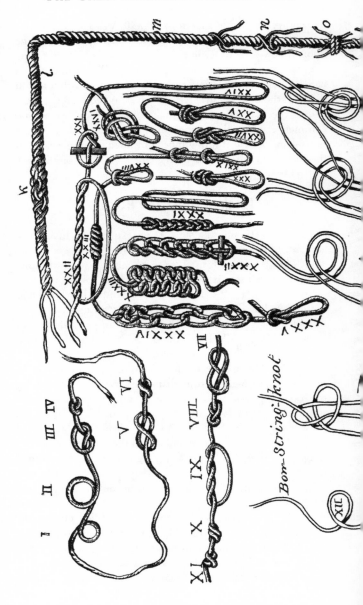

Bow-string-knot

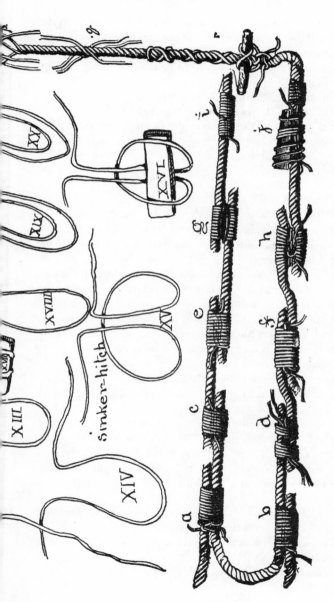

FIG. 91. KNOTS AND SPLICES

sail-boat you have occasion to throw a bucket over for water, you will find the anchor bend a very convenient and safe way to attach a line to the bucket handle.

FIG. 91, I and II are loops showing the elements of the simplest knots.

FIG. 91, III is a simple knot commenced.

FIG. 91, IV shows the simple knot tightened.

FIG. 91, V and VI show how the Flemish knot looks when commenced and finished.

FIG. 91, VII and VIII show a "rope knot" commenced and finished.

FIG. 91, IX is a double knot commenced.

FIG. 91, X is the same completed.

FIG. 91, XI shows a back view of the double knot.

FIG. 91, XII is the first loop of a "bowline knot." One end of the line is supposed to be made fast to some object. After the turn or loop (FIG. 91, XII) is made, hold it in position with your left hand and pass the end of the line up through the loop or turn you have just made, behind and over the line above, then down through the loop again, as shown in the diagram (FIG. 91, XIII); pull it tight and the knot is complete. The "sinker hitch" is a very handy one to know, and the variety of uses it may be put to will be at once suggested by the diagrams.

Lines that have both ends made fast may have weights attached to them by means of the sinker hitch (FIG. 90, D, D, D).

To accomplish this, first gather up some slack and make it in the form of the loop (FIG. 91, XIV); bend the loop back on itself (FIG. 91, XV) and slip the weight through the double loop thus formed (FIG. 91, XVI); draw tight by pulling the two top lines, and the sinker hitch is finished (FIG. 91, XVII).

The "fire-escape sling" previously mentioned, and illustrated by FIG. 90, E, is made with a double line.

Proceed at first as you would to make a simple bowline knot (FIG. 91, XVIII).

After you have run the end loop up through the turn (FIG.

91, XIX.), bend it downward and over the bottom loop and turn, then up again until it is in the position shown in FIG. 91, XX.; pull it downward until the knot is tightened, as in FIG. 90, E, and it makes a safe sling in which to lower a person from any height. The longer loop serves for a seat, and the shorter one, coming under the arms, makes a rest for the back.

FIG. 91, XXI is called a "boat knot," and is made with the aid of a stick. It is an excellent knot for holding weights which may want instant detachment. To detach it, lift the weight slightly and push out the stick, and instantly the knot is untied.

FIG. 91, XXII. Commencement of a "six-fold knot."

FIG. 91, XXIII. Six-fold knot completed by drawing the two ends with equal force. A knot drawn in this manner is said to be "nipped."

FIG. 91, XXIV. A simple hitch or "double" used in making loop knots.

FIG. 91, XXV. "Loop knot."

FIG. 91, XXVI shows how the loop knot is commenced.

FIG. 91, XXVII is the "Dutch double knot," sometimes called the "Flemish loop."

FIG. 91, XXVIII shows a common "running knot."

FIG. 91, XXIX. A running knot with a check knot to hold.

FIG. 91, XXX. A running knot checked.

FIG. 91, XXXI. The right hand part of the rope shows how to make the double loop for the "twist knot." The left hand part of the same rope shows a finished twist knot. It is made by taking a half turn on both the right hand and left hand lines of the double loop, and passing the end through the "bight" (loop) so made.

Whip-Lashes

FIG. 91, XXXII is called the "chain knot," which is often used in braiding leather whip-lashes. To make a "chain knot," fasten one end of the thong or line; make a simple loop and pass it over the left hand; retain hold of the free end with the right hand; with the left hand seize the line above the right hand and draw a loop through the loop already formed; finish the knot by drawing it tight with the left hand. Repeat the operation until the braid is of the required length, then secure it by passing the free end through the last loop.

FIG. 91, XXXIII shows a double chain knot.

FIG. 91, XXXIV is a double chain knot pulled out. It shows how the free end is thrust through the last loop.

FIG. 91, XXXV. Knotted loop for end of rope, used to prevent the end of the rope from slipping, and for various other purposes.

Splices, Timber-Hitches, etc.

Although splices may not be as useful as knots and hitches, for the benefit of those among our readers who are interested in the subject, We have introduced a few bands and splices on the cables partly surrounding Fig. 91.

FIG. 91, *a* shows the knot and upper side of a "simple band."

FIG. 91, *b* shows under side of the same.

FIG. 91, *c* and *d* show a tie with cross ends. To hold the ends of the cords, a turn is taken tinder the strands.

FIG. 91, *e* and *f.* Bend with cross strands, one end looped over the other.

FIG. 91, *g* shows the upper side of the "necklace tie."

FIG. 91, *h* shows the underside of the same. The advantage of this tie is that the greater the strain on the cords, the tighter it draws the knot.

FIG. 91, *i* and *j* are slight modifications of *g* and *h*.

FIG. 91, *p* shows the first position of the end of the ropes for making the splice *k*. Untwist the strands and put the ends of two ropes together as close as possible, and place the strands of the one between the strands of the other alternately, so as to interlace, as in *k*. This splice should only be used when there is not time to make the "long splice," as the short one is not very strong.

From *l* to *m* is a long splice, made by underlaying the

strands of each of the ropes joined about hail the length of the splice, and putting each strand of the one between two of the other; *q* shows the strands arranged for the long splice.

FIG. 91, *n* is a simple mode of making a hitch on a rope.

FIG. 91, *o* is a "shroud knot."

FIG. 91, *r* shows a very convenient way to make a handle on a rope, and is used upon large ropes when it is necessary for several persons to take hold to pull.

FIG. 92, A. Combination of half hitch and timber hitch.

FIG. 92, B. Ordinary half hitch.

FIG. 92, C. Ordinary timber hitch.

FIG. 92, D. Another timber hitch, called the "clove hitch.'

FIG. 92, E. "Hammock hitch," used for binding bales of goods or cloth.

FIG. 92, F. "Lark-head knot," used by sailors and boatmen for mooring their crafts.

FIG. 92, P shows a lark-head fastening to a running knot.

FIG. 92, G is a double-looped lark-head.

FIG. 92, H shows a double-looped lark-head knot fastened to the ring of a boat.

FIG. 92, I is a "treble lark-head." To make it you must first tie a single lark-head, then divide the two heads and use each singly, as shown in the diagram.

FIG. 92, J shows a simple boat knot with one turn.

FIG. 92, K. "Crossed running knot." It is a strong and handy tie, not as difficult to make as appears to be.

FIG. 92, L is the bowline knot, described by the diagrams XII and XIII. (FIG. 91). The free end of the knot is made fast by binding it to the "bight" or the loop. It makes a secure sling for a man to sit in at his work among the rigging.

FIG. 92, M, N, and O. "Slip clinches," or "sailors' knots."

FIG. 92, Q shows a rope fastened by the chain hitch. The knot at the left-hand end explains a simple way to prevent a rope from unravelling.

FIG. 92, R shows a timber hitch; when tightened the line binds around the timber so that it will not slip.

FIG. 92, S. Commencement of simple lashing knot.

FIG. 92, T. Simple lashing knot finished.

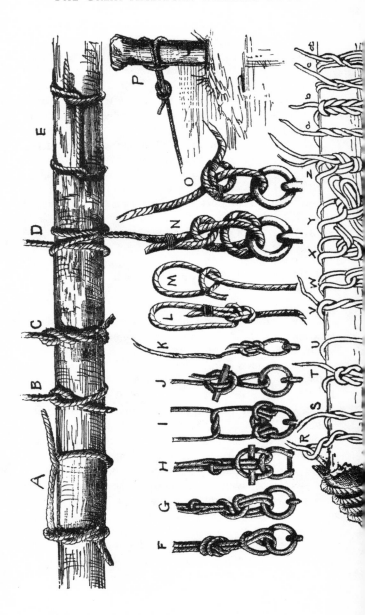

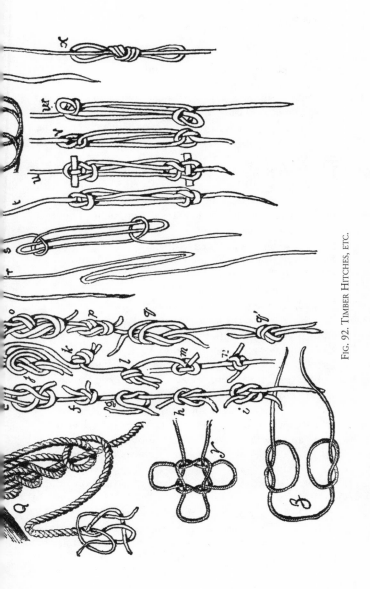

FIG. 92. TIMBER HITCHES, ETC.

165

Fig. 92, U. "Infallible loop;" not properly a timber hitch, but useful in a variety of ways, and well adapted for use in archery.

Fig. 92, V Same as R, reversed. It looks like it might give way under a heavy strain, but it will not.

Fig. 92, W. Running knot with two ends.

Fig. 92, X. Running knot with a check knot that can only be opened with a marline-spike.

Fig. 92, Y. A two-ended running knot with a check to the running loops. This knot can be untied by drawing both ends of the cord.

Fig. 92, Z. Running knot with two ends, fixed by a double Flemish knot. When you wish to encircle a timber with this tie, pass the ends, on which the check knot is to be, through the cords before they are drawn tight. This will require considerable practice.

Fig. 92, *a* shows an ordinary twist knot.

Fig. 92, *a'* shows the form of loop for builder's knot.

Fig. 92, *b*. Double twist knot.

Fig. 92, *c*. Builder's knot finished.

Fig. 92, *d* represents a double builder's knot.

Fig. 92, *e*. "Weaver's knot," same as described under the head of Becket hitch (Fig. 90, V).

Fig. 92, *f.* Weaver's knot drawn tight.

Fig. 92, *g* shows how to commence a reef knot. This is - useful for small ropes; with ropes unequal in size the knot is likely to draw out of shape, as in.

Fig. 92, *h* shows a reef knot completed.

Of all knots, avoid the "granny;" it is next to useless under a strain, and marks the tier as a "landlubber."

Fig. 92, *i* shows a granny knot; *n* shows a granny under strain.

Fig. 92, *j* shows the commencement of a common "rough knot."

Fig. 92, *k*. The front view of finished knot.

Fig. 92, *1*. The back view of finished knot. Although this knot will not untie nor slip, the rope is likely to part at one side if the strain is great. Awkward as it looks, this tie is very useful at times on account of the rapidity with which it can be made.

FIG. 92, *o* and *p*. Knot commenced and finished, used fot the same purposes as the Flemish knot.

FIG. 92, *q* and *q'*. An ordinary knot with the ends used separately.

FIG. 92, *s*. Sheep-shank, or dog-shank as it is sometimes called, is very useful in shortening a line. Suppose, for instance, a swing is much longer than necessary, and you wish to shorten it without climbing aloft to do so; it can be done with a sheep-shank.

FIG. 92, *r* shows the first position of the two loops. Take two half hitches, and you have a bend of the form shown by *s*. Pull tightly from above and below the shank, and you will find that the rope is shortened securely enough for ordinary strain.

FIG. 92, *t*. Shortening by loop and turns made where the end of the rope is free.

FIG. 92, *u*. A shortened knot that can be used when either end is free.

FIG. 92, *v*, w, and x. Shortening knots.

FIG. 92, *y* and *z*. A "true lover's knot," and the last one that you need to practise on, for one of these knots is as much as most persons can attend to, and ought to last a lifetime.

SCRAP-BOOK AND HOME-MADE BOOK-COVERS

THE FASHION OF COLLECTING PICTURED ADVERTISING CARDS, so much in vogue among the children a few years ago, seems to have run its course, and dying out, it has left on the young collectors' hands more cards than they know well what to do with. Many of the collections have been pasted in scrap-books, of which the children have long since tired. While examining one of these volumes with its row after row of cards, it occurred to us that these advertisements might be utilized in a new way by dividing and combining them. The experiment proved a success, and we will now try to show you how, with the aid of scissors and mucilage, the pictures which have become so familiar may be made to undergo changes that are indeed wonderful.

Mother Goose Scrap-book

The nursery scrap-books made of linen or paper cambric are, perhaps, familiar to most of our readers; but for the benefit of those who may not yet have seen these durable little books, we will give the following directions for making one: Cut from a piece of strong linen, colored paper cambric, or white muslin, four squares twenty-four inches long by twelve inches wide. Button-hole-stitch the edges all around with some bright-colored worsted, then place the squares neatly together and stitch them directly through the center with strong thread (FIG. 93). Fold them over, stitch again, as in FIG. 94, and your book is finished and ready for the pictures.

FIG. 93. SCRAP-BOOK OPENED AND STITCHED
THROUGH THE CENTER

FIG. 94. SCRAP-BOOK FOLDED
AND AGAIN STITCHED

It is in the preparation of these pictures that you will find the novelty of the plan we propose. Instead of pasting in those cards which have become too familiar to awaken much interest, let the young book-makers design and form their own pictures by cutting special figures, or parts of figures, from different cards, and then pasting them together so as to form new combinations.

Any subject which pleases the fancy can be illustrated in this way, and you will soon be deeply interested in the work and delighted at the strange and striking pictorial characters that can be produced by ingenious combinations.

Stories and little poems may be very nicely and aptly illustrated; but the "Mother Goose Melodies" are, perhaps, the most suitable subjects with which to interest younger chil-

Fig. 95. "Three Wise Men
of Gotham"

Fig. 98. "Little Jack
Horner"

Fig. 96. Figures cut from
Advertising Cards

Fig. 97. Figures cut from
Christmas Cards

dren, as they will be easily recognized by the little folk. Take, for instance, the "Three Wise Men of Gotham," who went to sea in a bowl. Will not Fig. 95 serve very well as an illustration of the subject? Yet these figures are cut from advertising cards, and no two from the same card. Fig. 96 shows the materials, Fig. 95 the result of combining them.

Again, the little man dancing so gayly (Fig. 97) is turned into "Little Jack Homer" eating his Christmas pie (Fig. 98), by merely cutting off his legs and substituting a dress-skirt and pair of feet clipped from another card. The Christmas pie in his lap is from still another card.

In making pictures of this kind, figures that were originally standing may be forced to sit; babies may be placed in arms which, on the cards they were stolen from, held only cakes of soap, perhaps, or boxes of blacking; heads may be ruthlessly torn from bodies to which they belong, and as ruthlessly clapped upon strange shoulders; and you will be surprised to see what amusing, and often excellent, illustrations present themselves as the result of a little ingenuity in clipping and pasting.

Transformation Scrap-Book

This will be found exceedingly amusing on account of the various and ever-changing pictures it presents.

Unlike any other, where the picture once pasted in must remain ever the same, the transformation scrap-book alters one picture many times. To work these transformations a blank book is the first article required one eight inches long by six and a half or seven wide is a good size.

Cut the pages of this book across, one-third of the way down. Fig. 99 shows how this should be done. The three-cornered piece cut out near the binding allows the pages to be turned without catching or tearing. Leave the first page uncut; also the one in the middle of the book.

Cut from picture-cards, or old toy-books which have colored illustrations, the odd and funny figures of men and women, boys and girls, selecting those which will give a variety of costumes and attitudes.

FIG. 99. TRANSFORMATION
SCRAP-BOOK WITH PAGES CUT

Paste a figure of a woman or girl on the first page, placing it so that when the lower part of the next page is turned, the upper edge of it will come across the neck of the figure where it is joined on to the shoulders.

Cut the heads from the rest of the pictured women, and choosing a body as different as possible from the one just used, paste it upon the lower part of the next page, directly under the head belonging to the first body. Upon the upper part of the same page paste any one of the other heads, being careful to place it so that it will fit the body. Continue in this way, pasting the heads upon the upper, and the bodies on the lower, part of the page, until the space allowed for the women is filled up; then, commencing at the page left in the middle of the book, paste upon it the figure of a man, and continue in the same manner as with the woman, until the spaces are all used and the book is complete.

The combinations formed in this way are very funny. Old heads with young bodies; young heads with old bodies; then one head with a great variety of bodies, and so on.

The first picture may represent a man, tall and thin, dressed in a rowing costume, as shown in the illustration. Turn the lower part of the next page, and no longer is he thin and tall, but short and stout, the position of this body giving the expression of amazement, even to the face. The next page turned shows him to be neither tall nor short, thick nor thin, but a soldier, well-proportioned, who is looking over his shoulder in the most natural manner possible.

The figures in the illustration were cut from advertising cards, and the head belongs to none of the bodies.

A curious fact in arranging the pictures in this way is that the heads all look as though they might really belong to any of the various bodies given them.

Instead of having but one figure on a page, groups may be formed of both men and women, and in the different arrangement of the figures they can be made very ludicrous indeed.

An Album

A scrap-book for older children, which might be termed more fitly an album can be made by mounting engravings, wood-cuts, photographs, and water-colors on pieces of thin card-board all of the same size. If any one subject be chosen, and such pictures selected as tend in some way to illustrate that subject, the book will prove more interesting in the making, and will be quite valuable when finished.

There will be no difficulty in mounting the pictures; simply paste them on the card-board with good flour-paste, and press under a heavy weight, keeping them perfectly neat and free from smears of paste on the edges. When two or more are mounted at the same time, place clean pieces of blotting-paper between, pile one upon another, and put the heavy weight on top.

Home-made Book-cover

Such a scrap-book should be bound in a home-made book cover which is made in this way:

Take two pieces of heavy card-board a trifle larger than the book you wish to cover, make three holes near the edge of each (FIG. 100) and corresponding holes in the edges of the book, which must not be too thick-that is, contain too many leaves; pass narrow ribbons through these holes and tie in bow-knots, as in FIG. 101. If the leaves of the book are thin, more holes can be made in the back and the covers laced together with silk cord (FIG. 102).

These book-covers may be beautifully decorated by anyone who can paint in water-colors, and tinted card-board can also be used for them. They are pretty, and suitable as covers for manuscript poems or stories, or for a collection of autographs.

Fig. 100. One Side of Book-cover with Holes cut near the Edge

Fig. 101. Book-cover Tied with Ribbons

Fig. 102. Book-cover Laced together with Silk Cord

Flour-paste

In making any kind of scrap-book it is very necessary that the paste used should be good. If the paste is poor, the pictures will peel off or the paste turn sour. We can recommend an excellent one for this recipe.

Mix one-half cup of flour with enough cold water to make a very thin batter, which must be smooth and free from lumps; put the batter on top of the stove—not next to the fire—in a tin sauce-pan, and stir continually until it boils; then remove from the stove, add three drops of oil of cloves, and pour the paste into a cup or tumbler. This will keep for a long time and will not become sour.

PRACTICAL TAXIDERMY

TO THE PRACTICAL NATURALIST A KNOWLEDGE OF TAXIDERMY is not only an interesting accomplishment from which to derive amusement, but is almost an absolute necessity, an indispensable adjunct to his profession. Probably there is no study the pursuit of which affords such opportunities for physical exercise and real healthy enjoyment as that of natural history. It is a study that, by broadening the horizon of thought, enlarges the capacity for pleasure. To the pride of the sportsman in exhibiting the results of his skill and success, the naturalist adds the intelligent pleasure of acquiring a more complete knowledge of the life and habits, nature and anatomy of his trophies, as well as the ability to detect at a glance any unknown genus or rare variety he may capture; and here the practical knowledge of taxidermy enables him to properly preserve the otherwise perishable specimen.

Do not suppose that after reading the following directions you can sit down, and, without any previous experience, set up a bird as neatly and perfectly as one of those you see in the museums or show windows. On the contrary, you must expect to make one or two dismal failures, but each failure will teach you what to avoid in the next attempt.

Let us suppose an owl has been lowering around suspiciously near the pigeon house or chicken coop, and that you have shot the rascal. Do not throw him away. What a splendid ornament he will make for the library! How appropriate that wise old face of his will be peering over the top of the book-case! (FIG. 103). He must be skinned and stuffed! With a damp sponge carefully remove any bloodstains there may be upon his plumage. Plug up the mouth and nostrils with cotton; also insert cotton in all the shot holes, to prevent any

FIG. 103. STUFFED AND MOUNTED

more blood oozing out and soiling the feathers. You may then lay him aside in some cool place until you are ready to begin the operation of skinning and stuffing the owl.

Measure the length of the bird, following the curves of the form, from root of tail to top of head, and its girth about the body; make a note of these figures.

Skinning

Place the bird on its back upon the table, in such a position that the head will be toward your left hand; then, with the knife in your right hand you are ready to make the incision.

With your left hand separate the feathers, left and right, from the apex of the breast-bone to the tail (FIG. 104). Cut a straight slit through the skin between these points, using the utmost care to prevent the knife penetrating the flesh or the inner skin which encloses the intestines. With a bird as large as the owl, you will find that you can easily separate the skin from the flesh with your fingers, though it may be best to use a blunt instrument, such as a small ivory paper-cutter, to reach the back by passing it underneath the skin. In removing the skin you must try to shove in lieu of pulling, lest you stretch it out of shape. Press as lightly as possible upon the bird, stopping occasionally to take a view to see that all is right and that the feathers are not being soiled or broken. When you come to the head do not let the skin dangle from your hand or its own weight will stretch it. Bearing these things in mind, you can commence removing the skin in the following manner: Press the skin apart at the incision, and dust the exposed part with Indian meal to absorb any fluids that may escape; carefully lift the skin on one side and separate from muscles of the breast with the point of your knife and a small ivory paper-folder alternately, as occasion may require, until the leg is reached and you have approached as near as possible to the wings. Having accomplished this, and dusted again with the Indian meal, the thighs must be pressed inward and the skin turned back far enough to allow you to use your knife and disarticulate the hip-joint. Bend the tail toward the back; keep down the detached skin upon each side of the incision with the thumb and first finger of the left hand; then with your knife make a deep cut, exposing the backbone at a point near the oil gland, which you will find near the root of the tail; sever the backbone near this point, but be careful to leave a large enough piece of it to support the tail feathers.

Take the part of the body which is now denuded of the skin in the left hand and peel the skin upward to the wings; during this operation your knife or small scissors may be used to cut any of the tendons which are met with. Separate the wings from the body at the shoulder-joint. Next turn your attention to the head and neck. Push the skin back toward the head, after the manner of removing a kid glove from the finger, until the back part of the skull is laid bare; then with your knife

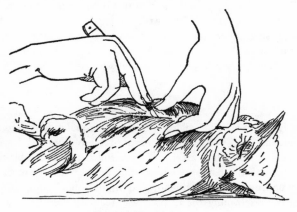

FIG. 104. THE INCISION

detach the vertebre (neck bone) from the head. This will sever all connection between the body and the skin. The dismembered, denuded carcass may be thrown aside and your attention turned to skinning the head, which remember in an owl is so large in proportion to the neck that care must be used in drawing the skin of the neck over it, lest you stretch the skin. A great deal depends upon the delicacy of your touch, especially when you reach the eyes. Work slowly; cut the ears close to the skull; do not cut either the eyelid or the eyeball, but separate them carefully; then remove the eyes, which can be done by breaking the slender bones which separate the orbits (eye-holes) in the skull from the top of the mouth. Cut away all flesh from the neck; at the same time remove a small portion of the base of the skull. Through the opening thus made extract the brains with a small spoon or some similar instrument, after which draw the tongue through the same cavity. After removing all fleshy particles from the head and neck, and scraping out the eye-holes, paint them with arsenical soap and stuff them tightly with cotton. Be careful not to detach the skin from the bill, as the skull must be left in place. Coat the interior of the skull with arsenical soap and fill it with tow.

The wings and legs still remain intact. Push back the wings to the first joint; lay the bones bare, removing all the meat. Paint with arsenical soap and return them to their places. Go through the same process with the legs and rump; and after all flesh and fatty matter have been removed, paint the whole interior of the skin thoroughly with arsenical soap, and you are ready to begin the operation of stuffing

Stuffing

Take a piece of straight wire (size 20) equal in length to the measurement you made from root of tail to top of head; wind about it a bunch of excelsior (straw will answer as a substitute for excelsior shavings); secure this to the wire by repeated wrappings of stout thread, and mould the bundle into a shape resembling the bird's body; regulate the girth by the measurement you noted down for that purpose before you

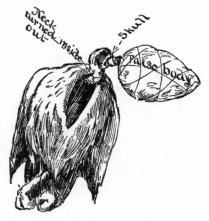

FIG. 105. OWL-SKIN AND FALSE BODY

commenced the skinning process. When you have completed the artificial body there will, of course, be a portion of the wire still bare, which represents the neck. File the extremity of this wire to a sharp point, then force it diagonally up through the skull to the top, where it must be clinched; wrap the neck wire between the artificial body and the head with cotton batting (FIG. 105). Now draw the skin back so as to cover the artificial neck and body.

The eyelids must be carefully pulled in place over the cotton in the eye-holes, or orbits; pull the eyelids up nicely, to make the parts about the eye appear plump and natural. Push more cotton down the throat until it has a round, real look. For the legs use two pieces of wire, each sharpened at one end. The taxidermist must shove the wire through the ball of the foot and guide it with the other hand up along the side of the bones of the leg, the skin being turned back for that purpose (FIG. 106). This figure shows the leg with skin turned back, as it appears

FIG. 106. WIRING THE LEG

FIG. 107. SHOWING HOW LEG-WIRE IS ATTACHED TO FALSE BODY

when the wire is pushed through.

Wind cotton around both wire and bone to the natural thickness of the thigh, and go through the same process with the other leg; then push the wires clear through the artificial body and bend the protruding ends into a hook form (FIG. 107). Taking hold at the part extending from the bottom of the foot, pull the wire of each leg down until the hooks fasten firmly into the body. The ends of the wires protruding from the foot are left to fasten the bird to its perch, which is done either by wrapping the wires around the perch or by thrusting them through holes made for the purpose and clinching the ends. With a few stitches sew up the hole in the breast. For small birds this is not necessary. After your owl is set up in this manner, gather the wings up close to the body and fasten them there by thrusting two wires, one from each side, diagonally through the skin of the second joint.

If you wish the tail to be spread you must push a wire across the body through each feather.

Eyes can be made of white marbles painted yellow with black centres, but glass eyes are better and cost very little. To fix the eyes, put a touch of glue upon the cotton in each orbit and insert the glass eyes, being careful to place them properly under the eyelids; with a sharp needle pull the lids nicely in place.

The stuffing of the bird is now finished, and it may be placed upon the branch in some natural position (see FIG. 103).

The attitude fixed, it only remains to put the feathers in their natural order as smoothly and regularly as possible, and to keep them in place by winding a thread over the body very loosely, beginning at the head and winding until all the feathers are secured (FIG. 108). The bird must be left in some dry place for several days. When it is perfectly dry the thread may be taken off and all protruding wires cut close to the body. The specimen is now ready for the parlor or library.

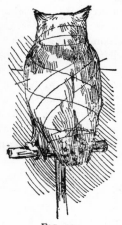

FIG. 108.

The above directions, with very little modification, will serve for any other bird. For practice, a chicken is the best subject, as it is easily obtained and large enough not to be readily damaged by the awkwardness of a beginner.

The more tools you have the better, but if our reader has carefully read the foregoing description he must have noticed that during the whole process of skinning and stuffing the owl the only tools used were such as are within the reach of every one—a penknife, a paper-cutter, small spoon (a mustard-spoon will answer), and a thread and needle. Arsenical soap is the only material used not likely to be easily procured. This preparation is of course very poisonous and should be so labelled. It can be procured of any taxidermist or made by any druggist from the following recipe of Bécœur:

Arsenic in powder	2 pounds
Camphor	5 ounces
White soap	2 pounds
Salt of tartar	12 ounces
Powdered lime	4 ounces

Mr. J. Wallace, the taxidermist, recommends the following recipe: "Dissolve ten pounds of finely cut, best white soap in warm water; add one pound of potash; thicken with pipe-clay and a little lime to give the preparation body; heat and stir well. When cooling add ten pounds of arsenic." Of course the young beginner will not need any such quantity as is represented in either of these recipes, but if he goes to the druggist that gentleman can make the soap in any quantity desired. The utmost care must be observed in handling this preparation and keeping it out of the reach of children and animals, although it is not very tempting in taste or looks and hence not as dangerous as other compounds might be.

A New Manner of Preserving Fish

The boys at school used to say, "You cannot eat your apple and keep it." Being not only fond of fishing and fish, but also taking an interest in the study of ichthyology, the question with us has been, How can we eat our fish and still preserve them for future reference? A few experiments and several failures suggested a plan which has proved partially successful.

Having caught a very large bass or trout that you would like to preserve as a trophy, or some odd-looking fish that you want to keep as a specimen, the following is the plan to adopt:

Place your fish upon a piece of paper of any kind you may have, or a piece of birch bark; spread out the fins and trace a careful and accurate outline; then with your pocket-knife remove the tail at a point just beyond its junction with the body of the fish; in the same manner cut off the fins, being careful not to injure them; a small portion of flesh will be attached to each; this must be removed with your knife. Put the fins in a safe place, and again taking your knife, insert the blade under the gill and cut up to the center of the top of the head; split the head down in a line exactly on the top to the upper jaw; carefully cut through this and the lower jaw to where the gill commences underneath; this will sever the whole side of the head. Cut away all the flesh from the inside and remove all the bony structures possible without injuring the outside. The eyes can be removed so as to leave the outside skin or covering unbroken. Wash the half of the head clean and put that with the fins in your note-book, taking care to leave a leaf of paper between each, to prevent their adhering together.

FIG. 109. PORTFOLIO OF FISH

When you reach home you can have the fish cooked, and while it is cooking trace the outline of the fish upon a clean sheet of white paper; take the fins, head and tail from your note-book, dampen them with a sponge or wet cloth, and with glue or mucilage fasten them in their proper places upon the outline drawing, distended by means of pins; the latter may be removed after the glue or mucilage is dry; write in one corner the weight of the fish, the date upon which it was caught, and the name of the place where it was captured. You can then frame it or number the sheet and place it in a

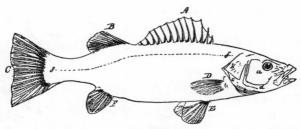

Diagram Showing the Parts of a Fish.—A, first dorsal fin ; B, second dorsal fin ; C, caudal fin ; D, pectoral fin ; E, ventral fin ; F, anal fin ; b, operculum or gill cover proper ; a, preoperculum or fore-gill cover ; d, interoperculum, or middle gill cover ; c, suboperculum, or under gill cover ; e, branchiostegous, or gill rays ; f, lateral line.

portfolio (FIG. 109). In the course of a season's fishing quite an interesting and valuable portfolio of fishes can be made. The writers have often caught fish whose names were unknown to him, and in this manner preserved them, or enough of them to identify the fish at some future period when we had time to look it up.

Preserving Insects

Great care must be taken in killing insects, intended for the cabinet, and death should be produced without disfiguring them or rubbing off the down or scales that covers the bodies and wings of some specimens. A convenient and successful way to kill insects is to drop them into a wide-mouthed bottle, the bottom of which is lined with blotting-paper that has been previously saturated with ether, benzine, creosote or chloroform. When a butterfly, bug, or beetle is put into a bottle prepared in this manner, and the bottle tightly corked, the insect expires without a struggle, and hence without injuring itself. From the bottle the specimens may be taken and pinned upon a mounting-board, consisting of two strips of wood resting upon supports at each end, a space being left between the strips for the body of the insect. Under this space or crack a piece of cork is fas-

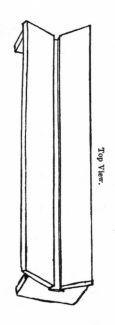

Top View.

End View.

FIG. 110. MOUNTING BOARD

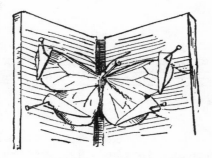

FIG. 111. BUTTERFLLY PINNED TO MOUNTING-BOARD

tened (FIG. 110) in which to stick the point of the pin. After pinning the specimen to the mounting-board, spread the wings and legs out in a natural position, and if it be a butterfly or moth, fasten its wings in position with bits of paper and pins, as shown in Fig. 111.

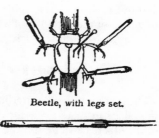

Beetle, with legs set.

FIG. 112. LEG-PIN

An ingenious and simple device for pinning the leg of an insect is illustrated by Fig. 112. It consists of two needles with their heads driven into a small pine stick.

Morse Insect Box

Mr. E. S. Morse gives probably the best device for arranging an insect box for the cabinet. It consists of a light wooden frame with paper stretched upon the upper and under surface. Dampen the paper and glue it to the frame; when the paper dries it will contract and become as tight as a drumhead. Inside the box upon two sides fasten cleats, and let their top edges be about one-quarter of an inch above the

FIG. 113. CROSS SECTION OF MORSE INSECT BOX

bottom. Rest the paper-covered frame upon these cleats and secure it in position. The bottom of the box should be lined with soft pine to receive the points of the pins. The space under the frame can be dusted with snuff and camphor to keep out such insects as delight to feed upon the prepared specimens of their relatives. FIG. 113 shows a cross section of a box upon Mr. Morse's plan.

The Lawrence Breeding Box

The best moths and butterflies are obtained by rearing the caterpillars in cages made for the purpose. We are indebted to Mr. Albert Lawrence for the accompanying plan of a larva box, invented and used by himself for several seasons (see FIG. 114). The Lawrence box, as may be seen by the diagram,

FIG. 114. MR. ALBERT LAWRENCE 'S BREEDING BOX

can be taken apart and packed away when not in use or during transportation.

The sides, ends, and top are wooden frames covered with wire netting; the bottom is a flat board. They are all joined by hooks and screw-eyes. To take them apart it is only necessary to unfasten the hooks.

Spiders

Spiders are very likely to lose their colors if placed in spirits, and if pinned and dried like beetles they will not only lose all color, but their bodies will shrivel up and change in form and proportion to such a degree as to make the specimens next to worthless. Mr. Ralph Hemingray, of Covington, Ky., sent the authors some spider bottles manufactured under his direction of very thick, clear, white glass, three inches high by one and one-quarter inch broad, and three-quarters of an inch thick. These bottles are convenient in shape, and when a spider is put in one and the bottle filled with glycerine, the spider looks as if it might be imbedded in a solid block of crystal.

We have had some brightly colored garden spiders preserved in this manner for two years, and they have not only retained their original shape but color also. In the place of corks, pieces of elastic are stretched over the tops of the bottles; this allows the glycerine to expand or contract. FIG. 115 represents a drawing of one of these bottles with a spider in it. A case of specimens preserved in this manner makes not only an interesting cabinet, but a very pretty one. Although many persons have a horror of spiders, they lose all their nervousness when the insects are seen neatly labelled and enclosed in pretty glass bottles.

FIG. 115. THE HEMINGRAY BOTTLE

How to Make Beautiful or Comical Groups and Designs of Insects

Many really beautiful, as well as some absurdly comical designs can be made of properly preserved insects by ingenious folks.

Butterflies may be made to have the appearance of hovering in mid-air by mounting them upon extremely fine wire.

Grasshoppers can be arranged in comical, human-like attitudes.

Beetles may be harnessed like horses to a tiny car made of the half of an English walnut-shell. A very pretty design can be made by seating a grasshopper in a delicate sea-shell of some kind, and glueing the shell to a bit of looking-glass; fine wires attached to the shell will answer the double purpose of a support and harness for a couple of flying beetles; a little moss glued around the sides so as to conceal the ragged edges of the glass will add greatly to the effect, and the whole will have the appearance of a fairy boat being drawn over the surface of the water by two flying beetles, guided by the long-legged imp in the shell.

Preserved insects are exceedingly brittle, the least touch will often break off a wing or leg or otherwise disfigure the specimen, hence it is necessary not only to be very careful in handling them, but to supply some sort of cover to protect them from accidents, dust, and injurious insects. Dome-shape glass-covers are best adapted for small groups or compositions, and these may be obtained from the dealers at moderate prices, or, if the budding taxidermist has acquired sufficient skill to make his work valuable, he can readily trade off duplicate specimens for glass-covers, as many amateurs as well as some professionals do.

Marine Animals

Starfish must be first placed in fresh water and allowed to remain there for several hours; they may then be removed and spread out upon a board, and held in position by pins or nails driven in the board alongside of the rays, but not into the creature. Put the board in a dry place out of the sun, and the air will absorb all the moisture in the specimens; the latter, as they dry, become hard and stiff.

We have several starfish preserved in this simple manner, and although no pickle or artificial preservative was used, they have kept in good condition for several years.

Small crabs may be dried in the same manner. The flesh must be extracted from the big pincers of the larger crabs and lobsters; this may be done by breaking off the points of the pincers and removing the meat with a crooked wire. The points of the claws should be saved and glued in place after the animal is dry. The smaller claws may be allowed to dry; small holes pierced in them will allow the air to enter and facilitate the drying process. The insides of both lobsters and large crabs must be removed from an opening made underneath. Wash them with cold water and inject carbolic acid and water into their extremities; place them upon a board to dry, with their legs spread out; after all moisture has evaporated, varnish them and fasten the bodies and legs of the specimens to a board with fine wires.

All soft-bodied animals, such as squids and slugs, can be preserved in spirits. Sea-urchins, such as are found upon our coast, may be dried like starfish, but it is best to remove the insides of the larger specimens.

With these suggestions, sufficient to help the new taxidermist, we will close this chapter. We have purposely avoided advising the use of expensive material or tools; where it was possible, We have not suggested the use of poisonous preservatives, but have given the most simple and safe methods of mounting specimens for the cabinet or for decorations.

EGG BLOW-PIPE AND DRILL

EXERCISES FOR WOMEN

EVERYONE *MUST* EXERCISE TO KEEP HEALTHY AND STRONG, for life is motion and activity. It is natural to be well and happy, and to keep so we must exercise all our muscles, as well as our moral and intellectual faculties, or they will dwindle and wither. The arm of the Hindoo devotee, not being used, at length becomes completely paralyzed, and fish in the Mammoth Cave having no use for eyes pass their life without them; so we find that *use* is the foundation of all things, otherwise they would cease to exist; then, readers, it lies within your power to become stronger and more graceful each day by regular and graduated bodily exercise, which will bring life and energy to every part of your system by causing the blood to circulate freely through all the body.

There are some simple methods of carrying this into effect in the most agreeable and salutary manner, but the exercises must be very light at first, and as you advance they may be increased a little each time, but always stop before you feel fatigued, for when the calisthenics cease to give pleasure it is doubtful if they are beneficial.

The best time for exercising is in the morning after having partaken of some light refreshments, though any time will do except directly after hearty meals. Try and have a regular time set apart each day for your physical culture. Commence by exercising five or ten minutes, then for a little longer period next time, and so on until you can exercise with ease for half an hour or longer. You will feel refreshed, invigorated, and better prepared for the duties and pleasures which await you. Your clothing must not incommode the free action of the body, and it is essential that it be comfortable. What is suitable for lawn tennis is also well adapted for the gymnasium. An ordinary bathing-dress answers the purpose very well, as it is made for exercise.

Exercise First

The Egyptian water-carrier, with the jug of water poised so prettily on her head, and her figure so straight and beautiful, has always challenged admiration; her carriage is dignified, erect, and graceful, something worth striving for, especially when we have the certainty of success if we will only be faithful and persevering. The peasantry of foreign countries who carry all their burdens balanced on their heads have their reward in healthy, strong, straight figures, even in old age they do not stoop. Witness the emigrants landing at Castle Garden who carry their possessions done up in huge bundles on their heads with the utmost ease; of this class, three generations—a grandmother, mother, and grown daughter—with baggage of the same weight on their heads, were lately seen at a New York ferry, each equally upright, strong, and vigorous.

A good straight back is an excellent thing; and when the head is properly carried and all the movements are buoyant and elastic, then we may walk as it was intended we should, every step bringing a glow to the cheek and a sparkle to the eye. It requires only a few minutes' regular daily exercise for any girl to attain a carriage equal to that of the Egyptian water-carrier, and the only apparatus needed for this is a roll of paper.

Now stand with your heels together, toes out, and shoulders well back; then place on your head the roll of paper; if your position is not perfectly erect the roll will fall off; keep your chin straight and back against your neck, for it is the *chin* which determines the poise of the body. You cannot stand straight unless the chin is straight; throw out your chin and your shoulders will stoop forward, have your chin straight and your back will be straight; bear this in mind in all your exercises. Now walk, keeping the roll balanced on your head (Fig. 116). Practice this walking back and forth until you can do so without the paper rolling off; then try a

FIG. 116. BALANCING A ROLL OF PAPER

tin cup full to the brim with water. Walk erect or the water will wash over, down on your head, and it will feel cold as it trickles through your hair; soon, however, you will be able to carry the cup of water with ease and no danger of its spilling. But do not discontinue the practice on that account; try something else in its place, until you are able to carry anything you wish on your head with no fear of it falling. The exercise affords amusement, and at the same time you will be acquiring a beautiful, dignified, and graceful carriage.

Exercise Second

This exercise is for gaining agility, suppleness, quickness of eye, hand, and foot. Standing as far from the wall as possible, take a common rubber hand-ball and toss it against the wall, catching it as it rebounds, and again toss it against the wall. Vary this by allowing the ball to strike the floor, catching it on the rebound; then try keeping the ball in constant motion by using first one hand and then the other as a bat for returning the ball to the wall. The exercise can also be changed by striking the ball against the floor, and on its return bound again striking it, thus keeping it in motion. You will find that activity is necessary, and the work so quick that it will keep you on the jump all through the exercise.

Exercise Third

This is exercise done with a broom-handle. Saw or cut off the broom and smooth down the sharp ends of the handle, and it will be ready for use. Stand erect, heels together, toes out, chin well back and straight, so as to throw out and expand the chest. Now grasp firmly each end of the broom-stick and bring it up over the head (FIG. 117); repeat this motion six or seven times; then change by carrying the broomstick over back of the head down across and back of the shoulders; then up above the head again, repeating this, and all other motions in your calisthenics, half a dozen times. Another exercise is holding the stick down in front of you with both hands and bringing it up over the head and down back of the shoulders without stopping.

The side motion is made by grasping the broomstick at each end, holding it down in front of you, and swinging it sideways, thus bringing the right hand up when the left is down, and *vice versa*. Another way is to hold the stick by both ends above your head and swing it from one side

FIG. 117. BROOM-HANDLE EXERCISE

to the other, which will cause the right arm to come in contact with the right side of the head, while the left arm is extended out horizontally to the left. Next carry the stick to the back of and against the shoulders; then swing it from right to left, which gives another side movement. Vary all the movements in as many different ways as you can think of.

Exercise Fourth

Stand erect always when in position for exercising, according to the directions given—heels together, toes out, etc. Now allow your arms to hang naturally down at your sides, raise your heels, and stand on your toes; now lower the heels and repeat the motion; then close your hands tightly and raise your arms out sideways at right angles with your body, next up straight above your head, and down again to the level of the shoulders, then back down to your sides as at first.

Again take position, close your hands tightly, and raise them up under the arms, bringing the elbows out to a level with the shoulders; then bring your hands down at your sides again and repeat the movement vigorously; resume position, firmly close your hands and carry them up to the shoulders, next extend them up straight above your head, down again to your shoulders, and back to the first position. A very good exercise is to extend both arms straight out in front of you, close your hands and bring them back to your chest, which will cause the bent elbows to project beyond your back.

Exercise Fifth

Assume position, close your hands, and take one long step forward with your right foot, bend the right knee and stand with your weight resting on the right foot; then extend your arms out sideways straight from the shoulders, now bring your hands together in front of you, still keeping the arms on a level with the shoulders, and while doing so throw the body back, straightening the right knee and bending the left so the weight of the body will rest on the left foot; repeat this and vary it by taking one step forward with the left foot and going through with the same motions.

Resume position, and place your hands on your hips, with your thumbs turned forward and fingers backward. Now take a long step forward with your right foot, throwing the weight on that foot, then back again in position, and in the same manner step forward with your left foot and back again;

next take a step backward with your right foot, resume position, and then with your left.

Again stand with your hands on your hips, thumbs turned forward, and without bending your knees move the body, first bending it forward, then backward, and resuming an upright position, bend over to the right and to the left.

Exercise Sixth

In this the broomstick is used for balancing; hold it in an upright position, and first try balancing it on the palm of your hand; then on the back of your hand, next on each of the fingers in succession, commencing with the first finger (FIG. 118);

FIG. 118. BALANCING A BROOM-HANDLE

be cautious, and when the stick wavers do not let it fall, but catch it with the other hand, and again balance it. This is an interesting, light, and diverting exercise, requiring all your attention, and, for the time being, your thoughts are concentrated on the effort to keep the broomstick properly balanced.

Exercise Seventh

Pure blood means good health, and to purify the blood and keep the complexion clear it is essential that you breathe a sufficient quantity of *pure air*, and you cannot take in a proper amount of air unless your lungs are wholly extended. So take position with your hands correctly placed on your hips; then very slowly draw in your breath until your chest and lungs are fully expanded; next slowly exhale your breath, and repeat the exercise.

Exercise Eighth

Screw in two large, *strong* hooks in the woodwork on each side of the doorway; place the hooks as far above your head as you can conveniently reach; slide the broomstick in so that it will extend across the doorway and be supported by the hooks; have the apparatus on that side of the doorway where it will not interfere with the opening and closing of the door, and be sure that it is perfectly secure before attempting to exercise each time before commencing a new movement examine the stick, and be certain that it is not in any danger of slipping from the hooks. Unless you can be perfectly safe from liability to hurts or falls, do not include this in your list of exercises.

For the first movement grasp the bar firmly with both hands and swing the body forward and backward, standing first on the toes, then on the heels; next, still grasping the bar, raise up on your toes, then back again. Change the movements in as many ways as you like, but do not try anything that may strain or hurt you. Now screw in two more hooks, on either side of the woodwork, below the first ones, placing them about two feet and eight inches from the floor; take the stick from its elevated position and slide it across the doorway so it will rest securely on the two lower hooks. Standing in front of it, grasp the bar firmly with both hands and try to raise yourself up, feet and all, from the floor by bearing your weight down on the bar; then let yourself gently back again. When you have finished exercising, remove the stick and put it away.

Exercise Ninth

In the top part of the framework of the doorway fasten a very strong hook by screwing it into the wood; then take a broomstick and, after shortening it so that when held in a horizontal position it will readily pass through the doorway, cut notches in each end and securely tie the two ends of a rope across the notches; suspend this swing by slipping the centre of the rope over the hook in the doorway (FIG. 119); have the apparatus strong and firm, capable of any amount of wear and tear. Stand facing the stick, which should be at the height of the chest, and take hold of it

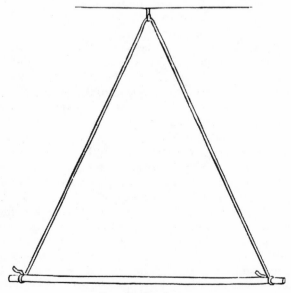

FIG. 119. THE SWING

with both hands; now bend the knees until they are within a short distance of the floor, then rise and repeat the exercise. Next, with both hands on the stick, take a long step forward with the right foot, throwing the weight on that foot; return to your position and go through the same exercise with your left foot. Try different movements which suggest themselves, and select those you like best. When not in use the swing can be slipped off the hook and put out of the way.

Exercise Tenth

To develop a strong voice and make it clear and sweet, and to strengthen the lungs, reading aloud is an excellent exercise; as it requires both mental and muscular exertion and performs a double duty, it should receive a full share of time and attention. Begin with something you are interested in, then you will find it much easier to read aloud than if you undertook a book or an article which might be full of merit, but lacks interest for you. When commencing this exercise read only ten minutes or less at a sitting, increasing the time as you practise and the reading grows less difficult. Do not be discouraged if your voice sounds a little husky while reading; stop a moment, and then go on again. After a few trials you will have no more trouble in that way, for your voice will grow clear and distinct, and the exercise will become a great pleasure as well as an attractive, useful accomplishment. Let your reading matter be very choice and of the best; do not condescend to waste your time on other writings.

From the ten different exercises given, select those best adapted to your size, age, and liking, and practise them for a short time daily; you can hardly realize the great advantage they will prove to be. In this way all parts of the system may be strengthened and harmoniously developed. But the constitution cannot be hurried: all must be accomplished little by little. Allow yourselves to be happy and merry; be ready to enjoy the little pleasures of life, and this, with kind and generous feelings for others, will do a great deal toward keeping you well and strong.

Out-of-door exercise is always to be preferred to indoor when one has a choice. Walking, tennis, archery, horseback, and swimming are some of the athletic sports for girls, and they all have their attractions. But there are times when we are denied the pleasure of these pastimes, and then we are glad of a little exercise indoors, which also affords enjoyment and recreation.

SOCIAL
AMUSEMENTS

SOCIAL AMUSEMENTS FOR EVENING PARTIES

I T IS CERTAINLY A SUBJECT FOR REGRET, THAT IN OUR GREAT cities, our towns, villages, and more scattered country houses, social gatherings are so apt to assume the character of "solemn occasions," where the perplexed hostess and equally perplexed guests hover about the room, trying vainly to solve the problem, "what shall we do?"

Dancing and music, varied by eating and drinking, are the standard amusements at evening parties; but there are many circles where dancing is excluded on principle, while amateur music has reached such perfection that it requires a decided and well-cultivated talent to make it endurable among people who have any pretensions to refinement and taste. There is really something pitiful in the sight of a company of intelligent and talented young folks, each one possessing an undeveloped fund of ready wit, mutely enduring an agonizing amateur performance of fine music; while the pianist, who has studied hard and can play well when alone, stumbles over the keys, blindly groping in all the torments of shyness, till a hideous discord is produced. Patiently the listeners sit, smiling under the torture with a politeness often springing from pure kind feeling, while each and all of them might be having a "jolly time" did they but know the best outlet for their wit and good-nature, their ingenuity or talent.

To supply the necessary information for such pleasure-seekers, the following collection of amusing pastimes is now offered.

Pity the Poor Blind

IT IS SURPRISING HOW HELPLESS A PERSON IS WHEN DEPRIVED of sight. As the proof of the pudding is in the eating, the truth of the foregoing remark may be easily tested.

Select a gentleman of the party, blindfold him carefully with a handkerchief, and place him three or four yards from, and facing, a table, near the edge of which is a lighted candle. Now bid him turn once entirely round, then advance toward the candle and try to blow it out. His vain attempts, oft repeated, will cause much amusement; he is in full pucker and not more than two yards away from the candle, and in momentary dread of burning his nose.

The Mysterious Release

This trick is so ingenious and interesting, that while it will probably require your closest attention to the explanation in order to comprehend it, will yet amply repay you for the trouble.

You get a string about three feet long, tie the ends together, and your preparations are complete.

First you require some one to hold up his finger. Place the string over it, winding it once around (the way of the clock, from right to left) forming a loop which completely surrounds the finger and clasps it tight. Then, with the right hand draw the remaining part of the string out straight, pulling it a little to show that it is securely fastened and cannot come off. You now propose to release the string from the finger, without taking it off over the top.

This seems an utter impossibility—and the uninitiated would undoubtedly so declare it. But it is not so. Holding the string out straight with the fingers of the right hand, lay the forefinger of your left hand across the double string, about half way between your right hand and the finger on which the string is fastened. Then, with the right hand, carry the end it holds forward, over the forefinger thus placed, laying it across the double string half way between your left hand and the fin-

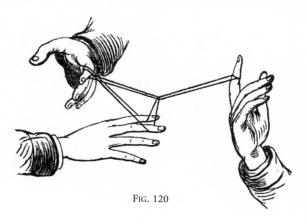

FIG. 120

ger to which it is attached. The single loop which you thus carry over, and lay across, being slack, hangs down on each side of the double string, forming two loops, or one on each side, so that you can pass your right hand, which is now free, underneath with the palm downward, and inserting the forefinger in the left-hand loop, and the second finger in the right-hand loop, pressing them down, the string being held across the top, you have the string in the position as represented in FIG 120.

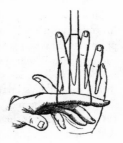

FIG. 121

In FIG. 121 the same position is shown as viewed from above by the operator.

As the string is thus held, you observe that the loops are precisely alike; that is, the inside strings pass under your forefinger, and the outside strings pass over it.

FIG. 122

What is wanted now is to change or reverse the right-hand loop.

To do this, pass the second finger from beneath, between the inside and outside strings of that loop (see FIG. 122), letting it off from the forefinger until it is fairly caught upon the second, (see Fig. 123), and then transferring it again back to the forefinger, and you will see that by these movements the loop has become reversed; that is, the *inside* string passes *over* your forefinger, and the *outside* string passes *under* it, the left-hand loop remaining as it was; so that now they are no longer alike (see FIG. 124).

FIG. 123

FIG. 124

Holding the loops on your forefinger thus arranged, and dropping your hand to a perpendicular position, keeping the palm toward you, carry the loops forward and pass them over the finger to which the string was attached at the beginning of the trick. This movement (see FIG. 125) twists the loops into a sort of cat's-cradle appearance as seen by the operator. Then request the party holding them to be careful not to let the string slip over the top of his finger; and, in order to make that impossible, place the forefinger of your disengaged left hand on the top of his finger.

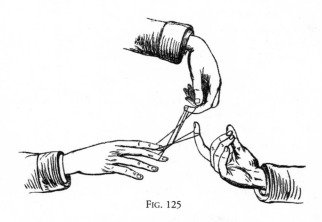

FIG. 125

To pull now with both fingers would not effect a separation, but the string would seem to be still more firmly fastened, and the release a far greater impossibility, but let go the loop on the forefinger and pull upon the loop held by the second finger, and as if by magic the string comes entirely free from the finger on which it was wound, and is exhibited to the gaze of the spectators entirely in your own possession.

If neatly and quickly performed, this trick can remain a mystery for a long time, if the *reversal of the loop* be rapidly and neatly effected. A smooth and flexible piece of cord is almost indispensable to a rapid performer.

My House, Your House

The ingenuity of the company having been expended in the attempt to guess the "Mysterious Release," a new game, requiring some thought, may be started, called My House, Your House. This game will afford considerable amusement for a party of five or six persons, or more, and requires but little preparation. Provide a piece of moderately stout cord about a yard in length; at one end make a small loop that will not slip, pass the other end of the cord through this loop, thus making a larger loop say six inches in diameter, which will slip easily; attach the end of the string to a cane or short stick, and we have a very respectable rod and line to go a-fishing to catch fingers.

The players are arranged around a small table—a round one is preferable—in the center of which a circle about five inches in diameter is marked; this may be drawn with a piece of chalk, or consist of a round piece of paper, as may be most convenient.

One of the players now takes the rod and line, arranges the loop around the circle in the centre of the table and holds the rod in his hand; he then explains to the rest of the players that when he says "my house," each must put his forefinger, promptly at the word of command, inside the circle, and keep it there. The fisherman then says, "your house," and the players must each promptly withdraw his finger and place it on the table immediately in front of him. The words of command "my house," "your house," should be given with sufficient frequency to confuse the players, a forfeit being attached to any failure to act promptly and correctly at the word. When the fisherman thinks he has a good chance he should jerk the string upward, and try to catch one or more of the fingers. The person whose finger is caught next takes the fishing-rod, and in his turn tries to catch somebody else's finger. The fisherman has perfect liberty to repeat the same command if he pleases; after having given the words "my house," and brought the fingers into the circle, he can again say "my house," and the party who withdraws his finger has to pay a forfeit.

Century Court

When the forfeits are all paid, some skillful necromancer may puzzle the probability increased number of guests by the following specimen of his cunning by playing Century Court. Have one person of the party leave the room and assigned a century to him during his absence, such as Sixth, Tenth, Nineteenth.

Upon his return he is charged with all the crimes and abuses of his century, which he must explain, extenuate or acknowledge, according to his wit; or he is praised for its redeeming events, noble examples or fine characters, all of which he must gracefully accept, trying at the same time to discover what century he represents.

When he succeeds, he selects the party whose last speech gave him the hint from which he gained his information, saying:

The Eighteenth (or other) Century, begs leave to retire, introducing Mr. —————— to the court," and the new victim leaves the room, while another century is selected.

EXAMPLE:
We will suppose a gentleman has left the room, and the company have agreed on assigning to him a certain century. Mr. Century is now called in, and proceeds to listen to the remarks made to him by the other.

MISS SMITH: Oh! How could you assassinate one of the best men that ever lived? *(William the Silent.)*

MR. JONES: Well! If he did, he produced one of the greatest poets. (*Shakespeare.*)

MRS. SMITH: Yes, and tried to introduce the inquisition into Holland.

MR. COYLE: That was nothing to compare with the fearful massacre he caused. (*St. Bartholomew.*)

MISS COLE: He was a good hand, too, at sinking ships—

MR. WELLS: Which made the most gentlemanly duck imaginable almost crow for joy. (*Admiral Drake.*)

MISS LAMB: Oh, yes; and laid the foundation for roast goose on Michaelmas-day.

MR. CENTURY: Thank you, Miss Lamb. I see. Roast goose, sinking ships, and Michaelmas. That means the Spanish Armada and Queen Elizabeth, thus making me represent the Sixteenth Century. Miss Lamb, you may take my place.

This game may be continued during the remainder of the evening.

Traveling Alphabetically

The players should be seated in a circle, and a leader chosen who asks the questions.

The answers must be given in regular alphabetical order, and should be original, and may be humorous if the spirit of fun moves the party speaking.

LEADER: Ladies and gentlemen, you are all invited to make a journey to any part of the world you may prefer, and tell me your mission; but you must name your destinations and errands in the order of the alphabet.

MISS A: Where are you going?

ANSWER: To Alexandria.

LEADER: What will you do there?

ANSWER: Apply for Amusing Anecdotes.

"I am going to Baltimore," says the next.

LEADER: What will you do there?

ANSWER: Bake Bacon and Beans.

Each one is asked in turn by the leader, "Where are you going?" and "What will you do there?"

C—goes to Constantinople to Call for Citron.

D—to Danforth, to Dress, Dine and Dance.

E—to Europe to Eagerly Enjoy Everything.

F—to Flanders to Fish for Flounders.

G—to Greenpoint to Garden and Groan.

H—to Hazlehurst to Hunt Hopping Hares.

I—to Ireland to Imitate Irishmen

J—to Jersey to Join in a Jubilee.

K—to Kinsington to Keep Kittens Kindly.

L—to Louisville to Love Loyally.

M—to Maryland to Marry a Musician.

N—to Newton to Nod Nervously.

O—to Ottawa to Own Outrageous Onions.

P—to Paterson to Patronize Pastry.

Q—to Queenstown to Quarrel Queerly.

R—to Rahway to Rove and Roam.

S—to Siam to Sell Seven Shawls.

T—to Toronto to Tell Tedious Tales.

U—to Uruguay to Upset a Usurper.

V—to Vienna to Vex a Vixen.

W—to Waterloo to Weep and Wail.

Y—to Yarmouth to Yawn.

Z—to Zante to Zig-zag Zealously

The Divided Tapes

To perform this trick, a little preparation is necessary. Provide two pieces of tape, each four feet long, and three ordinary cotton spools: or, if preferred, three of the barrel-shaped wooden foundations (FIG. 126) used by fringe-and-tassel manufacturers for making the upper part of window-

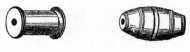

FIG. 126

tassels. Fold each of the tapes double, as shown in FIG. 127; pass about half an inch of the looped end of A through the loop of B, and fold it back on the tape A, which will thus be hooked into B. Pass the open ends of B through a spool, and

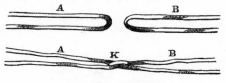

FIG. 127

draw the spool over the interlocked loop, as in FIG. 128; this spool must not be moved from its position at any time during the performance of the trick, as it conceals and holds the looped ends of the tape. Next, take the two remaining spools,

FIG. 128

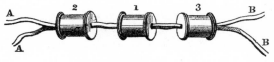

Fig. 129

and pass one on the tape B, and the other on A. as shown in Fig. 129. The whole contrivance is now ready for use. Request two persons to assist you; give the ends of the tape A (Fig. 129) to one of them, and the ends of B to the other, desiring them to hold the tape and spools out level between them. Now, explain that the spools are strung on to the tape, moving the two outer spools (not the middle one) to illustrate your explanation; then inform the spectators that you propose to remove the spools from the tape without passing them over the ends held by your assistants. Next, ask each of your aids to hand you one of the two ends held by him, either one of them, as it is quite immaterial which; you only desire to make the matter doubly sure, at the same time tie the ends that you have received with a double knot (see Fig. 130); thus drawing the three spools together, and appearing to secure them perfectly. This being done, grasp the spools

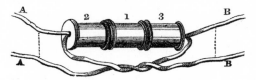

Fig. 130

with your right hand, and instruct your assistants to be ready, at the word "three," to pull the tapes with a sudden jerk. You then give the word, "one, two, three," and the spools will remain in your hand, the two tapes remaining in the assistants' hands, and joined in the middle by the knot which you tied. This trick is sometimes performed with thin twine instead of tapes, the looped ends being tied together with a piece of sewing thread, which breaks when pulled apart.

Five Minutes' Conversation

This is not exactly a game, although there are rules which must be obeyed in order to make it interesting.

A program with small pencil attached, like the one shown in FIG. 131, should be given to each guest upon her arrival. The engagements for five minutes' conversation are made by putting your name down on your friend's card opposite the time chosen for your conversation with her, Five minutes only are allowed for one conversation.

Two or more consecutive engagements with one person are not allowable. When engagements are made and programmes filled, the hostess, or anyone willing to be time-keeper, must ring a bell giving notice that the convers tion is to begin.

At the end of five minutes the bell is to be rung again,

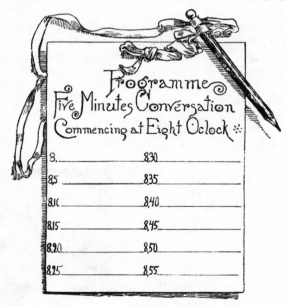

FIG. 131

when all talking must instantly cease, the exchange of positions be quickly made, and a new conversation be commenced.

The time-keeper should be strictly attentive to her duties, for the bell must be rung regularly at the end of every five minutes.

The hour allotted to this new mode of conversation will pass very quickly, and cannot become in the least tiresome, as the time spent in talking to any one person is so very short.

A Game of Noted Men

This game is played in this way: The hostess begins the game by saying, I know a celebrated poet; the first part of his name is very black, and the last is an elevation. Whoever gives the right name, which is COLERIDGE (coal, ridge), in her turn describes the name of some noted person. She may choose SHAKESPEARE and say, I give the name of a noted author and poet; the first part is something people are apt to do when they are cold, the last is a weapon of warfare.

There are quite a number of names which will do nicely for this game; a few of them are—

WORDSWORTH—words, worth.
SHELLEY—shell, lea.
CORNWALL—corn, wall.
WASHINGTON—washing, ton.
HOWITT—how, it.
FILLMORE—fill, more.
MILMAN—mill, man.
LONGFELLOW—long, fellow.

When giving a name to be guessed, the profession of the man, whether poet, author, statesman, or soldier, must be given, but nothing else should be told about him.

What will You Take to the Picnic?

This entertaining game can be played very nicely while the party are enjoying some light refreshments.

The hostess alone should be in the secret, and these directions are addressed only to her.

Commence the game by announcing that you propose to give a picnic, that it depends upon what your guests will bring for lunch whether they will be allowed to attend, and that each one must furnish two articles of food. Then ask the person nearest you, What will you take to the picnic? If the name of neither of the articles she mentions commences with the initial letter of her Christian name or surname tell her she cannot go, and put the question to the next person, asking each in turn, What will you take to the picnic?

For example, we will suppose that the name of one of the party is Susan Davis, and she says she will take crackers and lemons, she cannot go, as neither of her names commence with C or L; but if she proproses to take salmon and doughnuts, she will be doubly welcome, since S and D are both her initials. Should she say sugar and cream, she could go for one of her names commences with S.

Continue to put the question to each player until all, or nearly all, have discovered why their proposed contribution to the lunch secures them a welcome, or debars them from attending the picnic.

Assumed Characters

In this game some well-known novelist is selected—Dickens, for instance—and each player chooses one of his characters to personate, telling no one his choice. Then one of the players relates the life as though it were his own, and portrays with voice and gesture the character he has assumed. Of course no names must be mentioned.

The person who first guesses what character is being personated has the privilege of deciding who shall be the next to tell his story.

The game of Assumed Characters will prove to be very entertaining if each player does his part and makes his narrative as amusing and interesting as possible.

Shadow Verbs

A white sheet is fastened tightly across a French window, or doorway opening upon the piazza, and a large lamp set behind it.

The company separates into two parties; one enters the house, while the other remains seated upon the piazza facing the suspended sheet.

The outside party chooses a verb which the others are to guess and perform. When their decision is made they call the leader of the inside party and say, "The verb we have chosen rhymes with rake," or whatever it may rhyme with. The leader then joins his followers and consults with them what the first guess shall be. It is best to take the verbs which rhyme with the noun given in alphabetical order. Bake would come first for rake, and if it is decided that they shall act this, several of the party step before the lamp, which casts their shadows on the sheet and, without speaking, go through the motions of making and baking bread. If the guess is right (that is if to bake was the verb chosen) the spectators clap their hands; if wrong, they cry, No, no.

When they hear the no, no, the actors retire and arrange what to do next. Make, quake, take, wake are all acted in turn, until the clap of approval announces that they have been successful in guessing the verb. Then the actors take the seats vacated by the spectators, who in their turn enter the house to become shadows and act the verbs chosen by the other party, and the game goes on as before. A little ingenuity on the part of the players in producing funny and absurd shadows makes the whole thing very laughable and causes great amusement.

Melted Lead

We use this activity to ascertain what the occupation of one's future husband would be. The fortune is told in this way: Each girl, in turn, holds a door-key in one hand, while with the other hand she pours the melted lead, from an iron spoon or ladle, through the handle of the key into a pan of cold water.

In the fanciful shapes the lead assumes can be traced resemblances to all sorts of things. Sometimes it is a sword or gun, which indicates that a soldier will win the fair prize; again, traces of a ship maybe seen: then the favored one is to be a sailor; a plough suggests a farmer; a book, a professor, or perhaps a minister; and when the lead forms only drops, it seems to mean that the gentle inquirer will not marry, or if she does, her husband will be of no profession.

AMERICAN
ETIQUETTE

VALUE OF ETIQUETTE

Intrinsic Value

To ESTIMATE THE REAL VALUE OF ETIQUETTE, DECORUM, or good manners, is to measure the breadth and scope of modern civilization. That culture only is valuable which smooths the rough places, harmonizes the imperfections, and develops the pure, the good and the gentle in human character. The revenge of the savage, the roughness of the barbarous, and the rudeness of even some who claim to be civilized are all lost in the good will and suavity of gentle manners. The efficiency and usefulness of a liberal education are dwarfed unless developed under the genial influence of proper decorum. The actual worth, then, of politeness is such as to make every one who would be refined and cultured seek to cultivate it to such an extent as to make it practical in all the walks of life.

Exchangeable Value

"A man's manners are his fortune," is a saying as true as it is old, as valuable as it is true. Many commodities are exchangeable, and money is the pivot upon which they turn. This is not less true of good manners than it is of the theories of the political economist. Who will number the times fortune has smiled upon penniless men who have had a good countenance and a pleasing address at their command? Good manners are made a leading business qualification in all pursuits. Neither sex is exempt, and the best positions with the fattest salaries are always commanded by the best mannered, most courteous individuals. Then, as an avenue to wealth and position, good manners constitute a desirable acquisition.

Value to Society

What is called society would be impossible were it not for the laws and usages of etiquette. So many interests are to be served—some to be protected, others to be restrained, and still others to be allowed the privilege of growth and expansion—that all these could not be done without some acknowledged standard of action, of which all may acquire some information both on entering and while in society. The best manners are to be found in the society of *the good*, and they are only the outgrowth of what is actually essential to regulate intercourse among such people. Man can not do without society, and society can not be maintained without customs and laws; therefore we have only to think of the mistakes, the heart-burnings and the mortifications which are the experience of the unrefined and ill-mannered, to see how valuable to society is a knowledge of the rules of decorum.

Value to Gentlemen

The name gentleman indicates one who is gentle, mild, even-tempered. Some are born so, and will naturally exercise these qualities in having to do with their fellows. Many have these qualities to acquire, and some, at least, have to use them as a cloak to gain admission to circles otherwise closed against them. The polished way, smooth speech and easy bearing of a complete gentleman have a pleasurable affect on any company of persons, neither are they soon forgotten. Unconsciously we imitate them, and thus the grace of good behavior becomes an influence well worth the while of any one who would be a gentleman, to seek it.

Value to Ladies

Woman is peculiarly the organizer and refiner of elegant society. Men will seek the essential principles, but all the nicety and elegance of polished manners must and do come through woman. A woman rude and uncultured in her manners, however beautiful in person she may be, is like an uncut diamond, whose sparkle and luster, though like that of the dog-star, are lost by the roughness of the exterior. The graceful mien and pleasing address of a cultured and refined woman make her a favorite in every company, and the radiant of a courtesy as wide and as luminous as her manners are pleasing. Worthy men strive to please and honor noble, virtuous, amiable women. So that woman, who by her courtesy has acquired these attributes, has in her power the touch-stones which test and at the same time claim the best society among gentlemen.

Value to the Rich

Riches are desirable, but many a one who has had money at his command has been entirely unable to find ingress to good society. The basis of etiquette does not rest upon money, neither will money buy good manners. Yet the rich seek the culture and the courtesy of good society, because of the finish and the éclat thus given to their wealth and their homes.

Value to the Middle Classes

In society there is a large class of persons who, without being affluent, still have sufficient of this world's goods to enable them to enjoy much of the culture and refinement which may come of education and right training in the customs of courtesy. To these the practice of good manners is especially enjoyable, because it affords them the amenities and the pleasurable things of life, without its troubles and vexations. These persons hold, too, the balance of power in social life. Their culture and their courtesy give them admission to the houses of the rich, and at the same time permit them to elevate the society of their poorer friends. The great majority of our best writers and most cultured speakers have sprung from the ranks of this class. To these, more than any other class, are we indebted for the invention and application of those rules of conduct which serve to make social life more attractive and more desirable than it could otherwise be. To people of this class we look for a large application and a more liberal interpretation of the Golden Rule, upon whose principles all real etiquette must rest. Then, to those who must be the adjusters of the arrogance in the rich and the self-deprecation in the poor, a correct knowledge of the usages of polite society can not but be of inestimable value.

Value to the Poor

It is the birthright of an American citizen to rise from the ranks of poverty to the highest gift of the people, if he but possess the ability. Whatever the circumstances, no one likes to admit his poverty. Of all things which make us most easily forget a man's poverty, the practice of good manners is most efficient. One's clothing may be naught but rags and tatters, but if he bear the impress of a gentleman he is honored and respected by all. The graceful air and self-reliant feeling which belong to a well-bred man, are the most effectual antidotes for the stings of poverty. Many a poor man, not only in this but in other lands, has found his way into the society of the best, only on the favor granted because of his manners. One may be poor, yet if he possess good manners and an amiable style in his intercourse with people, his poverty is soon lost amid the good will and friendly feeling created among his associates. Therefore let the young man or the young woman of humble circumstances take courage and set to work at once to acquire a knowledge of the laws and usages of good society.

Value to Various Kinds of Business

Most of the laws of business are based upon the Golden Rule. One who has gained for himself a practical knowledge of this rule is fit for any business. What one of the learned professions would thrive without the aid of proper behavior in its practice? In the physician's efforts to alleviate pain and disease, how valuable to him is a knowledge of what is proper and right in his social treatment of patients. Who has not heard of a physician unsuccessful in his practice because he did not observe good manners? Every successful lawyer soon discovers the benefit of good breeding in his dealings with his clients. Who has not heard it asked about a minister, "Are his social qualities good?"—meaning nothing more nor less than an estimate of a pastor's ability to exercise good manners and genial behavior among his people. Such knowledge is equally useful to the teacher, who must in turn shape the manners of his pupils. Where do we find more agreeable or more polite men, women and boys, than in the clerks, sales-women and cash-boys of the large mercantile establishments of our cities and towns? Every business is pervaded, more or less, by the influence of good behavior and gentle manners. Hence, who can venture to undertake any business except he first acquaint himself with what is right as to his manners and conduct?

Value to Churches

As disciples of the great Master we would naturally expect the best manners to be found among Christians. This as a rule is true, and as a result these teachings are practiced to a greater or less extent in all places of worship. Besides this, various classes of persons collect in our churches. This calls for some plan of action and mode of intercourse which shall cause the least trouble and the easiest and most harmonious action among all interested. The minister has his rule of action, and so have the pews. Churches ought not to be places to which people go to see and be seen. Therefore a respectful and reverent manner is necessary to worship properly in any church. Quiet, and attention to proper behavior in church, are always marks of good breeding, and they are valuable in helping to make the services and the teachings of the sanctuary useful and beneficial to all engaging in them.

Value to Governments and Nations

France has long been considered the politest nation of the modern world. Greece held sway in this particular among the ancients. The two nations have stood foremost during their respective ages. The culture of Athens, the grace and gayety of Paris, have long been proverbial. The "free and easy" manners of America, as compared with the stiffness and severe propriety of England, strike a balance in favor of the Republic. French influence, language and manners have long moved the courts of the continent. French diplomacy only gave way to the energy and persistence of the Prussian Bismarck. Here we are confronted by the code of manners which governments have found it necessary to institute. Not even Republican America is exempt from this necessity. Washington etiquette stands side by side with that of the Court of St. James and St. Cloud. The decorum of a capital must necessarily influence the conduct of all officials belonging to the government. Without this formality and system the dignity and self-respect of a nation could not be preserved. As it is, the weakest nation claims recognition and honor at the hands of the strongest; and the mildest government as thoroughly influences the diplomacy and courtesy of the world as does the most severe. So thoroughly does the observance of propriety and etiquette pervade the actions of governments, that the Golden Rule is more thoroughly observed among nations than it is among individuals.

Summary

Good manners are great helps in the work of life. From individuals to governments, from nations to communities, their value is seen and appreciated. Politeness in the hourly intercourse of life pours oil upon the troubles and vexations of business, and smooths away most of the rudeness that otherwise might jar upon our nerves. "In honor preferring one another," is the great secret of good manners. An Indian Chief, at an official interview with President Jackson, was as graceful as Henry Clay. He was asked, "How is it that you are so graceful, never having studied etiquette?" "Ah," said the Chief, "I have no mad in me now." So it is with us all. With the good will of the Master in the heart, the practice of the rules of good breeding is easy. Study, observation, experiment, will make any one master of this great accomplishment.

DRESS

EXQUISITE TASTE AND GOOD COMMON SENSE ARE THE essential elements of dress. Elegant dressing is not found in expense; money without judgment may load, but never can adorn. A lady may be covered with jewels, and yet not show the slightest good taste. One has rightly said: "The result of the finest toilet should be an *elegant woman,* not an elegantly dressed woman."

Consistency in Dress

The only just principles of dressing are, simplicity, adaptation to your figure, your rank and your circumstances.

Consistency in regard to station and fortune is the first matter to be considered. A woman of good sense will not wish to expend in unnecessary extravagances, money wrung from an anxious, laborious husband; or if her husband be a man of fortune, she will not, even then, encroach upon her allowance. In the early years of married life, when the income is moderate, it should be the pride of a woman to see how little she can spend upon her dress, and yet present that tasteful and creditable appearance which is desirable. Much depends upon management, and upon the care taken of garments. She should turn everything to account, and be careful of her clothing when wearing it.

Extravagance in Dress

Dress, to be in perfect taste, need not be costly. It is unfortunate that in the United States, too much attention is paid

to dress by those who have neither the excuse of ample means, nor of social culture. The wife of a poorly paid clerk, or of a young man just starting in business, aims at dressing as stylishly as does the wealthiest among her acquaintances. The sewing girl, the shop girl, the chambermaid, and even the cook, must have their elegantly trimmed silk dresses and velvet cloaks for Sunday and holiday wear, and the injury done by this state of things to the morals and manners of the poorer classes is incalculable.

Indifference to Dress

Indifference to dress is a sign of indolence and slovenliness. Even if a lady's dress is of cheap material it must be neat. Poverty is no excuse for uncleanliness.

It is the duty of every lady to dress as well and as becomingly as her means will allow.

Appropriate Dress

The style of a lady's dress must assume a character corresponding with the wearer. Small ladies may wear delicate colors, while large and robust persons appear best in dark shades. A lady's complexion determines the colors that are most becoming for her. Dark rich shades harmonize with brunette complexion and dark hair, and persons of fair complexion and light hair look best in the delicate tints.

Gloves

Ladies and gentlemen wear gloves on the street, at evening parties, to the opera, or, theatre, at receptions, at balls, at church, when making a call, riding or driving; but not at a dinner.

White gloves should be worn at balls; delicate tints for evening parties, and any shade at church.

Evening Dress for Gentlemen

For evening a gentleman should wear a black dress suit, with white cravat, and kid gloves of white or pale hue. His shirt front should be spotless. He should give especial attention to his hair, and see to it that it is a becoming length and neither too long nor too short. Dress for a large dinner party, opera or ball may be the same. Morning dress is worn for church, and on Sunday no gentleman should appear in evening dress, either at church, at home or abroad.

Morning Dress for Gentlemen

The morning dress for gentlemen is a black frock coat, or a black cut-away, white or black vest, gray or colored pants, a high silk (stove-pipe) hat, and a black necktie. A black frock coat with black pants is not considered a good combination, nor is a dress coat and colored or light pants. The morning dress is suitable, for garden calls and receptions. It is not good taste for a gentleman to wear a dress coat, and white tie in day time.

Jewelry for Gentlemen

No well-bred gentleman will load himself with jewelry. He may wear one ring, a watch chain, studs and cuff buttons.

Evening Dress for Ladies

A lady's evening dress may be as rich, elegant and attractive as she wishes to have it. Full evening dress should be worn to parties and balls, and it may be worn to large dinners. A dress should not be cut so low in the neck as to cause remarks.

Fashions are too changeable to give directions as to how a party dress should be made.

Ball Dress

A fanciful and airy dress is most suitable for the ballroom. Rich and heavily trimmed silks are for those who do not dance. The brightest and most delicately tinted, silks, expensive laces, an elaborate display of diamonds and flowers for the hair all belong to the costume for a ball.

The Full Dinner Dress

A lady's dinner dress for winter may be of heavy silk or elegant velvet, and for summer, light, rich goods. Everything about her costume should be as complete and faultless as possible. The fan and gloves should be fresh. Diamonds are used as extravagantly as you wish. The flowers worn should be of the choicest variety. Black, dark blue, purple, dark green, garnet and light tints may be worn at dinner parties.

Dress of a Hostess at a Dinner Party

The dress of a hostess at a dinner party should be rich, but not more elegant than her guests. A rich silk dress, with lace at the neck and wrists, with plain jewelry by daylight, but diamonds by gaslight, must be worn by a young hostess.

Showy Dress

Black predominates over all colors. The showy costumes once worn have given way to more sober colors.

Dress for Receiving Calls

If a lady has set apart a special day for receiving calls, she should have a silk dress for the occasion. The quality may depend on her position. Laces and jewelry may be worn with this dress. A lady who attends to her morning domestic affairs, may receive calls in her morning dress, which must be neat, with white collar and cuffs. Upon receiving New Years calls, a lady should be dressed as elegantly as she can afford. If she darkens her parlors and lights the gas, she should be dressed in full evening dress.

Carriage Dress

A dress for a drive through the streets of a city, along fashionable drives, or in parks, can not be too elegant. It may or may not have a trail. For a country drive the material should be of a dark color as it is not so likely to be soiled.

Visiting Costumes

Costumes for visiting, funeral occasions, and informal calls should be of richer material than walking suits. The bonnet may be rich or simple. For winter, the jacket, mantle, and shawl or cloak worn should be rich. Whatever is worn in summer should be comfortable and pleasant to look at.

Dress for Morning Calls

For morning calls one may wear a walking suit if they are walking, if not, a carriage dress should be worn. A silk dress should be worn with laces, light gloves and jewelry. Diamonds are more preferable for evening than daylight. A dark dress is most appropriate for morning calls.

Morning Dress for the Street

A morning dress for the street should be neat and plain. It should be walking length. Gloves to suit the weather should be worn. Neat linen collars and cuffs are most suitable. The hat or bonnet should match the dress. For rainy weather a large waterproof with hood is more convenient than an umbrella.

A morning dress for a visit or breakfast in public may be of plain woolen goods, if it is winter. If it is summer, it may be white or figured wash goods. The hair should be neatly combed without ornaments.

The Promenade Dress

The dress for the promenade should be in perfect harmony with itself. All the colors worn should harmonize, if they are not strictly identical. The bonnet should not be of one color and parasol of another, the dress of a third, and the gloves of a fourth. Nor should one article be new and another shabby. The collar and cuffs should be of lace, the kid gloves should be selected to harmonize with the color of the dress, a perfect fit. The jewelry worn should be bracelets, cuff buttons, plain gold earrings, a watch, chain, and brooch.

Some Hints on Dress

Dress should, above all things, be appropriate and becoming.

Dress should always be made subordinate to the wearer; that is, the clothes should not attract more attention than the person they clothe.

Care should be taken to select only such materials and styles of dress as are suited to the figure, height, and complexion. To reproduce what looks well on others is frequently disastrous.

The colors worn on the street should be in keeping with the season.

A stout person should wear dark colors, and the thin, light.

Neatness and simple elegance are the signs of a well dressed woman. The French have a genius for dress, due in a great measure to their artistic temperaments, and their infallible judgment of the fitness of things. In that country, an old or middle-aged woman understands how to subdue the inroads of advancing years without suggesting the loss of youth by too great an effort.

In Paris the stage sets the fashions and it is at the leading theatres that the latest creations of Worth or Pingat are first seen.

In the days of the French emigration the ladies escaped from Honfleur with the full-skirted overcoats of their husbands about them, and these gave rise to a distinct style of dress.

A stout woman should never wear a loose sleeve, nor one coming only to the elbow. Neither the very stout nor very thin should appear in low-necked dresses.

Opera Dress

Opera dress for matinees may be as elegant as for morning calls. A bonnet is always worn unless she dresses in evening costume, then she may wear ornaments in the hair and leave off the bonnet. Since the effect of light colors is more brilliant in the opera house, they should be worn.

The Riding Dress

A lady's riding habit should fit perfectly. The skirt must be full, and long enough to cover her feet. She should wear stout shoes and gloves with gauntlets. The material for the riding dress may be of broadcloth or waterproof. Lighter goods maybe used for summer, and a row of shot should be stitched at the bottom of the breadths of the left side to prevent the skirt from being blown by the wind. The riding dress should button nearly to the throat, and a linen collar with a bright necktie should be worn. Coat sleeves should come to the wrist with linen cuffs beneath them. No lace or embroidery should be worn when riding. The waist must be attached to a skirt of usual length, and the long riding skirt fastened over it, so that

if an accident occurs obliging her to dismount, she can remove the long skirt and still be properly dressed. The hair should be tucked up very compactly, and no veil must be allowed to stream in the wind. Fashion will determine the shape of the hat, and the trimming should be fastened very securely.

A Walking Suit

A walking suit may be rich or plain. It should be neatly made and not shabby. Flashy colors may be used for trimmings. Black is the most becoming for a street dress. The walking dress must be short enough to clear the ground.

Dress for Ladies of Business

Ladies who are employed as sales women, teachers, or those occupied in literature, art or business of any kind should wear a dress different from the usual walking suit. The material should be serviceable and of a sober color. It should be plainly trimmed. Plain collar and cuffs should be worn; gloves that can be easily removed. Jewelry may be worn in a small quantity. The hat should be neat. Waterproof makes a good serviceable cloak for winter wear.

241

Ordinary Evening Dress

Silk is the most becoming for an evening dress. Woolen dresses may be worn in winter; and lawns or white dresses elegantly made, in summer. Much jewelry may be worn if desired. For winter the colors should be rich, and knots of bright ribbon should he worn at the throat and in the hair. Diamonds and artificial flowers are not in good taste. One may make a casual call in an ordinary evening dress. A dress bonnet or hood may be worn. If the latter is worn it must be removed during the call.

Dress for a Social Party

Choose your colors, material and trimmings to suit your taste. The neck and arms must be covered. Light gloves may or may not be worn.

Dress for Church

A church dress should be the plainest promenade costume; of dark color and no superfluous jewelry.

Dress for the Theatre

A rich promenade dress with a handsome cloak or shawl is suitable for the theatre. A bonnet or hat may be worn. Gloves should harmonize with the dress.

Dress for Lecture and Concert

A silk dress with laces and jewelry is a suitable costume for a lecture or concert. A rich shawl or an opera cloak is an appropriate outer garment. Light kid gloves should be worn.

Croquet, Archery, and Skating Costumes

Croquet and archery costumes may be similar, and they admit of more brilliancy in coloring than any of the out-of-door costumes. They should be short, displaying a handsomely fitting but stout boot, and should be so arranged as to leave the arms perfectly free. The gloves should be soft and washable. Kid is not suitable for either occasion. The hat should have a broad brim, so as to shield the face from the sun and render a parasol unnecessary. The trimming for archery costumes is usually of green.

An elegant skating costume may be made of velvet, trimmed with fur, with fur bordered gloves and boots. Any of the warm, bright colored wool fabrics, however, are suitable for the dress. If blue or green are worn, they should be relieved with trimmings of dark furs. Silk is not suitable for skating costume. To avoid suffering from cold feet, the boot should be amply loose.

Bathing Costume

The best material for a bathing costume is flannel, and the most suitable color is gray, and may be trimmed with bright worsted braid. The loose sacque, or the yoke waist, both to

be belted in, and falling about midway between the knee and ankle, is the best form for a bathing costume. An oil-skin cap to protect the hair from the water, and merino socks to match the dress, complete the costume.

Traveling Dress

Comfort and protection from dust and dirt are the requirements of a traveling dress. For an extensive journey a traveling suit is a great convenience, but for a short trip an ordinary dress may be worn with a duster or a waterproof cloak, as the season demands. A variety of materials may be used for a traveling dress. Soft neutral tints, and smooth surface, which does not retain the dust, may be used. The dress should be made plain and quite short. The underskirts should be colored, woolen in winter and linen in summer. The hat or bonnet must be plainly trimmed and protected by a thick veil. Collar and cuffs should be worn. The hair should be put up in the plainest manner. A waterproof and warm woolen shawl are necessary, and may be carried in a shawl strap when not needed. A satchel should be carried, in which may be kept a change of collars, cuffs, gloves, handkerchiefs, toilet articles and towels. A traveling dress should be well supplied with pockets. The waterproof should have large pockets, and there should be one in the underskirt, in which to carry such money and valuables as are not needed for immediate use.

The Wedding Dress

A full bridal costume should be white from head to foot. The dress may be of silk, heavily corded satin, or plain silk, merino, alpaca, crape, lawn or muslin. The veil may be of lace, tulle or illusion, but it must long and full. It may or may not cover the face. Orange blossoms or other white flowers and maiden blush rosés should form the bridal wreaths and bouquets. The dress is high, and the arms covered. Slippers of white satin and white kid gloves complete the dress.

Dress of the Bridesmaids

The bridesmaids should not be so elaborately dressed as the bride. Their dresses must be of white, but they may wear delicately colored flowers and ribbons. They may not wear veils, but if they do, they must be shorter than that of the bride.

Traveling Dress of a Bride

Silk or any of the fine fabrics for walking dresses are suitable for a bride's traveling dress. The shade may depend upon the latest style. Bonnet and gloves should match the dress in color. It may, if she wishes, be more elaborately trimmed than an ordinary traveling dress. It is very customary now for the bride to be married in a traveling costume, and the bridal pair at once set out upon their journey.

Dress at Wedding Receptions

Full evening dress should be worn by the guests at evening receptions. No one should attend in black or mourning dress, which should give place to grey or lavender. At a morning reception of the wedded couple, guests should wear the richest street costume with white gloves.

Mourning

In the United States no prescribed periods for wearing mourning garments have been fixed upon. When the grief is profound no rules are needed. But where persons wear mourning for style and not for feeling, there is need of fixed rules. For deep mourning one should wear the heaviest black of serge, bombazine, lustreless alpaca, delaine, merino or similar heavily clinging material, with crape collar and cuffs. Mourning dresses should not be trimmed. No ruffles, bows, or flounces are admissible. The bonnet is of black crape; a hat should never be worn. The veil is of crape or barege with heavy border; black gloves are worn and black bordered handkerchiefs should be used. Black furs may be worn in winter. Jewelry is forbidden; jet pins and buckles should be used. Black silk and alpaca trimmed with crape may be worn for second mourning with white collars and cuffs. The crape veil is laid aside for net or tulle, but the jet jewelry is still retained. A less degree of mourning is worn of black and white, purple and gray, or a combination of these colors. Crape is retained in bonnet trimming and crape flowers may be added. Light gray, white and black, and light shades of lilac indicate a slight mourning. A black lace bonnet, with white or violet flowers, supersedes crape, and jet or gold jewelry is worn.

Periods of Wearing Mourning

The deepest mourning is that worn by a widow for her husband. It is worn two years, sometimes longer. Widow's mourning for the first year consists of solid black woolen goods, collar and cuffs of folded untrimmed crape, a simple crape bonnet, and a long, thick, black crape veil. The second year, silk trimmed with crape, black lace collar and cuffs, and a shorter veil may be worn, and in the last six months gray, violet and white are permitted. A widow should wear her hair perfectly plain, and should always wear a bonnet; never a hat.

The mourning for a father or mother is worn for one year. The first six months the proper dress is of solid black woolen goods trimmed with crape, black crape bonnet with black crape facings and black strings, black crape veil, collar and cuffs of black crape. Three months, black silk with crape trimming, white or black lace collar and cuffs, veil of tulle and white bonnet facings; and the last three months in gray, purple and violet. Mourning worn for a child is the same as that worn for a parent.

Mourning for a grandparent is worn for six months. Three months black woolen goods, white collar and cuffs, short crape veil and bonnet of crape trimmed with black silk or ribbon; six weeks in black silk trimmed with crape, lace collar and cuffs, short tulle veil; and six weeks in gray, purple, white and violet.

Mourning worn for a friend who leaves you an inheritance, is the same as that worn for a grandparent.

Mourning for a brother or sister is worn for six months, two months in solid black trimmed with crape, white linen collar and cuffs, bonnet of black with white facing and black strings; two months in black silk, with white lace collar and cuffs; and two months in gray, purple, white and violet.

Mourning for an uncle or aunt is worn for three months, and is the second mourning named above, tulle, white linen and white bonnet facings being worn at once. For a nephew or niece, the same is worn for the same length of time.

The deepest mourning excludes kid gloves; they should be of cloth, silk or thread; and no jewelry is permitted during the first month of close mourning. Embroidery, jet trimmings, puffs, plaits—in fact, trimming of any kind—is forbidden in deep mourning, but worn when it is lightened.

Mourning handkerchiefs should be of very sheer fine linen, with a border of black, very wide for close mourning, narrower as the black is lightened.

Mourning silks should be perfectly lustreless, and the ribbons worn without any gloss.

Ladies invited to funeral ceremonies should always wear a black dress, even if they are not in mourning; and it is bad taste to appear with a gay bonnet or shawl, as if for a festive occasion.

The mourning for children under twelve years of age is white in summer and gray in winter, with black trimmings, belt, sleeve ruffles and bonnet ribbons.

PRESENTS

OUR PRESENTS SPRING FROM ONE OF TWO SOURCES. EITHER they are the manifestation of a pure, unselfish affection, or they are given with the expectation of receiving something in return. In the latter case they partake of the nature of bribes, and are a violation, not only of the rules of propriety, but even of the principles of morality. A true present must be a token of affection already existing, not a means of winning favor.

Costly Presents

Rich and costly presents should rarely if ever be made. A present ought to be valuable from what it signifies, rather than on account of what it really is. A wealthy father may, of course, make a costly gift to a son or daughter; but in most cases where there is not some close relationship, the propriety of such a gift would be extremely questionable.

Most Suitable Presents

Says Emerson: "Our tokens of love are for the most part barbarous, cold, and lifeless, because they do not represent our life. The only gift is a portion of thyself. Therefore, let the farmer give his corn; the miner, his gem; the sailor, his corals and shells; the painter, his picture, and the poet, his poem."

In other words, it is always best to give something of your own production or discovery. If the recipient have any love for you, the value of the gift will be enhanced many fold by being the offspring of your effort and skill. But if he have no true affection for the giver, nothing can be valuable as a gift.

A person sometimes comes into possession of a thing which is of no special value to himself, but which to another, on account of his calling, studies, or tastes, may be very desirable. Under such circumstance it is always proper to make a present of the thing in question, even to a stranger.

Gifts for Ladies

As a rule a young unmarried lady should not receive a present, above all a costly present, from a gentleman; unless he be a relative, or is engaged to her. A costly gift from a gentleman to a young lady would be indelicate, as having the appearance of a bribe upon her affections. A married lady may receive a gift from a gentleman who is under obligations to her for hospitality.

Gifts by Ladies

Gifts by ladies should be of a delicate nature, usually some dainty product of their own taste and skill. If a married lady makes a present to a gentleman she should give it in the name of both herself and her husband.

A Gentleman's Present to his Bethrothed

Even to the lady to whom he is engaged a gentleman should not, as a rule, make very costly gifts. Neither is it the best of taste to present her ornaments for her person.

Gifts Beyond One's Means.

Avoid giving a present that may seem inconsistent with your means. The recipient will be apt to think, even if his good taste prevents him from saying so, that you should have kept the gift, or its cost, for yourself.

Receiving a Gift

Always accept with expressions of gratitude any present offered you in the spirit of kindness, unless the circumstances are such that you can not with propriety take the gift. Never say to one who makes you a present, "I fear you rob yourself," nor anything to imply that the gift is beyond his means.

Refferring to Gifts

After a present has once been received and acknowledged, it is in bad taste for either party to refer to it again.

If you have made a present and the recipient praises it, do not be given to depreciate its value; but say that you are glad to know that it has given pleasure, or something to that effect.

Rand. McNally Co.

GAMES, SPORTS AND AMUSEMENTS

A BOOK DESIGNED TO TREAT OF SOCIAL ETIQUETTE, WOULD not be complete unless all departments of social life were discussed. Whenever men and women meet, there the rules of etiquette and good manners are found in force. Sports and games are a very important part of social life, and ladies and gentlemen will be as careful while engaged in them, as at any other time, that their conduct may manifest politeness and refinement. While the same fundamental principles of politeness, unselfishness and regard for others, govern here as elsewhere, yet the formality of etiquette—if there be, any—should be relaxed, and ladies and gentlemen should engage in games and sports with perfect freedom and ease. There should be no rules of propriety to make one feel restrained, and thus make his actions seem awkward and his speech halting. Games should be entered into with mirth and cheerfulness, with the greatest gayety and liveliness—never with restraint. It is not our purpose here to lay down a set of rules governing the games we wish to mention; the full rules may be found accompanying the implements of each game. But we may properly describe some of the more popular and common games and amusements, and give suggestions as to what is customary, or what are regarded as improprieties.

Chess

This is the most popular intellectual game. It is called the game of the kings. It affords much amusement, sometimes intense excitement, to those who become practiced players. It is the most profitable of all indoor games. Requiring thought and quiet it is improper for either player to make a disturbing noise. A gentleman playing with a lady, should first assist her in arranging her pieces, and then arrange his own. He is not expected to give her advantages which the rules of the game do not accord to her. It is regarded by the rules of the game, as improper to whistle, or hum, or drum with the fingers, or keep time with the feet. The game should be conducted as nearly as possible in silence. You should not manifest impatience at your opponent taking his time to make a move. See that you play strictly according to the rules adopted, and if victor, play again if your opponent desire it.

Archery

Perhaps the most popular outdoor amusement which can be indulged in by ladies and gentlemen, is that found with the bow and arrow. In many villages and cities throughout the country archery clubs have been formed, and with American young people the practice of archery has become one of the most delightful and profitable of sports.

Implements for Archery

The implements required for archery are the bow, arrows, target, a quiver pouch and belt, an arm-guard or brace, a shooting glove or finger tip and a scoring card.

The bow is from five to six feet long, made of lancewood or locust. Spanish yew is considered the choicest, next comes the Italian, then the English yew; lancewood and lancewood backed with hickory are used more than any other. In choosing a bow, you will find that the best you can afford will prove the cheapest in the end. Men should use bows six feet long, pulling from forty to sixty pounds; and ladies, bows of five feet or five feet six inches in length, pulling from twenty-five to forty pounds. The target consists of a circular, thick mat of straw, from two to four feet in diameter, covered with canvas, painted in a series of circles. The inner circle is a gold

color, then comes red, white, black and the outer circle white. The score for a gold hit is nine; the red, seven; the inner white, five; the black, three; and the outer white, one. The arrows should be of uniform thickness throughout, being generally made of pine; the finest grades are made of white deal, and every arrow should have a sharp point of iron or brass; they are from twenty to thirty inches in length. The quiver-belt is worn around the waist and contains the arrows which are being sued. A shooting glove is worn on the right hand to protect the fingers from soreness in drawing the string of the bow.

Archery Clubs

It is by organization into clubs, that archery is made a game. The clubs are about equally divided as to ladies and gentlemen, and have their prescribed officers and rules. Each member of the club is expected to furnish his own implements, and to attend all the card practice meetings and prize shootings. Besides the officers usual to all other organizations, the club has a field marshal, whose duties are to place the targets, measure the shooting distances and have a general supervision of the field; a scorer, who shall keep a score of each individual member, and a lady paramount, who acts as umpire, and, as highest officer in the club, is judge of all disputes. In practice meetings there should be one target for every six or eight persons. The targets may be placed at any required distance, from thirty to one hundred yards,—ladies being generally allowed about one-fourth the distance in shooting. An equal number of ladies and gentlemen occupy one target, and each shoot a certain number of arrows, from three to six, a score being kept as the target is hit.

Ladie's Costume

May be more brilliant than the ordinary walking dress, and should be made short enough for convenience in movement, and so as to give free and easy motion of the arms.

Boating

Where there is water to admit of it, boating is found an enjoyable and profitable recreation. It may be pursued by both ladies and gentlemen. As there is considerable danger in sailing, no gentleman should think of inviting ladies to ride with him on the water, unless he is thoroughly capable of managing the boat. This requires tact and experience. Rowing is safer and is a healthful and delightful exercise, and many ladies become experts at the art. But care should be taken in not overloading the boat. Every gentleman should know how to row, as it is a knowledge easily acquired. If one inexperienced in rowing goes out with others in a boat, he should refrain from any attempt to row, as it may render the ride uncomfortable to his companions. It is polite to offer a friend the "stroke" oar, as it is regarded as the post of honor.

A lady's dress in rowing should give perfect freedom to her arms; she should have a short skirt, stout boots, and a hat with sufficient brim to protect her from the sun.

Lawn Tennis

This is one of the most ancient of games. The ancient Greeks and Romans played it, and ever since, with varying intermissions, it has been a favorite game in many countries of Europe. There are many points in favor of tennis to commend it to popular favor. It is a game for both ladies and gentlemen, with equal chances in favor of the ladies carrying off the palm. The exercise is not of an exhausting character, and affords ladies a training in easy and graceful movements.

The requisites for playing are, a lawn of level surface about forty-five by one hundred feet, as the "court," upon which

the playing is done, is twenty-seven by seventy-eight feet; a net four or five feet high and twenty-seven feet long, which divides the court a ball of india rubber and a "racket."

The uses of the net, the ball and the racket, may be found in the rules which accompany the implements.

Picnics

At picnic while ladies and gentlemen will not forget to be polite and courteous, forms and ceremonies are thrown aside. Men and women engage in these days of pleasure that they may escape, for a time, the cares of business, and the restraints of formal society, so at such times it is the duty of

all to make the occasion one of gayety and mirth. Formal introductions and ceremonies should not stand in the way of enjoyment. The ladies should provide the luncheon or dinner, and invent whatever they can in the way of enjoyment for the gentlemen. The gentlemen at such times are not only the guides and escorts of the ladies, but their servants as well, and they should perform such services for the ladies, in the way of procuring flowers, carrying baskets, etc., as may be requested. It is their duty to provide conveyances to and from the place of the festivities, to make all arrangements necessary in the way of providing music, games, boats, and whatever else is needed to add to the pleasure of the day.

Etiquette of Card Playing

We will note here some of the ordinary rules of politeness to be observed in card playing:

Never urge any one, who seems to be unwilling, to play a game of cards. They may have conscientious scruples in the matter, which should be respected.

If you do not understand the game it is proper to refuse to play. But if you know how, and have no scruples of conscience, you should not refuse, if a game can not be made up without you.

Guests should not call for cards. It is the privilege of the host or hostess to suggest them.

Never finger the cards while they are being dealt, nor take them up until they are all dealt out.

Never hurry any one who is playing. In endeavoring to play their best, they should be allowed their own time without interruption.

Betting at cards is vulgar; it is nothing less than gambling, and should be always scrupulously avoided.

If the players wish quiet, that they may play well, do not suggest, or keep up a conversation, or make any noise which will distract your own mind, or the minds of others, from the game.

WASHINGTON ETIQUETTE

AT OUR NATIONAL CAPITOL, WHERE social standing is determined by official rank, there are some special rules of etiquette which we shall briefly notice in this chapter.

The President

The President is regarded as "the first man in the nation," socially as well as officially. There is no special set of formalities necessary for forming his acquaintance. He receives calls, but is not required to return them. He is addressed as "Mr. President" or "Your Excellency."

When the President gives up the morning hours to receiving calls, those who have business with him take precedence over those who have not. In either case the caller is summoned into the room occupied by the President's secretaries. Here he presents his card and is shown in to the President. The person who has no business with the President simply pays his respects and withdraws. On a private call it is always better to secure the services of some official, or friend of the President, to go with you and introduce you.

Receptions at the White House

While congress is in session, stated receptions are given at the White House which all are permitted to attend. The caller gives his name to the usher upon entering the reception room. The usher announces the name, and as the caller approaches the President, he is introduced by an official appointed for that purpose. Having been presented to the President and the members of his family, the guest passes on and mingles in the social intercourse of those assembled. A caller may leave his card if he wishes.

Presidential State Dinners

At state dinners given by the President, the same rules prevail as at any other formal dinner, but precedence is given to the guests according to official station. An invitation from the President can not be refused, and it affords a sufficient excuse for breaking any other engagement; but the parties with whom you may shave other engagements should be informed of your invitation from the President.

Members of the Presidential Family

The wife of the President is not obliged to return calls, though she may visit those who are special friends, or whom she wishes to honor by her company.

The other members of the President's family may receive and return calls.

New Year's Receptions at the White House

New Year's receptions are the most ceremonious occasions which occur at the White House. Ladies appear in the most elegant toilets suitable for a morning reception, and members of foreign legations appear in the court dress of their respective nationalities.

Order of Official Rank

Next in rank to the President are, the Chief Justice, the Vice-President, and Speaker of the House of Representatives. These receive the first visits from all others. Next in order are the General of the Army, and the Admiral of the Navy. All these, so far mentioned, receive the first call from the representatives. The wife of any official is entitled to the same social precedence as her husband. Among officers of the army and navy, the Lieutenant-General corresponds to the Vice-Admiral, the Major-General to the Rear Admiral, Brigadier-General to Commodore, Colonel to Captain in the navy, and so on.

Cabinet Officers

On all ordinary occasions the cabinet officers take equal rank. When it becomes necessary in state ceremony to have some order of precedence, it is as follows:

Secretary of State, of the Treasury, of War, of the Navy, the Postmaster-General, Secretary of the Interior, Attorney-General.

The wives of the cabinet officers, or the ladies of the household, give receptions on every Wednesday during the season, from the first of January till Lent. On these occasions, all who wish to do so, are at liberty to call, and refreshments are served. The ladies of the family are under obligations to return these calls and leave the cards of the cabinet officers, with an invitation to an evening reception.

Cabinet officers are expected to entertain, by dinners and otherwise, senators, representatives and other high officials and distinguished visitors at Washington, as well as the ladies of their respective families. Hours for calling at the capital are usually from two till half past five.

Senators and Representatives

It is, optional with senators, representatives and all other officials, except President and cabinet officers, whether they entertain.

FOREIGN TITLES

I N THIS COUNTRY WHERE TITLES ARE NOT HANDED DOWN from father to son, but won, if at all, by each for himself, we naturally know but little of hereditary titles. In Europe it is quite different, and, as many of our citizens go abroad, it will be well that they be informed upon this subject. For, in Europe, to fail to give a person his or her proper title is a serious breach of manners, and one not readily overlooked.

Royalty

The head of the social structure in England is the King and Queen. They are addressed under the form "Your Majesty." Second in rank is the Prince of Wales, heir apparent to the throne. The other children while in their minority are all known as princes and princesses. The eldest of the princesses is the crown princess. When they attain to their majority the

princes become dukes, and the princesses retain their former title, adding that of their husbands when they marry. Members of the royal house are all designated as "Their Royal Highnesses."

The Nobility

A duke who inherits the title from his father is one grade below a royal duke. The wife of a duke is a duchess. They are both addressed as "Your Grace." The eldest son of a duke is styled a marquis until he comes into possession of his father's title. His wife is marchioness. The younger sons of a duke are by courtesy called lords, and the daughters have the title of lady, prefixed to their Christian names. An earl or a baron is spoken of as a lord, and his wife as a lady, though to the lady the title of countess or baroness would rightly belong. The daughters of an earl are ladies, the younger sons of both earls and barons are honorables. Bishops receive the title of lord, but with them it is not hereditary.

The Gentry

Baronets are addressed as "Sirs," and their wives receive the title of lady; but they are only commoners of a higher degree. A clergyman by right of his calling stands on an equality with all commoners, a bishop with all peers.

Esquire

In England the title of Esquire is not merely an empty compliment, as it is in this country. The following have a legal right to the title:

The sons of peers, whether known as lords or honorables.

The eldest sons of peers' sons, and their eldest sons in perpetual descent.

All the sons of baronets.

All esquires of the Knights of the Bath.

Lords of manors, chiefs of clans, and other tenants of the crown *in capite*, are esquires by prescription.

Esquires, created to that rank by patent, and their sons in perpetual succession.

Esquires by office, such as justices of the peace while on the roll, mayors of towns during mayoralty, and sheriffs of counties.

Members of the House of Commons.

Barristers at law.

Bachelors of divinity, law and physic.

All who in commissions signed by the sovereign are ever styled esquires, retain that title for life.

Imperial Rank

Emperors and empresses rank higher than kings and queens. The sons and daughters of the Emperor of Austria are styled archdukes and archduchesses.

European titles

Titles in continental Europe are so common and so often unsustained by landed or moneyed interests, that they have not the same significance which they hold in England. Many who have inherited high titles have nothing but the empty name. This is frequently the case in Germany, and still more often so in Italy.

TOILET RECIPES

TOILET RECIPES

To Beautify the Hair

THE HAIR MAY BE MADE MORE BEAUTIFUL OR DARKENED by taking four ounces of good bay rum, two ounces of olive oil, and one dram of the oil of almonds; mix and shake well and apply frequently.

To Cleanse the Hair

Beat up the yolk of an egg with a pint of soft water; apply it warm; rub briskly for several minutes, and then rinse with clean soft water.

Another method is to take one ounce of borax and half an ounce of camphor. Powder these ingredients fine and dissolve in one quart of boiling water. When cool, the solution will be ready for use. Dampen the hair with this frequently. It is claimed that this not only effectually cleanses and beautifies, but strengthens the hair, preserves the color and prevents baldness.

To Remove Dandruff

Take a piece of gum camphor as large as a chestnut and place it in one pint of alcohol. This camphorizes the alcohol. The mixture may be perfumed to suit the individual. Wet the scalp with this daily. It will stimulate the scalp, promote the growth of the hair, and in many instances prevent it from falling out.

To Preserve the Hair

Men should have their hair cut short if it begins to fall out, give it a good brushing with a moderately stiff brush while the hair is dry; then wash it well with a suds of castile soap and tepid water, and rub into the scalp, about the roots of the hair, a little bay rum, brandy or camphor water, twice a month. It is well to brush the scalp twice a week. Dampen the hair with pure soft water every time the toilet is made.

To Prevent the Hair from Turning Gray

One-half ounce sugar of lead, one-half ounce lao sulphur, one ounce glycerine, one quart rain water. Saturate the hair and scalp with this two or three times per week and you will soon have a head free from gray hairs and dandruff, while the hair will be soft and glossy.

The head should be kept cool by using, occasionally, sage tea with a little borax added. Apply with a small sponge to every part of the head just before dressing the hair.

Cure for Baldness

If the head has become bald, and the hair will grow at all, it may be restored by washing the head well every morning with the following: Four large handfuls of the stem and the leaves of the garden-box, boiled in three pints of water in a closely covered vessel for fifteen minutes, and allowed to stand in an earthen jar ten hours or more; then strain the liquid and add one ounce and a half of cologne.

To Restore Gray Hair

Hair may be restored to its natural color and beautified by the daily use of the following: Five grains sulphurate of potassium, half an ounce glycerine, one ounce tincture of acetate of iron and one pint of soft water. Mix and let the bottle stand open until the smell of potassium has disappeared, and then add a few drops attar of roses. The hair should be rubbed with a little of this daily.

Bathing the head in a weak solution of ammonia, an even teaspoonful of carbonate of ammonia to a quart of water, washing the head thoroughly with this, and brushing the hair while wet, is said to restore color.

A strong solution of rock-salt has restored gray hair. Take two tablespoonfuls to a quart of boiling water, and let it stand until cool before using.

Hair Removed by Fevers

If the hair has been removed by fevers, it may be made to grow by washing the scalp two or three times a day with a strong decoction of sage leaves.

Tonic for the Hair

Two ounces of French brandy, two of bay rum and one ounce of the best castor oil well mixed, is an excellent tonic for the hair.

Curling and Crimping the Hair

Most all curling fluids are mere impositions, but with a weak solution of isinglass a firm and perpetual form may be given to the hair. This solution is inoffensive.

Brushing the Hair

The hair should be well brushed every day in order to keep it in perfect condition. Always use the best brushes; they are the cheapest in the end. Use the brush very rapidly and for about five minutes. A celebrated beauty said, "the hair should receive one hundred strokes a day, and they should be applied in three minutes time."

The German's Treatment of the Hair

German women are noted for their luxuriant hair. Once every two weeks they wash the head thoroughly with a quart of soft water in which a handful of bran and a little white soap has been dissolved; then the yolk of an egg, slightly beaten, is rubbed into the roots of the hair; this is let remain a few minutes, and then washed and rinsed carefully in soft water. The hair is then wiped and dried thoroughly, combed up from the forehead, and parted with the fingers. After drying, apply a little pomatum made of beef marrow boiled in a small quantity of olive oil slightly perfumed. Do this near the fire in the winter or in a very warm room.

Hair Dye

A liquid that will color the human hair black and not stain the skin may be had by taking one part of bay rum, three parts of olive oil, and one part of good brandy by measure. Wash the hair with this mixture every morning. In a short time the hair will be a beautiful black, and not injured in the least. Mix in a bottle, and shake well before applying. The articles must be of the best quality.

A French hair dye is made as follows: Melt together in a bowl set in boiling water, four ounces of white wax in nine ounces of olive oil, stirring in when melted two ounces of burnt cork in powder. To apply, put on old gloves, cover the shoulders carefully, and spread on like pomade, brushing in well through the hair. Give it a brown tint by steeping an ounce of walnut black, tied in coarse muslin, in the almond oil, one week before boiling.

Hair Oils and Pomades

Mix equal parts sweet oil and cold pressed castor, oil, and to each pint of the mixture add one-fourth pint brandy and the same of cologne.

Procure a tall glass vessel, dip cotton wool in clear olive oil, and lay the cotton alternately with jessamine or other flowers. Let this stand several days, and when the flowers have imparted their perfume to the oil, squeeze the oil out of the cotton for use. The cotton may be laid in drawers or bandboxes where perfume is required.

Melt one dram of white wax, one of spermaceti, and two ounces of olive oil; add two ounces of rose water, and half an ounce of orange flower water.

Six ounces of unsalted lard, four of beef marrow, and half an ounce of yellow wax melted together and perfumed while cooling with oil of bergamot or attar of roses, makes a good and excellent pomatum for the hair.

Four ounces of spermaceti and one of lard melted together and perfumed with bergamot and rose water.

Coconut oil melted with a little olive oil and scented as preferred.

Melt together an ounce of spermaceti, one of hog's lard, one of beef marrow, and add the oil of roses, bergamot, or any other perfume.

For Inflamed Eyelids

Cut a slice of bread as thin as possible; toast both sides well, but do not burn it; soak it in cold water until cold, then put it between a piece of old linen, changing when it gets warm. This may be applied as often as desired.

Inflamed lids may be reduced by tying a small piece of ice in the corner of a thin handkerchief, and passing it back and forth over the closed eye, resting at intervals, when the cold is intense. This has been found very efficacious.

Burned Eyebrows

If the eyebrows are burned off by the fire, they may be caused to grow by applying five grains sulphate of quinine dissolved in an ounce of alcohol.

How to Make Bandoline

Simmer an ounce of quince seed in a quart of water for forty minutes, strain, and when cool add a few drops of scent, bottle and cork tightly.

Boil one-fourth of an ounce of Iceland moss in a quart of water, and add a little rectified spirits to make it keep well.

Mix one and a half drams of gum tragacanth and three ounces of rectified spirits with an equal quantity of water, and add half a pint of water. Add perfume, let the mixture stand two days and then strain.

For the Care of the Teeth

Never allow a particle of food of any kind to remain between the teeth.

Use the brush before breakfast and after each meal.

Brush lengthwise of the teeth, or up and down, as well as across.

The brush should not be too stiff nor too soft. The one will wear the teeth in the course of time, and the other will not thoroughly cleanse them.

Pure castile soap is better than prepared powders.

Use a goose quill toothpick freely after each meal.

Take two ounces of myrrh in fine powder, two table-spoonfuls of honey, and a little sage in fine powder. Mix them well together, and wet the teeth and gums with a little every night and morning. This will keep the teeth and gums clean.

To Clean Black Teeth

Pulverize equal parts of salt and cream of tartar, and mix them thoroughly. After washing the teeth in the morning, rub them with this powder, and after a few such applications the blackness will disappear.

To Clean the Teeth and Gums

Mix a little finely powdered green sage, one ounce of myrrh in fine powder, with two tablespoonfuls of honey. Every night and morning, wet the teeth and gums with a little of this preparation.

To Beautify the Teeth

Dissolve two ounces of borax in three pints of boiling water, and add one teaspoonful of spirits of camphor before it is cold; bottle for use. A teaspoonful of this with an equal quantity of tepid water may be used every time the teeth are washed.

Toothache Preventive

Use flour of sulphur as a tooth powder every night, rubbing the teeth and gums with a rather hard tooth brush. If used also after dinner, all the better. It preserves the teeth, and does not communicate any smell whatever to the mouth.

Wash for the Teeth

The safest, cheapest and most effective tooth wash is pure soft water and the finest quality of castile soap; apply with a moderately stiff brush, morning and evening.

To Make Lip Salve

Place a jar in a basin of boiling water. Melt an ounce each of white wax and spermaceti, flour of benzoin fifteen grains, and half an ounce of oil of almonds. Stir till the mixture is cold, and color red with a little alkanet root.

Remedy for Chapped Lips

Melt in a glass vessel, and stir with a wooden spoon one ounce of white wax, four ounces of oil of roses, and one-half ounce of spermaceti. Pour into a glass or china cup. Add ten drops of carbolic acid to one ounce of glycerine, and apply freely at night.

Lotion to Remove Freckles

Dissolve three grains of borax in five drams of rose water, and orange flower water. A very simple and harmless remedy is equal parts of pure glycerine and rose water, applied every night and allowed to dry.

To Remove Sunburn

A good article to remove sunburn is made by pouring a quart of boiling water upon a handful of bran, letting it stand an hour and then strain. Put it in a pint of bay rum when cold, and wash the face with it three times every day.

Milk of almonds is recommended as a good remedy.

One pound of ox gall, two drams of borax, one dram of camphor, one dram of alum, and half an ounce of sugar candy, mixed and stirred well for ten minutes, and strained through blotting paper when transparent, is also recommended. Bottle for use and stir several times a fortnight.

Tan

One-half pint of new milk, one-half ounce of white brandy, and one-fourth ounce of lemon juice boiled together, skimmed clean from scum, and used night and morning, will remove tan.

Freckles

Freckles may be removed by applying with a linen rag, a mixture of one pint of pure alcohol, two gallons of strong soapsuds, and a quarter of an ounce of rosemary.

Horse-radish, grated into sweet milk and let stand ten hours, may be used for the same purpose.

Finely powdered nitre applied to the freckles with the moistened finger is very, effective.

One ounce of honey mixed with one pint of luke-warm water, and applied when cold, is said to be a good freckle lotion.

For the Complexion

Mix in a vial one pint of cherry wine, one dram of benzoin gum in powder, one dram of nutmeg oil, six drops of orange-blossom tea. Bathe the face morning and night; this will give a beautiful complexion.

Apply with a fine linen rag, a mixture of eight ounces emulsion of almonds, two grains of muriate of ammonia, and two grains of cascarilla powder.

Mix one spoonful of the best tar in a pint of olive or almond oil by heating the two together in a tin cup set in boiling water. Stir till completely mixed and smooth, putting in more oil if the compound is too thick to run easily. Rub this on the face when going to bed, and lay patches of soft cloth on the cheeks and forehead to keep the tar from rubbing off. The bed linen must be protected by old sheets folded and thrown over the pillows. The black, unpleasant mask washes off easily with warm water and soap. The skin comes out after several applications, soft, moist, and tinted like a baby's. It effaces the marks of age by affecting incipient wrinkles.

Purchase one-fourth pound of best Jordan almonds, slip off the skin, mash in a mortar and rub together with the best white soap for fifteen minutes, and gradually add one quart of rose water. When the mixture looks like milk, strain through fine muslin and apply with a soft rag after washing.

The whites of four eggs boiled in rose water, half an ounce of oil of almonds, and half an ounce of alum, beat together until a consistent paste is formed, spread upon a silk or muslin mask and worn at night makes a "mask of beauty."

Pimples on the Face

To remove pimples, wash the face just before going to bed, with sour milk or buttermilk, and rub thoroughly with wheat flour when dry. Wash the face next morning in soft water, and rub vigorously with coarse towel. Continue this treatment for ten or twelve days.

Wet the face slightly with a mixture of one dram of sulphate of zinc and two ounces of rose water. Let it dry and then rub cream on the affected part.

Dissolve a piece of pulverized alum, the size of a large hickory nut, in an ounce of lemon juice, and add an ounce of alcohol. This applied to the face twice a day will eventually remove pimples.

Two gallons of strong soapsuds, one pint of pure alcohol, and a quarter of an ounce of rosemary, well mixed, and applied with a linen rag, is an excellent remedy for removing pimples, blotches, freckles and warts.

A half pint of water to which has been added one tablespoonful of borax, is highly recommended for ringworm and canker.

Flesh Worms

Wash the face in tepid water, rub thoroughly with a towel, and apply a lotion made of half an ounce of liquor of potash, and three ounces of cologne. Make the application with a soft flannel rag.

Soft Skin

Coarse and stippled skin may be made beautifully soft by wearing, at night, a mask made of quilted cotton, wet with cold water. The old skin will be softened and a new one formed. It takes several weeks to accomplish this, and patience is required. If the skin is oily, bathe it in camphor.

The milky juice of the broken stems of coarse garden lettuce rubbed over the face at night, and washed off in the morning with a solution of ammonia, is highly recommended.

Complexion Wash

A good and perfectly harmless wash for the complexion can be made by adding one ounce of powdered gum of benzoin to a pint of whisky; add water until it becomes milky, and wash hands and face, allowing it to dry without wiping.

Rub a little warm water and castile soap on the face with a flannel, once or twice a week, then wash it off carefully; with the same flannel rub the face gently every morning, and a great improvement in the complexion will soon be noticed.

To Prevent the Face from Chapping after Shaving

Apply a little diluted vinegar or other acid, or cologne water, immediately after shaving.

One ounce of sweet oil, one ounce of lime water, and one drop of oil of roses, is a good preparation. Shake well before using and apply with the forefinger.

To Make Cold Cream

Twenty grains of white wax, two ounces pure oil of sweet almonds, one-half ounce pure glycerine, six drops of oil of roses; melt the first three ingredients together in a shallow dish over hot water, and as it begins to cool add the glycerine and oil of roses, and strain through a piece of muslin. Beat with a silver spoon until cold and snowy white.

To Remove Wrinkles

Mix thirty-six grains of turpentine and three drams of alcohol. Apply and allow it to dry on the face. The wrinkles will be made less apparent, and possibly removed.

To Remove Stains from the Hands

Stains made by fruit may be removed by washing the hands without soap, and holding them over the smoke of burning matches or sulphur.

When the hands are stained with nitrate of silver, wash them in a solution of chloride of lime.

For Chapped Hands

Half an ounce of rice flour, three ounces of sweet almonds. Melt these over a slow fire, keep stirring until cool, and then add a few drops of rose oil.

Apply freely at night a mixture of one ounce of glycerine and ten drops of carbolic acid.

An excellent remedy for chapped hands is pure mutton tallow.

Rub the hands long and well with a thick mixture of vinegar and Indian meal, dry them near the fire without washing, and rub them thoroughly with glycerine.

Cold cream is good for chapped hands.

To Whiten the Hands and Arms

Melt together, in a dish over boiling water, four ounces of honey, two ounces of yellow wax and six ounces of rose water. Add one ounce of myrrh while hot. Before going to bed, rub this thickly over the skin.

A good way to keep the hands white is to wear at night large cloth mittens filled with wet bran or oat meal, tied closely at the wrists. A lady can do a great deal of house work, and by wearing bran mittens every night, may keep her hands white and soft.

Whiten the Finger Nails

Mix in a bottle four ounces of spring water, two draws of dilute sulphuric acid, one of the tincture of myrrh. Dip the fingers in the mixture, after washing the hands. Before using this mixture, remove rings with pearls or stones in them.

A fine color may be given to the nails by lathering and washing the hands and fingers well with a scented soap; then rub the nails with equal parts of cinnabar and emery, followed by oil of bitter almonds.

Remedy for Ringworm

Dissolve a piece of sulphate of potash, the size of a walnut, in ounce of water. Apply night and morning for a couple of days, and it will disappear.

Apply a solution of the root of common narrow-leafed dock. The vinegar for the solvent.

Wash the eruption with a mixture of boiled tobacco leaves, strong lye and vinegar.

Moisten with saliva and then apply the ashes of a cigar, repeating frequently until cured.

Perspirations

The unpleasant odor produced by perspiration is often the source of vexation to persons who are subject to it. Instead of using costly ingredients and perfumes, wash the face, hands and arms with water to which has been added two table-spoonfuls of the compound spirits of ammonia. It will leave the skin as clean, sweet and fresh as one could wish. It is very cheap, perfectly harmless, and is recommended on the authority of an experienced physician.

To Ward Off Mosquitoes

Apply to the skin a solution made of fifty drops carbolic acid to an ounce of glycerine. Mosquito bites may be instantly cured by touching them with this solution. Add two or three drops of the attar of roses to disguise the smell. The pure, crystallized form of the acid has a less powerful odor than the common preparation.

For Soft Corns

Soft corns between the toes may be healed with a weak solution of carbolic acid.

To Remove Corns

Take a lemon, cut a piece of it off, then nick it so as to let in the toe with corn, the pulp next the corn; tie this on at night so that it can not move, and the next morning a blunt knife will remove the corn to a great extent. Two or three applications will cure.

A strong solution of pearlash applied to corns will soften them so that they may be easily drawn out.

Ingrowing Toe Nails

Cut a notch in the centre of the nail, or scrape it thin in the middle.

Put a small piece of tallow in a spoon and heat it over a lamp until it becomes very hot. Drop two or three drops between the nail and granulations. The pain and tenderness will be at once relieved, and in a few days the granulations will all be gone. One or two applications will cure the most obstinate cases. If the tallow is properly heated, the operation will cause little, if any, pain.

To Remove Warts

Dissolve two or three cents worth of sal ammoniac in a gill of soft water, and wet the warts frequently with this solution. They will disappear in a week or two.

Apply a weak solution of potash in the same manner.

Wash the warts two or three times a day with strong brine.

Remedy for Chilblains

Apply common tar to the parts affected, and bind It up with cloth, so as not to interfere with wearing the stocking. Wear this five or six days.

Dissolve one ounce of white vitriol in a pint of water, and bathe the *afflicted parts* very often.

Dissolve three handfuls of common salt in warm water, and bathe the hands and feet in this three times a week.

Bathe the chilblains in strong alum water, as hot as can be borne.

When indications of chilblains first present themselves, take three ounces of vinegar, one ounce of camphorated spirits of wine, mix and rub the parts affected.

To Remove Stains from Bile

A fluid for removing greasy stains from silk, may be prepared by mixing two ounces of rectified spirits of turpentine, one-fourth ounce of absolute alcohol, and one-fourth ounce of sulphuric ether.

Apply spirits of ammonia with a soft rag to remove acid stains from silks.

To Remove Stains and Spots from Silk

If the soiled part is washed with ether, the grease will disappear.

Faded color may be restored by passing the silks through a mixture of fine soap lather and pearlash.

Boil five ounces of soft water and six ounces of powdered alum for a short time, and pour it into a vessel to cool. Warm it for use, and wash the stained part with it and leave it to dry.

To Remove Spots of Pitch and Tar

Scrape off all the pitch or tar you can, then saturate the spots with sweet oil or lard, then rub in well, and let it remain in a warm place for an hour.

To Extract Paint from Garments

Chloroform is an excellent medium for the removal of stains of paint from clothes, etc. It is found that' portions of dry white paint, which resisted the action of ether, benzole, and bi-sulphide of carbon, are at once dissolved by chloroform. If the paint is fresh, turpentine or alcohol will remove it.

Saturate the spot with turpentine, let it remain a number of hours, then rub between the hands; it will crumble away without injury either to the texture or color of any kind of woolen, cotton or silk goods.

To Remove Stains from White Cotton Goods

Common salt rubbed on ink or fruit stains before they become dry will extract them.

Apply scalding water, or hartshorn diluted with warm water, several times to remove fruit stains.

To remove mildew rub in salt and some buttermilk, and expose to the hot sun. Chalk and soap or lemon juice and salt are also good. As the spots become dry rub more on and keep the garments in the sun until the spots disappear.

Colored cotton goods that have ink spilled on them, should be soaked in lukewarm sour milk.

To Remove Grease Spots

Saturate carbonate of magnesia with benzole, and spread upon a grease spot to about one-third of an inch in thickness. A sheet of porous paper should be spread upon the benzonated magnesia, and a flat iron, moderately warm, put upon the top of all. The heat of the iron passes through and softens the grease which is then absorbed by the porous magnesia. Remove the iron in an hour and brush the magnesia off.

To Remove Grease Spots from Woolen Goods

Pulverize one ounce of borax, put into a quart of boiling water, and bottle for use. This is excellent.

To Remove Ink Spots from Linen

If the spots are comparatively fresh, apply the juice of lemons and wash out with warm water.

Muriatic acid is a powerful extractor of ink stains, but is unsafe in the hands of others than experts.

Apply salt immediately, and ink stains may be prevented.

To Remove Stains

Soak the spot some time in a mixture of ammonia and spirits of wine.

Moisten fruit stains and hold over the fumes of a brimstone match.

To Take Mildew Out of Linen

Moisten the linen with soft water, and rub the parts affected with white soap; then rub powdered chalk well into the linen, lay it on the grass, and from time to time, as it becomes dry, wet a little.

Mix soft soap with powdered starch, half as much salt and the juice of a lemon; apply it to the stain with a brush, on both sides of the linen. Let the stained articles lie on the grass day and night till the stain comes out.

To Clean Silks and Ribbons

Take equal quantities of soft lye soap, alcohol or gin, and molasses. Put the silk on a clean table without creasing; rub on the mixture with a flannel cloth. Rinse the silk well in cold, clear water, and hang it up to dry without wringing. Iron it on the wrong side before it gets dry. Silks and ribbons treated in this way will look very nicely.

The water in which pared potatoes have been boiled is very good to wash black silks in; it stiffens and makes them glossy and black.

Ribbons may be cleaned and grease taken out, without changing their color, by using camphene. Dry in the open air and iron when pretty dry.

To Wash Lace Collars

Cover a quart bottle with the leg of a soft, firm stocking, sewing it tightly above and below. Then wind the collar or lace smoothly around the covered bottle; sew very carefully around the edge of the collar or lace with a fine needle and thread, making every loop fast to the stocking. Shake the bottle up and down in a pailful of warm soapsuds, and rub the soiled places occasionally with a soft sponge. Rinse well the same way in clean water. When the lace is clean, apply a weak solution of gum arabic and place the bottle in the sunshine to dry. Take off the lace carefully when perfectly dry. Instead of ironing, lay it between the leaves of a heavy book; or, iron on flannel between a few thicknesses of fine muslin. If lace collars are done up in this way they will wear longer, remain clean longer, and have a rich, new, lacy look.

How to Whiten Linen

Fruit stains, iron rust and other stains may be removed by applying a weak solution of the chloride of lime after the cloth has been well washed. Rinse in soft, clear, warm water, without soap, and immediately dry in the sun.

Oxalic acid diluted with water will accomplish the same result.

To Clean Woolens

Immerse the garment in three gallons of cold water, into which has been put one ox-gall, and squeeze or pound (not wring) it, until the spots are removed; then thoroughly wash in cold water to remove the odor of gall.

To Clean Kid Gloves

Put the gloves on and wash them as if you were washing your hands in a basin of turpentine. Hang them up in a current of air, or in a warm place, where the smell of the turpentine may be carried away.

Mix one-fourth of an ounce of fluid chloroform, one-fourth ounce of carbonate of ammonia, one-fourth ounce sulphuric ether, and one quart distilled benzine. Pour out a small quantity into a saucer, put on gloves, and wash as if washing hands, changing solution until gloves are clean; take off, squeeze them, replace on hands, and with a clean cloth rub fingers until they are perfectly fitted to the hand. This solution is excellent for cleaning clothes, ribbons and silks. Apply with soft sponge, rubbing gently until spots disappear. Do not use close to the fire, a the benzine is very inflammable.

To Clean Kid Boots

Mix a little white of egg and ink in a bottle so that it may be well shaken up when required for use. Apply to the boot with a piece of sponge, and rub dry. It is better to rub with the palm of the hand. When the boot shows signs of cracking, rub in a few drops of sweet oil. Polish the soles and heels with common blacking.

To Clean Patent Leather Boots

Remove all the dirt upon the boots with a sponge or flannel, then rub them with a paste consisting of two spoonfuls of cream and one of linseed oil. Warm both before mixing. Polish with a soft cloth.

For Burnt Kid or Leather Shoes

While still hot, spread soft soap upon them. When cold, wash it off. The leather may thus be made nearly as good as ever. The soap softens the leather and prevents it drawing up.

To Clean Jewelry

The best way to clean gold ornaments is to wash them with warm water and soap, using a soft nail brush to scrub them with. Dry them in box sawdust, and let them remain in a bed of this before the fire for awhile. Treat imitation jewelry in the same manner.

For Cleaning Silver and Plated Ware

Use the finest impalpable whitening with a little soft water. Next, wash with rain water, dry and polish with a piece of soft leather, some rough powder or fine whitening, and finally rub down with the hand. Avoid all violent rubbing, also the use, in cleaning it, of any ingredient which would wear the silver.

How Ladies Can Make Their Own Perfumes

If we spread fresh, unsalted butter upon the inside of two dessert plates, and then fill one of the plates with gathered fragrant blossoms of clematis, covering them over with the second greased plate, we shall find that after twenty-four hours the grease has become fragrant. The blossoms, though separated from the parent stem, do not die for some time, but live to exhale odor, which is absorbed by the fat. To remove the odor from the fat, the fat must be scraped off the plates and put into alcohol; the odor then leaves the grease and enters into the spirit, which thus becomes "scent," and the grease again becomes colorless. The flower farmers of the

Var follow precisely this method on a very large scale, making but a little practical variation, with the following flowers: rose, orange, acacia, violet, jasmine, tube rose and jonquil.

Tincture of Roses

Take the leaves of the common rose (centifolia) and place, without pressing them, in a common bottle; pour some good spirits of wine upon them, close the bottle, and let it stand till required for use. This tincture will keep for years, and yield a perfume little inferior to attar of roses; a few drops of it will suffice to impregnate the atmosphere of a room with a delicious odor. Common vinegar is greatly improved by a very small quantity being added to it.

Pot-Pourri

Take three handfuls of orange flowers, three of cloves, carnations or pinks, three of damask roses, one of marjoram, one of lemon thyme, six bay leaves, a handful of rosemary, one of myrtle, half a handful of mint, one of lavender, the rind of a lemon, and a quarter of an ounce of cloves. Chop these all up, and place them in layers, with bay salt between the layers, until the jar is full. Do not forget to throw in the bay salt with each new ingredient put in, should it not be convenient to procure at once all the required articles. The perfume is very fine.

How to Make Rose Water

Take two drams of magnesia and one-half an ounce of powdered white sugar. Mix with these, twelve drops of attar of roses; add two ounces of alcohol, and a quart of water; mix gradually and filter through blotting paper.

Putting Away Furs for the Summer

Sun them well and sprinkle with ground black pepper. Pack them securely in paper flour sacks and tie them up well.

Protection Against Moths

Clothes closets that have been infested with moths should be well rubbed with a decoction of tobacco, and repeatedly sprinkled with spirits of camphor.

A few pieces of paper smeared with turpentine, and placed in drawers where furs and woolens are kept, will completely prevent their ravages.

The odor of turpentine is deadly poison to moths and their grubs.

One ounce of gum camphor, and one ounce of powdered red pepper, macerated in eight ounces of strong alcohol for several days, then strained. Sprinkle the clothes or furs, and roll them up in sheets.

To Remove a Tight Ring

If a ring should get tight on the finger, wind a well soaped string around the finger. Commence at the point of the finger, and wind the cord as tight as can be borne until the ring is reached, then force the end of the cord between the ring and finger; unwind the string, and the ring will come off with it.

To Loosen Stoppers of Toilet Bottles

Let a drop or two of pure oil flow around the stopper, and stand the bottle a foot or two from the fire. After a time tap the stopper smartly, but not too hard, with the handle of a hair brush. If this is not effectual, use a fresh drop of oil and repeat the process. It will certainly succeed.

THE LANGUAGE
OF FLOWERS AND
GEMSTONES

THE LANGUAGE OF FLOWERS

LANGUAGE MEANS, IN A GENERAL SENSE, ANY, METHOD OF communicating thought. Man commonly accomplishes it through the organs of sight and hearing, and sometimes by the sense or touch, but it is especially sight which conveys the most intelligence to the mina, and by its medium are the greatest impressions made. What more pleasing to our senses than beautiful flowers—their form, their great variety, and. sometimes sharp but harmonic contrast of color, and their fragrance! And how attractive to the youngest as well as the oldest—the well or sick—in trouble or in happiness! To the person of leisure, or to one utterly weary in body or mind, what more welcome than some sweet, fragrant flower—a pansy, or a carnation, even!—and it is an elegant custom, by which flowers, the beautiful part of creation, are made to express sentiments of love, tributes of affection, and premiums of honor, valor and fame.

The following is the language of flowers:

ACACIA. Concealed love.
ACACIA, ROSE. Friendship.
ACANTHUS. Arts. Adonis
VERNALIS. Bitter memories,
AGNUS CASTUS. Coldness.
AGRIMONY. Thankfulness.
ALMOND. Hope.
ALOE. Superstition.
ALTHEA. Consumed by love.
ALYSSUM, SWEET. Worth beyond beauty.

AMARANTH. Immortality.
AMARYLLIS. Splendid beauty.
AMBROSIA. Love returned.
ANEMONE. Expectation.
ANEMONE, GARDEN. Forsaken.
ANGELICA. Inspiration.
APOCYNUM, (DOGBANE). Inspiration.
APPLE. Temptation.
APPLE BLOSSOM. Preference.
ARBOR VITÆ. Unchanging friendship.
ARBUTUS, TRAILING. Welcome.
ARNUI. Ardor.
ASH. Grandeur.
ASH, MOUNTAIN. Prudence.
ASPEN TREE. Lamentation.
ASPHODEL. Regrets beyond the grave.
AURILICA. Avarice.
AZALEA. Romance.
BACHELORS' BUTTON. Hope in love.
BALM. Sympathy.
BALM OF GILEAD. Healing
BALSAM. Impatience.
BARBERRY. Sharpness; satire.
BASIL. Hatred.
BAY LEAF. No change till death.
BEECH. Prosperity.
BEE OPHRYS. Error.
BEE ORCHIS. Industry.
BELL FLOWER. Gratitude.
BELVIDERE, WILD (LICORICE). I declare against you

BILBERRY. Treachery.
BIRCH TREE. Meekness.
BLACK BRYONY. Be my support.
BLADDER-NUT TREE. Frivolous amusements.
BLUE BOTTLE. Delicacy.
BORAGE. Bluntness.
BOX. Constancy.
BRIERS. Envy.
BROKEN STRAW. Constancy.
BROOM. Neatness.
BUCKBRAN. Calm repose.
BUGLOSS. Falsehood.
BURDOCK. Importunity.
BUTTERCUP. Riches.
CACTUS. Thou lovest me.
CALLA LILLY. Feminine beauty.
CALYCANTHUS. Benevolence.
CAMELIA. Pity.
CAMOMILE. Energy in action.
CANDYTUFT. Indifference.
CANTERBURY BELL. Gratitude.
CAPE JASMINE GARDENIA. Transport; ecstasy.
CARDINAL FLOWER. Distinction.
CARNATION, YELLOW. Disdain.
CATCHFLY (SILENE), RED. Youthful love.
CATCHFLY, WHITE. I fall a victim.
CEDAR. I live for thee.
CEDAR OF LEBANON. Incorruptible.
CELANDINE. Future joy.
CHERRY TREE. Good education.
CHICKWEED. I cling to thee.
CHICKORY. Frugality.

CHINA ASTER. I will think of thee.
CHINA, PINK. Aversion.
CHRYSANTHEMUM, ROSE. In love.
CHRYSANTHEMUM, WHITE. Truth.
CHRYSANTHEMUM, YELLOW. Slighted love.
CINQUEFOIL. Beloved child.
CLEMATIS. Artifice.
CLOVER, RED. Industry.
COBŒA. Gossip.
COXCOMB. Foppery.
COLCHIUM. My best days fled.
COLTSFOOT. Justice shall be done you.
COLUMBINE. Folly.
COLUMBINE, PURPLE. Resolved to win.
COLUMBINE, RED. Anxious.
CONVOLVULUS MAJOR. Dead hope.
CONVOLVULUS MINOR. Uncertainty.
CORCHORUS. Impatience of happiness.
COREOPSIS. Love at first sight.
CORIANDER. Hidden merit.
CORN. Riches.
CORNELIAN CHERRY TREE. Durability.
CRONILLA. Success to you.
COWSLIP. Pensiveness.
COWSLIP, AMERICAN. My divinity.
CROCUS. Cheerfulness.
CROWN IMPERIAL. Majesty.
CURRANTS. You please me.
CYPRESS. Mourning.
CYPRESS AND MARIGOLD. Despair.
DAFFODIL. Chivalry.
DAHLIA. Forever thine.

DAISY, GARDEN. I share your feelings.
DAISY, MICHAELMAS. Farewell.
DAISY, RED. Beauty unknown to possessor.
DAISY, WHITE. Innocence.
DAISY, WILD. I will think of it.
DANDELION. Coquetry.
DAPHNE MEZEREON. I desire to please.
DAPHNE ODORA. I would not have you otherwise.
DEAD LEAVES. Sadness.
DIOSMA. Usefulness.
DITTANY. Birth.
DOCK. Patience.
DODDER. Meanness.
DOGWOOD FLOWERING (CORNUS). Am I indifferent to you?
EBONY. Hypocrisy.
EGLANTINE. I wound to heal.
ELDER. Compassion.
ELM. Dignity.
ENDINE. Frugality.
EPIGNEA, REPEUS (MAY FLOWER). Budding beauty.
EUPATORIUM. Delay.
EVENING PRIMROSE. Inconstancy
EVERGREEN. Poverty.
EVERLASTING (GRAPHALIUM). Never-ceasing memory.
FILBERT. Reconciliation.
FIR TREE. Elevation.
FLAX. I feel your kindness.
FLORA'S BELL. Without pretension.
FLOWERING REED. Confide in heaven.
FORGET-ME-NOT. True love.
FOXGLOVE. Insincerity.
FRAXINELLA. Fire.

FRITTILLARIA, (GUINEA-HEN FLOWER). Persecution.
FURZE. Anger.
FUCHSIA. The ambition of my love thus plagues itself.
FUCHSIA, Scarlet. Taste.
GARDENIA. Transport; ecstacy.
GENTIAN, Fringed. Intrinsic worth.
GERANIUM, APPLE. Present preference.
GERANIUM, IVY. Your hand for next dance.
GERANIUM, NUTMEG. I expect a meeting.
GERANIUM, OAK. Lady, deign to smile.
GERANIUM, ROSE. Preference.
GERANIUM, SILVER LEAF. Recall.
GILLYFLOWER. Lasting beauty.
GLADIOLUS. Ready armed.
GOLDEN ROD. Encouragement.
GOOSEBERRY. Anticipation.
GOOSEFOOT. Goodness.
GORSE. Endearing affection.
GRAPE. Charity.
GRASS. Utility.
GUELDER ROSE (SNOWBALL). Writer.
HAREBELL. Grief.
HAWTHORN. Hope.
HEART'S EASE. Think of me.
HEART'S EASE, PURPLE. You occupy my thoughts.
HAZEL. Reconciliation.
HEATH. Solitude.
HELENIUM. Tears.
HELIOTROPE, PERUVIAN. I love; devotion.
HELLEBORE. Scandal.
HENBANE. Blemish.
HEPATICA. Confidence.

HIBISCUS. Delicate beauty.
HOLLY. Foresight.
HOLLYHOCK. Fruitfulness.
HOLLYHOCK, WHITE. Female ambition.
HONESTY (LUNARIA). Sincerity.
HONEYSUCKLE. The bond of love.
HONEYSUCKLE, CORAL. The color of my fate.
HONEYSUCKLE, MONTHLY. I will not answer hastily.
HOP. Injustice.
HORNBEAM. Ornament.
HORSE-CHESTNUT. Luxury.
HOUSE-LEEK. Domestic economy
HOUSTONIA. Content.
HOYA (WAX PLANT). Sculpture.
HYACINTH. Jealousy.
HYACINTH, BLUE. Constancy.
HYACINTH, PURPLE. Sorrow.
HYDRANGEA. Heartlessness.
ICE PLANT. Your looks freeze me.
INDIAN CRESS. Resignation.
IPOMACO. I attach myself to you.
IRIS. Message.
IRIS, GERMAN. Flame.
IVY. Friendship; matrimony.
JESSAMINE, CAPE. Transient joy.
JESSAMINE, WHITE. Amiability.
JESSAMINE, YELLOW. Grace; elegance
JONQUIL. Return my affection.
JUDAS TREE. Betrayed.
JUNIPER. Perfect loveliness.
KALAMIA, (MOUNTAIN LAUREL). Treachery.
KENNEDIA. Intellectual beauty.

LABURNUM. Pensive beauty.
LADY'S SLIPPER. Capricious beauty.
LAGERSTRŒMA, (Cape Myrtle). Eloquence.
LANTANA. Rigor.
LARCH. Boldness.
LARKSPUR. Fickleness.
LAUREL. Glory.
LAURESTINE. I die of neglect.
LAVENDER. Distrust.
LEMON BLOSSOM. Discretion.
LETTUCE. Cold hearted.
LILAC. First emotion of love.
LILAC, WHITE. Youth.
LILY. Purity; modesty.
LILY OF THE VALLEY. Return of happiness.
LILY, DAY. Coquetry.
LILY, WATER. Eloquence.
LILY, YELLOW. Falsehood.
LINDEN TREE. Conjugal love.
LIVE OAK. Liberty. Liverwort. Confidence.
LOCUST. Affection beyond the grave.
LONDON PRIDE. Frivolity.
LOTUS. Forgetful of the past.
LOVE IN A MIST. You puzzle me.
LOVE LIES BLEEDING. Hopeless, not heartless.
LUCERNE. Life.
LUNGWORT (PULMONARIA). Thou art my life.
LUPINE. Imagination.
LYCHNIS. Religious enthusiasm
LYTHRUIN. Pretension.
MADDER. Calumny.
MAIDEN'S HAIR. Discretion.

MAGNOLIA, CHINESE. Love of nature.
MAGNOLIA, GRANDIFLORA. Peerless and proud.
MAGNOLIA, SWAMP. Perseverance.
MALLOW. Sweetness.
MANDRAKE. Honor.
MAPLE. Reserve.
MARIGOLD. Cruelty.
MARIGOLD, AFRICAN. Vulgarminded.
MARIGOLD, FRENCH. Jealousy.
MARJORAM. Blushes.
MARSHMALLOW. Beneficence.
MARVEL OF PERU, (FOUR O'CLOCK). Timidity.
MEADOW SAFFRON. My best day's gone.
MEADOW SWEET. Usefulness.
MIGNONETTE. Your qualities surpass your charms.
MIMOSA. Sensitiveness
MINT. Virtue.
MISTLETOE. I surmount all difficulties.
MOCK ORANGE, (SYRINGA). Counterfeit.
MONKSHOOD. A deadly foe is near.
MOONWORT. Forgetfulness.
MORNING GLORY. Coquetry
MOSS. Material love.
MOTHERWORT. Secret love.
MOURNING BRIDE, (SCABIOUS). Unfortunate attachment.
MOUSE-EAR Chickweed. Simplicity.
MULBERRY, BLACK. I will not survive you.
MULBERRY, WHITE. Wisdom.
MULLEN. Good nature.
MUSHROOM. Suspicion.
MUSH PLANT. Weakness.
MUSTARD SEED. Indifference.

MYOSOTIS. Forget me not.
MYRTLE. Love; Narcissus; Egotism.
NASTURTIUM. Patriotism.
NETTLE. Cruelty; slander.
NIGHT BLOOMING CEREUS. Transient beauty.
NIGHTSHADE. Bitter truth.
OAK. Hospitality.
OATS. Music.
OLEANDER. Beware.
ORANGE. Generosity.
ORANGE FLOWER. Chastity.
OROHIS. Beauty.
OSIER. Frankness.
OSMUNDA. Dreams.
PANSY. Think of me.
PARSLEY. Entertainment.
PASQUE FLOWER. Unpretentious.
PASSION FLOWER. Religious fervor.
PEA. Appointed meeting.
PEA, EVERLASTING. Wilt go with me?
PEA, SWEET. Departure.
PEACH BLOSSOM. My heart is thine.
PEAR TREE. Affection
PEONY. Anger.
PENNYROYAL. Flee away.
PERIWINKLE. Sweet memories.
PERSIMMON. Bury me amid nature's beauties.
PETUNIA. Am not proud.
PEASANT'S EYE. Sorrowful memories.
PHLOX. Our souls united.
PIMPERNAL. Change.

PINE. Time.
PINE APPLE. You are perfect.
PINE, SPRUCE. Farewell.
PINK. Pure affection.
PINK, CLOVE. Dignity.
PINK, DOUBLE-RED. Pure, ardent love.
PINK, INDIAN. Aversion.
PINK, MOUNTAIN. You are aspiring.
PINK, VARIEGATED. Refusal.
PINK, WHITE. You are fair.
PINK, YELLOW. Disdain.
PLANE TREE. Genius.
PLEURISY ROOT (ASCLEPIAS). Heartache cure.
PLUM TREE. Keep promise.
PLUM TREE, WILD. Independence.
POLYANTHUS. Confidence.
POPLAR, BLACK. Courage
POPLAR, WHITE. Time.
POPPY. Consolation.
POPPY, WHITE. Sleep of the heart.
POMEGRANATE. Foolishness.
POMEGRANATE FLOWER. Elegance.
POTATO. Beneficence.
PRIDE OF CHINA (MELIA). Dissension.
PRIMROSE. Early youth.
PRIMROSE, EVENING. Inconstancy.
PRINT. Mildness.
PUMPKIN. Coarseness.
QUINCE. Temptation.
RAGGED ROBIN (LYCHNIS). Wit.
RANUNCULUS. Radiant with charms.
REEDS. Music.

RHODODENDRON. Agitation.

ROSE. Beauty.

ROSE, AUSTRIAN. Thou art all that is lovely.

ROSE, BAROLINA. Love is dangerous.

ROSE, BRIDAL. Happy love.

ROSE, BURGUNDY. Unconscious beauty.

ROSE, CABBAGE. Love's ambassador.

ROSE, CAMPION. Only deserve my love.

ROSE, CHINA. Grace.

ROSE, DAILY. That smile I would aspire to.

ROSE, DAMASK. Freshness.

ROSE, DOG. Pleasure and pain.

ROSE, HUNDRED LEAF. Pride.

ROSE, INERMIS. Ingratitude.

ROSE, MAIDEN'S BLUSH. If you do love me you will find me out

ROSE, MOSS. Superior merit.

ROSE, MULTIFLORA. Grace.

ROSE, MUSK-CLUSTER. Charming.

ROSE, SWEETBRIAR. Sympathy.

ROSE, TEA. Always lovely.

ROSE, UNIQUE. Call me not beautiful.

ROSE, WHITE. I am worthy of you.

ROSE, WHITE (WITHERED). Transient impression.

ROSE, WILD. Simplicity.

ROSE, YELLOW. Decrease of love.

ROSE, YORK AND LANCASTER. War.

ROSES, GARLAND OF. Reward of virtue.

ROSEBUD. Young girl.

ROSEBUD, MOSS. Confessed love.

ROSEBUD, WHITE. The heart that knows not love.

ROSEMARY. Your presence revives me.

RUE. Disdain.

RUSH. Docility.

SAFFRON. Excess is dangerous.

SAGE. Esteem.

SARDONIA. Irony.

SATINFLOWER (LUNARIA). Sincerity.

SCABIOUS, MOURNING BRIDE. Widowhood.

SENSITIVE PLANT. Timidity.

SERVICE TREE. Prudence.

SNAPDRAGON. Presumption.

SNOWBALL. Thoughts of heaven.

SNOWDROP. Consolation.

SORREL. Wit ill timed.

SOUTHERNWOOD. Jesting.

SPEARMINT. Warm feelings.

SPEEDWELL, NEREVICA. Female fidelity.

SPINDLE TREE. Your image is engraved on my heart.

STAR OF BETHLEHEM. Reconciliation.

STARWORT, AMERICAN. Welcome to a stranger.

ST. JOHN'S WORT (HYPERICUM). Superstition.

STOCK, TEN-WEEK. Promptitude.

STRAMONIUM, COMMON. Disguise.

STRAWBERRY. Perfect excellence.

STRAWBERRY TREE (ARBUTIS). Esteemed love.

SUMAC. Splendor.

SUNFLOWER, FALL. Pride.

SUNFLOWER, DWARF. Your devout admirer.

SWEET SULTAN. Felicity.

SWEET WILLIAM. Artifice.

SYCAMORE. Curiosity.

SYRINGA. Memory.

TANSY. I declare against you.

Teasel. Misanthropy.

Thistle. Austerity.

Thorn Apple. Deceitful charms.

Thorn, Black. Difficulty.

Thorns. Severity.

Thrift. Sympathy.

Throatwood (Pulmonaria). Neglected beauty.

Thyme. Activity.

Tiger Flower. May pride befriend thee.

Touch-me-not, Balsam. Impatience.

Truffle. Surprise.

Trumpet Flower. Separation.

Tuberose. Dangerous pleasures.

Tulip. Declaration of love.

Tulip Tree. Rural happiness.

Tulip, Variegated. Beautiful eyes.

Tulip, Yellow. Hopeless love.

Turnip. Charity.

Valerian. Accommodating disposition.

Venus' Flytrap. Caught at last

Venus' Looking Glass. Flattery.

Verbena. Sensibility.

Vine. Intoxicating.

Violet, Blue. Love.

Violet, White. Modesty.

Violet, Yellow. Modest worth.

Virgin's Bower. Filial love.

Wall Flower. Fidelity.

Walnut. Stratagem.

Weeping Willow. Forsaken.

Wheat. Prosperity.

Woodbine. Fraternal love.

Wood Sorrel. Joy.

Wormwood. Absence.

Yarrow. Cure for heartache.

Yew. Sorrow.

Zennæ. Absent friends.

GEMSTONES

ROMANCE AND IMAGINATION HAVE ASCRIBED TO THE VARIOUS precious stones different significations. Many curious and interesting things might be said of the esteem in which various persons hold this custom. For instance, some people are very solicitous to secure appropriate stones for presents, lest the health, life or prosperity of the donee should thereby be injured.

JANUARY	Garnet. *Constancy and Fidelity.*
FEBRUARY	Amethyst. *Sincerity.*
MARCH	Bloodstone. *Courage.*
APRIL	Sapphire. *Repentance.*
MAY	Emerald. *Success in love.*
JUNE	Agate. *Health and long life.*
JULY	Ruby. *Forgetfulness of, and exemption from vexations caused by friendship and love.*
AUGUST	Sardonyx. *Conjugal Fidelity.*
SEPTEMBER	Chrysolite. *Freedom from evil passions and sadness of the mind.*
OCTOBER	Opal. *Hope and Faith.*
NOVEMBER	Topaz. *Fidelity and friendship.*
DECEMBER	Turquoise. *Prosperity.*
DIAMOND:	*Innocence.*
PEARL:	*Purity.*
CORNELIAN:	*Contented mind.*
MOONSTONE:	*Protects from danger.*
HELIOTROPE:	*Causing the owner to walk Invisible.*

PICNICS

CORN ROAST

PICNICS

TRACES OF FOREIGN ANCESTORS ARE APPARENT OCCASIONALLY in most of us, true Americans though we be. It is perhaps a spice of gypsy blood in our veins that sets our pulses throbbing with pleasant excitement when, seated in an old haywagon, we go bumping and thumping down the road prepared for a delightful holiday.

With camp-kettle swinging beneath, and coffee pot stowed safely away within the wagon, do we not feel able to provide as savory dishes for our picnic dinner as any concocted by the gypsies themselves? Surely no coffee is ever so delicious as that cooked over the campfire, albeit it tastes somewhat smoky when prepared by hands inexperienced in the art of outdoor cooking; but if the fish we broil is a little burned, and the baked potatoes rather hard in the middle, who cares? Hearty, healthy appetites, which the early morning drive through the fresh, exhilarating air has developed, laugh at such trifles and dinner is voted a success in spite of sundry mistakes and mishaps in its preparation.

There are picnics and *picnics*. When one drives out in a fine carriage to meet a fine company, and partake of a fine lunch prepared by fine servants, is one kind.

When one goes with a large party, on a boat, and takes a lunch of sandwiches, cake, pickles, hardboiled eggs, etc., which is spread on the grass at the landing and eaten as quickly as possible, is another kind; but the picnic most enjoyed by young people who are not afraid of a little work, which is only play to them, is the one where the raw materials for the dinner are taken and the cooking, or most of it, is done, gypsy fashion, by the picnickers themselves.

A pleasant innovation in the ordinary routine of a picnic is

A Burgoo

Thirty or forty years ago the men of Kentucky, in celebration of a holiday, would get up what they called a burgoo. In character it was very much like the clambake of today, but instead of chowder, or baked clams, the company prepared and partook of a soup or stew made of almost everything edible. Early in the morning the party would meet at the appointed place and decide what each should contribute toward the making of this most delectable stew.

Those who were fond of hunting would go forth in search of birds, squirrels, rabbits, and game of all kinds, with which the woods were filled. Some caught fish, and others provided fowl, pork, vegetables, and condiments.

As the ingredients were brought in, those who had charge of the cooking prepared and dropped them into an immense pot which, half full of water, was suspended over a roaring fire.

When everything of which the stew was composed was cooked to shreds, the burgoo was pronounced done, and was served in tin cups, and eaten with shell spoons, made by splitting a stick and wedging a mussel-shell in the opening.

That this was a most appetizing feast I know from an old gentleman who has frequently attended the burgoos and partaken of the stew. Of course at a picnic composed of girls and boys, it would not do to depend upon the game which might be shot and the fish which might be caught, for the dinner, but the burgoo should be adapted to the ways and means of the party, and each member should provide something for the stew. The following recipe will make enough for fifteen or twenty persons.

Burgoo Stew

Two pounds of salt pork, the same of lean beef; two good-sized chickens, or fowls of any kind; two quarts of oysters, the same of clams; twelve potatoes, four turnips, one onion, two quarts of tomatoes, and any other vegetables which may be obtainable. Make a bouquet of parsley, celery, and a very little bay-leaf, thyme and hyssop, tied together with thread.

Put the beef, fowl, pork, oysters, clams and a handful of salt in a large iron kettle, three-quarters full of water; skim it before it begins to boil hard, and add the other ingredients; keep the kettle covered and boil until the bones fall from the meat. Serve hot with crackers. Wild game and fish may also be added to the recipe. When a burgoo is decided upon, it is best to prepare a light lunch to be eaten about eleven o'clock, and have the heartier meal at four or five in the afternoon, as it requires some time for the stew to cook.

Our illustration shows four ways of suspending the kettle over the fire. While the girls are preparing the ingredients for the stew, the boys will build a fire in some such fashion as is shown in FIG. 133 on the following page, and put the kettle on. The best way to boil coffee is to make or build a kind of little stove of stones and mud, and set the coffeepot on top, as shown in FIG. 132; this will prevent the smoky taste it is apt to have when placed directly on the fire.

FIG. 132

FIG. 133

A Corn-roast

During the season when green corn is plentiful, there is no better way of having a real jolly time than by getting up a corn-roast. It is not as elaborate an affair as the burgoo. Some green corn, a long pole sharpened at one end, for each member of the party and a large fire built in some open space where there will be no danger of causing conflagration makes us ready for the corn-roast.

Several summers ago a gay party of friends from New York and vicinity took possession of and occupied for a few months a little cottage at a place on the coast of Maine called Ocean Point.

Toward the end of August, when all places of interest had been explored, when the stock of shells, starfish, and such like treasures had grown beyond the accommodation of an ordinary trunk, and the minds of the sojourners were beginning to be filled with thoughts of a speedy return home, green corn, for the first time that summer, made its appearance. This was hailed with delight, and a farewell lark, in the form of a corn-roast, was promptly proposed and almost as promptly carried into execution.

The place selected on which to build the fire was a large rock jutting out into a little cove called "Grimes Cove." Here the party met about three o'clock in the afternoon, each member bringing only such dishes as were considered necessary for his or her own use. It is needless to say that the supply was not very plentiful, many limiting themselves to a cup and spoon; still as the supper was to consist merely of roasted corn, bread and coffee, these answered every purpose.

Not only was the corn roasted on the ends of the long poles, but bread was toasted, and in true American fashion it was eaten piping hot. One of the gentlemen, much to the amusement of the rest of the party, produced a piece of breakfast bacon, which he fastened, on to the end of his pole and toasted over the glowing embers, declaring that it was better cooked in that way than in any other.

Yes, corn-roasts are great fun, and they can be held almost any place where a large fire can be safely built. It is best to allow the fire to burn down until it is a glowing pile of coals then sticking the sharp end of a pole into an ear of corn (FIG. 134), and standing as far from the fire as the length of the pole will permit, it can be held close to the hot embers until thoroughly cooked; then with butter and salt this roasted corn is excellent eating.

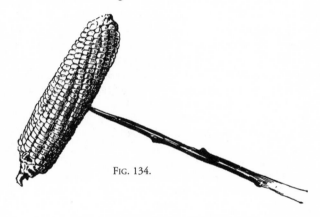

FIG. 134.

Enough corn should be provided to allow several ears to each member of the party, as mishaps are liable to occur, and the tempting ear of corn may be devoured by the flames, instead of the person for whom it was intended.

The poles, about six feet in length, should be as light as possible, for if too heavy they will tire the hands and arms of those holding them.

RECIPES

BREAD

"'Bread,' says he, 'dear brothers, is the staff of life.'"

Boston Brown Bread

One level pint cornmeal scalded, one level tablespoonful salt, one cup New Orleans molasses, two teaspoonfuls soda over which pour a little boiling water, one pint sour milk; put half the soda in the molasses and the remainder in the milk. Stiffen with Graham flour. Steam four hours, and brown in oven for about fifteen minutes.

Kentucky Corn Bread

One pint thick, sour milk, two teaspoonfuls salt, one egg. Mix with this enough cornmeal to make a batter not stiff. Use meal of medium fineness—not the very fine sold in most groceries. Beat well; add last one level teaspoonful soda dissolved in a little water. Allow a tablespoonful of lard to become very hot in baking pan; pour into the batter, stir, and turn into pan. Bake until cooked through.

CEREALS, BREAKFAST FOODS

"Look up! the wide extended plain?
Is billowy with its ripened grain,?
And on the summer winds are rolled
Its waves of emerald and gold."

Hominy

This is very good when well cooked, and may be simply boiled until done in salted water, and served with pepper and butter. It is good fried like mush.

S O U P S

"La soupe fait le soldat." ("The soup makes the soldier.")

Cream of Celery Soup

A pint of milk, a tablespoonful of flour, one of butter, a head of celery, a large slice of onion and a small piece of mace, a little salt. Boil celery in one pint of water from thirty to forty-five minutes; boil mace, onion and milk together; mix flour with two tablespoonfuls of cold milk. Cook ten minutes. Mash celery in water it has been cooked in and stir in boiling milk. Strain and serve.

Mixed Vegetable Soup

Fifteen-cent soup bone, three quarts water, half a small cabbage cut very fine, three large potatoes, two good-sized carrots, two turnips, one medium-sized onion, three teaspoonfuls salt, one-half teaspoonful pepper, a little celery and green pepper. Put on in cold water with all vegetables except potatoes. Cook very slowly one hour. Do not cover closely. At the end of one hour add potatoes and cook an hour longer. Put in two or three tomatoes when potatoes are added, if liked.

Mock Bisque

One-half can tomatoes strained, one quart milk, one-third cup butter, one tablespoonful cornstarch, one teaspoonful salt, one salt-spoon pepper, heat milk in double boiler. Mix smoothly one tablespoonful butter, cornstarch and seasoning, add hot milk slowly. Boil ten minutes and add remainder of butter and strained tomatoes. Serve immediately.

F I S H

"Fools lade water, and wise men catch the fish."

Codfish Balls

Boil and mash as many potatoes as desired, using about one-half pound of soaked and drained codfish to a pound of potatoes. Have fish picked apart, and after soaking and drying mix thoroughly with potatoes, adding, for one-half pound of codfish, one tablespoonful butter, yolks of two eggs, one-half teaspoonful salt and a dash of pepper. Make into balls, dip in beaten egg and bread crumbs and fry in hot fat.

Oyster Cocktail

Mix one tablespoonful tomato catsup, one-half tablespoonful vinegar or lemon, two drops Tabasco sauce, one-half teaspoonful salt, one teaspoonful finely chopped celery and one-half teaspoonful Worcestershire sauce. Chill these ingredients thoroughly, pour over eight oysters and serve in cocktail glasses.

S A L A D S

"Salads and eggs and lighter fare."

More progressive Americans now understand the value of the salad, and in this way use many vegetables, fish and meats that heretofore have not been extensively used for that purpose. There is room for much interesting experimenting in the making of salads. Almost endless variety may be had by ingenious mixing and combining of suitable ingredients. Used sparingly, they give a zest to the plainest meal, and the olive oil which is used so frequently in the preparation of salads is of immense value in promoting health.

The greens used in making salad, lettuce, dandelion and water cress should always be most carefully washed, and served only when fresh, crisp and cold. Many canned vegetables and left-overs may be used in salad, which would not be nearly so appetizing prepared in any other way.

Asparagus Salad

Use either fresh or canned asparagus. If fresh, of course it should be cooked in the usual way and allowed to cool. Only very tender asparagus is suitable for salad. Cut green or red peppers into rings, put four stalks in each ring. Place these bundles on lettuce leaves and serve with usual French dressing. A little pat of Philadelphia cream cheese may be put on edge of each plate.

Beet Relish

One quart chopped beets, one quart chopped cabbage, one cup ground horseradish, one cup brown sugar, salt and pepper to taste. Pour over enough vinegar to moisten well about three cups. Heat and seal.

Cold Slaw

One-half cup vinegar boiled, two teaspoonfuls sugar, one-half teaspoonful salt and mustard, one-half teaspoonful pepper, one-quarter cup butter to a cream, one teaspoonful flour; pour into boiling vinegar, cook five minutes. One well-beaten egg, with the cabbage chopped fine; pour vinegar over while hot.

Fruit Salad

Bananas sliced lengthwise in quarters; over this put pineapple in cubes. Boil the pineapple a few minutes, to make it more tender. Then large strawberries and English walnuts. Over it put a spoonful of mayonnaise. Make the mayonnaise as you would a filling for lemon pie, with two lemons. Add whipped cream to it before serving.

Mayonnaise

Two tablespoonfuls butter, one teaspoonful mustard, one tea-spoonful salt, four teaspoonfuls sugar, one-half cup vinegar, one cup cream, yolks of four eggs. Beat yolks together, add butter, mustard, salt and sugar. Boil cream and add to mixture. Boil vinegar and add. Then put on fire and stir until it thickens.

New England Potato Salad

One pint of cream, yolks of two eggs, one-half teaspoonful dry mustard, one-half teaspoonful salt, one-half teaspoonful pepper. Beat yolks for a few minutes, add mustard, salt and pepper, then mix with the cream and put in double boiler; let come to a boil. Put pepper and salt (more, if deemed necessary) and vinegar over potatoes or cabbage about ten minutes before putting in the dressing.

MEAT

"Meat was made for mouths."

While it is undoubtedly true that raw meat is, as a rule, more easily digested than cooked, our present state of civilization demands that it be cooked, and we can only comply with the demand, preparing the food in question so that it may be not only attractive to the eye, but in a manner that will render it pleasing to the taste and readily assimilated. Cooking softens the tissues, making the act of eating more enjoyable, and also destroys parasitic growths.

To boil meat when broth is not desired, plunge into boiling water. The water should be allowed to boil for about ten minutes and then be permitted to fall somewhat below boiling point and kept at even heat for a long time. The juices and flavors are thus retained.

It is not desirable that fish should be treated in this manner, as the boiling water would break it into little pieces.

To stew meat, put small portions into cold water and raise temperature slowly, until very hot, but not quite boiling. Let it remain thus for some hours, and a rich broth, as well as juicy and tender meat, will result.

In roasting meat it is well to remember that the smaller roast requires the hotter fire. Intense heat produces a semi-solid condition of the exterior, and prevents the drying up of the meat juices. Great heat would be inapplicable to large cuts, the exterior of which would be burned to a coal under such treatment before the heat could reach the interior.

Young housekeepers and others who are not familiar with the various cuts of meat obtainable in most of our markets will do well to consider thoughtfully the accompanying illustrations.

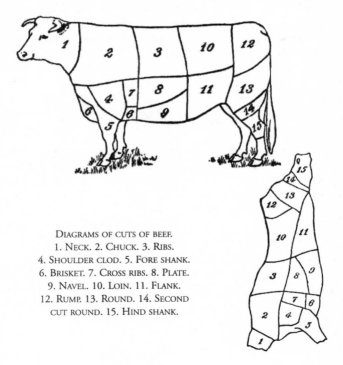

DIAGRAMS OF CUTS OF BEEF.
1. NECK. 2. CHUCK. 3. RIBS.
4. SHOULDER CLOD. 5. FORE SHANK.
6. BRISKET. 7. CROSS RIBS. 8. PLATE.
9. NAVEL. 10. LOIN. 11. FLANK.
12. RUMP. 13. ROUND. 14. SECOND
CUT ROUND. 15. HIND SHANK.

In selecting beef we must remember that color is of great importance. The surface of a fresh lean cut should be a bright red, while the fat should be clear white. After being exposed to a warm atmosphere the surface will of course become darker in color.

The loin commands a higher market price than any other cut, on account of its tenderness and quality. The names applied to different parts of the loin vary in different localities. The part nearest the ribs is often called the "short steak," the other end the "sirloin."

It is interesting in this connection to recall the story which has been told regarding the origin of the word "sirloin." It is said that this steak found such favor with some epicurean king of olden times that he, in a spirit of jocularity and good humor, bestowed upon it the honor of knighthood, to the great delight of his assembled court, and as "Sir Loin" it was thereafter known. It is a pity to spoil so good a story, but the fact is that the word is derived from the French "sur" (upon) and "longe" (loin), and the preferable orthography would therefore be "surloin." However spelled, and whatever its history, the sirloin is deservedly popular.

Between the short and sirloin is the portion usually called the tenderloin, the name of which indicates its prevailing characteristic, the tenderness which makes it a much-to-be-desired cut in spite of its lack of juiciness and flavor as compared with other cuts.

The rib is the cut between the loin and chuck, and contains the best roasts. The fat on the best grade of ribs should be about one-half inch deep.

Round steaks are rather popular, but as Americans have a preference for loin and rib cuts, a large share of the lower grades of "rounds" are used otherwise, being converted into Hamburger, used as sausage trimmings and disposed of in many other ways.

Chucks are used extensively as shoulder steak, boiling pieces, and make very good roasts. Pot roasts are cut from the lower side, and stews or soup meat from the neck. The better grade of chucks should have a complete covering of fat, thickest at the rib end of the cut.

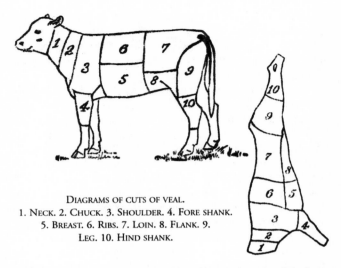

DIAGRAMS OF CUTS OF VEAL.
1. NECK. 2. CHUCK. 3. SHOULDER. 4. FORE SHANK.
5. BREAST. 6. RIBS. 7. LOIN. 8. FLANK. 9.
LEG. 10. HIND SHANK.

Quality in veal is determined by color and grain of flesh. It should be light pink, nearly white, and should contain a quantity of fat. The many ways of cooking and serving veal are so well known as to need but passing mention; veal loaf, veal cutlets, chops, pie, stew, curry of veal and many others are all favorite dishes in many homes.

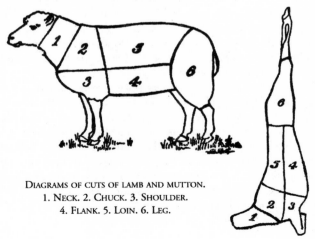

DIAGRAMS OF CUTS OF LAMB AND MUTTON.
1. NECK. 2. CHUCK. 3. SHOULDER.
4. FLANK. 5. LOIN. 6. LEG.

In selecting mutton or lamb we should be guided by color, fineness of grain, thickness of flesh and amount of fat. Mutton of a dull brick red is preferable, though the color varies from that to dark red. Lamb on account of its superior flavor is more popular than mutton. The flesh of lamb should be light in color, of fine grain and the fat evenly distributed. The nutritive value of mutton and lamb is practically the same as beef.

DIAGRAMS OF CUTS OF PORK.
1. HEAD. 2. SHOULDER. 3. BACK.
4. MIDDLE CUT. 5. BELLY. 6. HAM.
7. RIBS. 8. LOIN.

The larger share of dressed pork is almost entirely clear fat, which should be white, firm and evenly distributed. Skin should be thin and smooth. Any detailed description of the various cuts of pork would be superfluous here. Not all our eloquence could adequately picture the delight with which an epicure gazes upon a ham boiled or baked by an experienced Kentucky or Virginia cook. The "roasting pig" is also a favorite in many places, and long has been, for, according to Washington Irving, it was much prized by Ichabod Crane of Sleepy Hollow, and it has been mentioned by so great and learned a poet as Shakespeare.

Regarding all meats, we wish to say that as a rule the cheaper cuts have as much food value as the more expensive ones. Careful cooking will render the less expensive cuts delightfully appetizing. It is an advantage to housekeepers to know that meat need not be the highest in price to be nutritious and palatable.

Beef Tenderloin

Take tenderloin of beef and lard it with pork. Put one can of mushrooms with the beef and cook in oven twenty minutes. Then cut the meat in slices one and one-half inch thick. On top of each slice place a few of the mushrooms and a little of the gravy, and set back in the oven five minutes to keep hot. Serve the slices on a chop plate, forming a circle, and filling in the center with peas.

Blanketed Ham with Sweet Potatoes and Apples

Cut off the fat close to the edge of a slice of ham one-half inch thick. Put fat through meat chopper, spread on top of ham, then sprinkle one-half cup of brown sugar and wineglass of sherry over it. Peel and quarter four large sweet potatoes and four large apples. Put ham in oven in covered roasting pan. After it has cooked a quarter of an hour add apples and sweet potatoes. Now cook all of it three-quarters of an hour. This makes a delicious and savory dish, and is so substantial that little else is required for a meal.

Brown Stew

Thirty-five-cent beef off the shoulder; cut in pieces, cover with water and stew two hours until tender. Add one tablespoonful butter, and thicken with flour. Cook until brown.

Chicken (or Veal) Croquette

One-half pound chicken or veal, chopped very fine; season with one-half teaspoonful salt, one-half teaspoonful celery salt, one-fourth teaspoonful onion juice, one teaspoonful chopped parsley, one teaspoonful lemon juice, one saltspoonful white pepper, one-fourth saltspoonful cayenne. Mix with enough cream sauce to be easily handled; let cool, then shape into rolls. Roll on fine bread crumbs, dip in beaten egg, then roll in bread crumbs and fry in smoking-hot fat, drain on tissue paper. Boil meat in three quarts hot water, cold for soup, season with one teaspoonful salt, four grains pepper.

Veal Loaf

Three pounds of veal chopped fine, one-half pound salt or fresh pork, one cup powdered crackers, one cup water, two eggs, three teaspoonfuls salt, three teaspoonfuls sage, one teaspoonful pepper. Bake in rather quick oven.

VEGETABLES

"Perhaps if we could penetrate Nature's secrets we should find that what we call weeds are more essential to the well-being of the world than the most precious fruit or grain."
—NATHANIAL HAWTHORNE.

The simplest methods of cooking and serving vegetables are generally the best. The most common method of cooking them is in boiling water. All green vegetables, bulbs and tubers should be crisp and firm when put on to cook, and should, of course, be thoroughly cleaned before being cooked.

Almost all vegetables may be served in the form of salad. Our most common green salad plant is lettuce; celery is next, but endive, chicory and dandelion, with many others, may be used to advantage in this way, and furnish pleasing variety to the menu.

Nearly all vegetables are good canned, and if care is taken in preparing and canning, it is possible to have fresh-tasting fruits and vegetables through all seasons.

Thorough sterilization is necessary in canning or preserving. In the first place, use good jars. Glass jars will be found the most satisfactory. Those with glass top and rubber ring held in place by a wire spring are the cheapest in the long run, although the initial expense may be somewhat high. Never use defective rubbers, as vegetables often spoil after being sterilized, because of bad rubbers.

A clothes boiler makes a good container to use in sterilizing. A false bottom made of wire netting cut to fit or strips of wood may be used, as the jars will break if set flat on the bottom of the boiler.

Select vegetables that have not begun to harden or decay. Always can as soon as possible after gathering. Some vegetables are best cooked before putting in jars; among these are beets, pumpkins and turnips, but most of them may be packed while raw in jars and cooked as follows:

Pack jar full, adding salt as desired, fill with cold water to the top of the jar. Put the rubber on the jar and place the glass top on, but do not press down the spring at the side of the jar. Put as many jars in the boiler as it will hold without crowding. Pour into the boiler enough water (cold) to prevent it from going dry during the boiling. Put the cover on the boiler and bring the water to a boil and keep it boiling for an hour. (Hour and a half for half-gallon jars.) At the end of this time remove the boiler cover, and let the steam escape. Press down the spring on each jar, which clamps on the top, and no outside air can enter.

On the next day raise the spring at the side of the jar and boil as on the first day, clamping on the top as before at the end of operation. Repeat this on the third day. All meats, fruits and vegetables are sterilized on this principle.

Never subject jars to a draft of cold air when removing them from the boiler, as this will be likely to crack them. If, after sterilization seems complete, any jars spoil, increase the time of boiling.

Asparagus

Cut the tender part into short pieces. Cover with boiling water, and boil until done. Season with salt and pepper, and serve with most of juice; or, if preferred, serve with a cream dressing.

Beets

Wash the beets carefully without breaking the skin. Cover with boiling water and boil until tender. Take from the boiling water and drop into cold. Rub off the skin, cut in thin slices and serve at once with salt and butter.

Cincinnati Baked Beans

Measure beans (marrowfat are best), put them in cold water and parboil fifteen minutes and drain; use the Boston bean pot. For three pints of dried beans add three level teaspoonfuls salt, one-quarter pound pickled pork cut fine, six tablespoonfuls New Orleans molasses or six tablespoonfuls of C sugar, one tablespoonful standard mustard. Mix the above well and put in a three-quart bean pot, and fill within one inch of top with boiling water. May be kept in oven several days, but must never be allowed to get dry, adding boiling water as needed.

Corn

Cook ears of corn five minutes in boiling water. Then cut through the center of each row of grains and press the grains from the hulls with the back of a knife. Put corn in saucepan and season with butter, salt, pepper and sugar. Add enough hot milk to moisten, and cook ten minutes.

When succotash is desired, add to a pint of corn cooked as above the same amount of cooked and seasoned shelled beans.

Creamed Cauliflower

One pint cooked cauliflower, one pint milk, one teaspoonful salt, one-third teaspoonful pepper, one tablespoonful butter, one-half teaspoonful flour, three slices toasted bread. Break cooked cauliflower into branches and season with half of the salt and pepper. Put butter in a saucepan on the fire. When hot add flour and stir until frothy and smooth. Add gradually the milk, constantly stirring. When sauce boils add the salt, pepper and cauliflower. Cook ten minutes and serve very hot on the slices of toast.

Potatoes au Gratin

First prepare your white sauce of one-half pint milk, one tablespoonful butter, two tablespoonfuls flour. Cream butter and flour and add to boiling milk. Cook about ten minutes in double boiler. Slice or chop cold boiled potatoes, put in baking dish. One layer of potatoes. Cover thickly with layer of white sauce and grated cheese. Season with salt, pepper, mustard and cayenne pepper to suit taste. Put in other layers in same manner and bake twenty minutes.

Scalloped Celery

Chopped celery, bread or cracker crumbs, butter, salt and pepper, milk. Place a layer of crumbs in bottom of buttered dish, then a layer of celery, dot with butter, season and continue alternately until pan is full, having crumbs on top, cover with milk, bake slowly until milk is absorbed, about one-half hour. Serve in bake dish.

DESSERTS

"The little sweet doth kill much bitterness."
—KEATS

Chocolate Pudding

One pint milk, four tablespoonfuls sugar, one teaspoonful vanilla, salt, two tablespoonfuls cornstarch, one tablespoonful cocoa, cinnamon. Thoroughly blend together the dry cornstarch and cocoa, then dissolve with a little cold milk and reduce to a pouring state, add vanilla. Heat the milk in a double boiler, add sugar and a pinch of cinnamon and salt; when scalding hot, pour in cornstarch and cocoa mixture and stir carefully until it thickens well. Turn into wet molds. Serve with plain or whipped cream. Garnish with Maraschino cherry.

Apple Pie

Pare, core and cut five sour apples into eighths; place evenly in a pie plate lined with the usual pie pastry. Mix one-third cup sugar, one-fourth teaspoonful grated nutmeg, one-third teaspoonful salt, teaspoonful lemon juice and a few gratings of lemon rind and sprinkle over apples. Dot over with little lumps of butter, wet edges of under crust, cover with upper crust and press edges together. Bake forty-five minutes in a moderate oven.

HOW TO MAKE A HAMMOCK

NDERNEATH THE SPREADING BRANCHES OF THE COOL, shady tree swings our hammock.

Through the intertwining boughs the golden sunlight is sifted in bright little dashes on the leafy foliage below. Lying ensconced in its lacy meshes idly listening to the hum of the busy bumble bees at work among the red clover, or gazing up through the leafy canopy to the blue heavens where now and then fleecy white clouds float softly past, or watching a flight of birds skim o'er the distant horizon, who would not be lulled by the harmony of the summer day! A delightful languor steals over us and we unconsciously drift into the land of dreams where perfect rest is found. We awaken refreshed, to again gently swing back and forth and vaguely wonder who could have first thought of this most delightful invention. It is said that we owe the luxury to the Athenian, General Alcibiades, who, in 415 B.C. first made the swinging bed. The word hammock is taken from hamacas or hamac, an Indian word which Columbus relates as being used by the Indians to signify a hanging bed composed of netting. What these uncivilized red men made with their rude implements, we ought to be able with our modern facilities to accomplish very easily and quickly.

It is not difficult to make a hammock; anyone can soon knit one that is strong and comfortable, and it should not cost more than fifty cents. The materials required will be one hammock-needle about nine inches long (this can be whittled out of hickory or ash, or purchased for ten cents); two iron rings two and one-half inches in diameter, which will cost about five cents each; two mesh-sticks or fids, one twenty

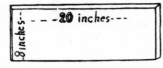

FIG. 135.

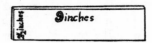

FIG. 136.

FIG. 137.

inches long and eight inches wide bevelled on both edges (FIG. 135) : the other nine inches long and two and one-half inches wide, bevelled on the long edge (FIG. 136); these you can easily make yourself from any kind of wood.

One pound of Macremé cord number twenty-four, or hammock twine of the same number, which can be had for less than thirty cents; colored cord comes five cents extra.

Wind the cord in balls, as it is then more convenient to handle, and begin making your hammock. First, thread the needle by taking it in the left hand and using the thumb to hold the end of the cord in place, while looping it over the tongue (FIG. 137); pass the cord down under the needle to the opposite side and catch it over the tongue; repeat this until the needle is full.

Next, make a loop of a piece of cord two yards long and fasten this to any suitable place (FIG. 138)—a doorknob will do very well; then tie the cord on your needle three inches from the end to this loop. Place the small fid under the cord, the bevelled edge close to the loop (FIG. 139). With your thumb on the cord to hold it in place while you pass the needle around the fid, and with its point toward you, pass it through the loop from the top, bringing it over the fid, so forming the first half of the knot (FIG. 140). Pull this taut, holding it in

FIG. 138.

place with your thumb while throwing the cord over your hand, which forms the loop as in (FIG. 141). Then pass the needle from under through the loops, drawing it tight to fasten the knot. Hold it in place with your thumb, and repeat the operation for the next knot. FIG. 142 shows a number of these knots finished. A is a loosened knot, making plain its construction. B, in FIGS. 140, 141, and 142, is the cord running to the needle, and D is the fid. When thirty meshes are finished shove them off the fid (FIG. 143), as this number will make the hammock sufficiently wide.

FIG. 139.

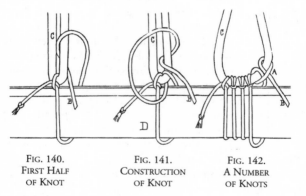

FIG. 140.	FIG. 141.	FIG. 142.
FIRST HALF	CONSTRUCTION	A NUMBER
OF KNOT	OF KNOT	OF KNOTS

Commence the next row by again placing the fid under the cord, and take up the first mesh, drawing it close to the fid; hold it in place with your thumb while throwing the cord over your hand; pass the needle on the left hand-side of the mesh from under through the loop thrown over your hand

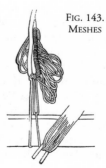

FIG. 143.
MESHES

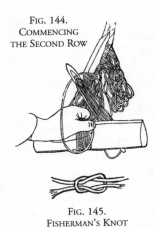

FIG. 144.
COMMENCING
THE SECOND ROW

FIG. 145.
FISHERMAN'S KNOT

(FIG. 144); pull this tight and you will have tied the common knitting-knot; proceed in like manner with all the loops in rotation until the row is finished. When it is necessary to thread or fill your needle, tie the ends of the cord with the fisherman's knot shown in FIG. 145, which cannot slip when properly tightened. Wrap each end of the cord from the knot securely to the main cord with strong thread to give a neat appearance to the hammock.

Continue knitting until thirty rows are finished.

Then use the large fid, knitting one row on the short side first, next one on the long side. This accomplished, knit the meshes to the ring by passing the needle through it from the top, knitting them to the ring in rotation as if they were on the mesh-stick or fid (FIG. 146). When finished tie the string securely to the ring, and one end of your hammock is finished.

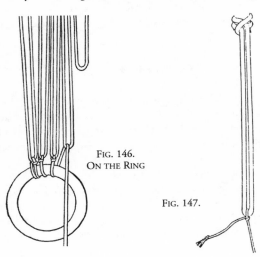

FIG. 146.
ON THE RING

FIG. 147.

Cut the loop on which the first row was knitted, and draw it through the knots. Tie the end of the cord on your needle to the same piece used in fastening the end of the first needleful to the loop (FIG. 147), and knit the long meshes to the other ring as described. This completed, the hammock is finished.

To swing it, secure two pieces of strong rope and fasten them firmly to the iron rings, the length of the rope depending upon the space between the two points from which you wish it to hang. These should be if possible twelve or fifteen feet apart and at least ten feet high, to give your hammock sufficient room to swing freely.

This suspended bed will furnish a welcome retreat when the weather is too warm to admit of games, walks, or other amusements. Then, with some favorite book, or if even reading is too much of an exertion, simply to lie indolently in the hammock is a comfort, so restful and quiet that the time quickly passes, and we are made better and brighter for our short, passive repose.

Very decorative nets, and useful ones of many kinds, including fishnets and minnow-seines, are made with the same stitch as that used in the hammock. The size of the mesh is regulated by the circumference of the fid, and the twine used is fine or coarse, according to the style of net desired.

Barrel Hammock

When in the Catskills last summer we saw for the first time a hammock made of a barrel. It was painted red and looked very cheery and inviting hanging under the green boughs; the two colors, being complementary, harmonized beautifully.

This hammock was made of a piece of strong rope twenty feet long threaded in and out of barrel staves, and was substantial and durable. The construction of such a hammock is very simple. Remove the top and bottom hoops and nails from a firm, clean barrel. Then before taking off the remain-

Fig. 148.

ing hoops draw a pencil-line around both ends of the barrel, being careful to have the marking three inches from and parallel to the edges; this is for a guide when making the two holes in each end of all the staves. Bore the holes with a five-eighth of an inch augur or a red-hot poker, using the pencil-line as a centre; leave an equal margin on both sides of the staves, and at the same time enough space in the centre to preclude all danger of breakage.

Fasten the staves together by threading the rope through the hole from the outside of the first stave, then across the inside of the stave down through the other hole (see FIG. 148). Continue threading until one side is finished, then in like manner thread the other side. Knock off the remaining hoops and the staves will appear as shown in FIG. 149. Tie the two ends of the rope together and fasten loops of rope on

FIG. 149.

both ends; these should be of sufficient length to conveniently swing the hammock. When threading the staves let the rope be loose enough to leave a space of an inch or so between each stave when the barrel is spread out in the form of a hammock.

In this way you can have a serviceable hammock, the cost of which will be about twenty-five cents and a little labor.

POEMS, SONGS, AND COWBOY DANCING

POEMS

Flowers and Weeds

Have you ever heard what the fairies say,
    Little girl, little boy?
    Oh, hear and heed!
For each smile you wear on your face to-day
    There's a flower grows;
    For each frown, a weed.

So to make this world like a garden bright,
    Little girl, little boy,
    Keep frowns away,
Oh, the loving lips that can say to-night,
"We've scattered flowers o'ver the earth to-day."

What They Caught

Four mischievous youngsters,
    On a summer day,
Just to go a-fishing
    Slyly ran away.

Willows, worms and tackle
    To their work they brought,
But, if you'll believe me,
    This is what they caught.

Tommy caught a wetting,
    He was overbold;
Jimmy caught a scolding,
    Johnny caught a cold.

Harry caught a whipping-
    Much against his wish-
But, with all their trouble,
    No one caught a fish!

Little Flowers

(*All*)
We are little flowers
    Coming with the spring,
If you listen closely
    Sometimes you'll hear us sing.

(*First Girl*)
I am the Honeysuckle,
    With my drooping head,
And early in the springtime
    I don my dress of red.
I grow in quiet woodlands,
    Beneath some budding tree;
So when you take a ramble
    Just look for me.

(*Second Girl*)
I am the Dandelion,
    Yellow as you see,
And when the children see me
    They shout with glee.
I grow by every wayside,
    And when I've had my day,
I spread my wings so silvery
    And fly away.

(*Third Girl*)
I am the gay Nasturtium,
    I bloom in gardens fine,
Among the grander flowers
    My slender stalk I twine.
Bright orange is my color-
    The eyes of all to please-
I have a tube of honey
    For all the bees.

(*Fourth Girl*)
I am the little Violet;
    In my purple dress
I hide myself so safely
    That you'd never guess
There was a flower so near you,
    Nestling at your feet;
And that's why I send you
    My fragrance sweet.

May Day

One day, all in the sweet spring weather,
Two little maids went out together-
    Oh, the bright May day!
Sun was shining, birds were singing,
Flowers blooming, May bells ringing-
    Oh, the glad May day!

So they too went forth a-Maying
Laughing, dancing, singing, saying-
    Oh, the bright May day!
What care we for mother's warning?
Who would bide at home this morning?
    Oh, the glad May day!

Mother peeps from the lattice crying,
Wise birds back to their nests are flying-
　　Oh, the fickle May!
Silly maidens, where do ye wander?
Storm clouds gather thickly yonder!
　　Oh, the false May day!

Hark, the rain comes patter, patter!
Garlands gay the wild winds scatter-
　　Oh, the fickle May!
Now the maidens, helter skelter,
Hasten back to mother's shelter
　　From the false May day!

Sunny skies may oft deceive us,
Mother's love can never leave us-
　　Oh, no more we'll stray!
Home for maidens is the meetest,
Brightest, safest, dearest, sweetest;
　　So at home we'll stay!

Little Foxes

Among my tender vines I spy
A little fox named "By and By,"
Then set upon him quick, I say,
The swift young hunter, "Right Away."

Around each tender vine I plant
I find a little fox, "I Can't!"
Then fast as ever hunter ran,
Chase him with bold and brave "I Can."

"No Use in Trying," lags and whines,
This fox among my tender vines;
Then drive him low and drive him high
With this good hunter named "I'll Try."

Among the vines in my small lot
Creeps in the young fox "I Forgot,"
Then hunt him out and to his den
With "I Will Not Forget Again."

A little fox is hidden there
Among my vines named "I Don't Care,"
Then let "I'm Sorry," hunter true,
Chase him afar from vines and you.

A Game of Tag

A grasshopper once had a game of tag
    With some crickets that lived near by,
When he stubbed his toe and over he went,
    In the twinkling of an eye.

The crickets leaned up against a fence
    And laughed till their sides were sore,
But the grasshopper said, "You are laughing at me
    And I shan't play any more."

So off he went, tho' he wanted to stay
    For he was not hurt by his fall,
And the gay little crickets went on with the game
    And never missed him at all.

A bright-eyed squirrel called out as he passed,
    Swinging from a tree by his toes,
"What a foolish fellow that grasshopper is,
    Why he's bit off his own little nose."

The Chestnut Burr

A wee little nut lay deep in its nest
Of satin and down, the softest and best;
And slept and grew while its cradle rocked,
As it hung in the bows that interlocked.

Now the house was small where the cradle lay,
As it swung in the wind by night and day,
For a thicket of underbrush fenced it round,
This little lone cot, by the great sun browned.

The little nut grew, and ere long it found
There was work outside on the soft green ground,
It must do its part so the world might know
It had tried one little seed to grow.

And soon the house that had kept it warm
Was tossed about by the autumn storm;
The stem was cracked, the old house fell,
And the chestnut burr was an empty shell.

But the little seed as it waiting lay
Dreamed a wonderful dream day by day,
Of how it should break its coat of brown,
And live as a tree to grow up and down.

October's Bright Blue Weather

Oh, suns and skies and flowers of June,
And clouds of June together,
Ye cannot rival for one hour
October's bright blue weather.

When loud the bumble-bee makes haste,
Belated, thriftless, vagrant,
And goldenrod is dying fast,
And lanes with grapes are fragrant;

When gentians roll their fringes tight,
To save them for the morning,
And chestnuts fall from satin burrs
Without a word of warning;

When on the ground red apples lie
In piles, like jewels shining,
And redder still, on old stone walls,
Are leaves of woodbine twining;

When all the lovely wayside things
Their white-winged seeds are sowing,
And in the fields, still green and fair,
Late aftermaths are growing;
When springs run low, and on the brooks,
In idle, golden freighting,
Bright leaves sink noiseless in the hush
Of woods, for winter waiting;

Oh, suns and skies and flowers of June,
Count all your boasts together;
Love loveth best of all the year
October's bright blue weather.

Points of the Compass
(DIALOGUE FOR FOUR BOYS.)

(*In concert*)
Whenever we go from place to place
We go in some direction-
No matter what part of the country it is,
'Tis the same in every section.

(*First pupil*)
This is the North, and we are told
That in the far North it is very cold;
There is nothing but snow and icebergs there,
'Tis the home of the great white polar bear.

(*Second pupil*)
Down South the weather is warm and fair,
The little birds always find summer there;

And people there have fruit and flowers
That cannot grow in this climate of ours.

(*Third pupil*)
This is the East where the great round sun
Tells us another day has begun;
He sends out his golden beams ahead
To say to us all, "Jump out of bed."

(*Fourth pupil*)
West is the place where the great round sun
Sinks to rest when the day is done;
As he goes to sleep in his bed so bright,
He says to us all, "Good-night, Good-night!"

If I Knew

If I knew the box where the smiles were kept,
No matter how large the key,
Or strong the bold, I would try so hard,
'Twould open, I know, for me.
Then over the land and the sea, broadcast,
I'd scatter the smiles to play,
That the children's faces might hold them fast
For many and many a day.

If I knew a box that was large enough
To hold all the frowns I meet,
I would like to gather them, every one,
From nursery, school, and street;
Then folding and holding, I'd pack them in,
And turning the monster key,
I'd hire a giant to drop the box
In the depths of the deep, deep sea.

MUSIC

Musical Merry-go-round

This affords an excellent opportunity for one individual, who has a clear voice, to add largely to the hilarity and amusement of all present. It is conducted by a gentleman, who explains to the rest of the company that each will in turn be requred to sing one complete verse of any song, himself volunteering to be the first, and the others to follow in the order in which they are seated. The conductor commences by singing an introductory verse as follows:

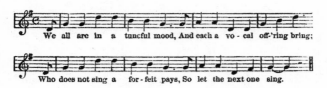

We all are in a tuneful mood, And each a vo-cal off-'ring bring; Who does not sing a for-feit pays, So let the next one sing.

He then sings one verse of any song, sentimental or comic, as he may think most suitable. At the close, the whole company sing in chorus, under the direction of the conductor:

Right well sung, {he} {she} has {his} {her} du-ty brave-ly done, 'Tis right well sung. We all are in a, &c.

This leads to a repetition of the introductory verse, which is used as a refrain between each regular versus sung, the pause being filled up by a single, simultaneous clap of the hands by all the company present.

The next person must then sing a verse of his own selection, to be followed by the company in chorus, "Right well sung." etc., and the refrain, as before. Each member of the company should be ready to sing when his or her turn comes; if, however, after a reasonable but short pause, any one should fail to "come to time," the conductor and whole company sing:

After the forfeit has been decided upon by the conductor, the company sing, instead of "Right well sung," etc. the following couplet:

followed by the refrain, as before. The word "Fie" should be given short and with a will, the second and third beats of the bar being filled up by the syllable "oh!" instead of clapping the hands, this latter being the reward of the successsful vocalist. Under an efficient conductor, this pastime is very amusing, the company falling easily into the couplets and refrain after two or three verses have been song.

The Emperor of Austria

The great requisites for this funny performance are, some knowledge of music and the keeping of *perfect* time.

The tune should be monotonous, but well accented, and the song consists of the repetition, four times, of one line, as follows:

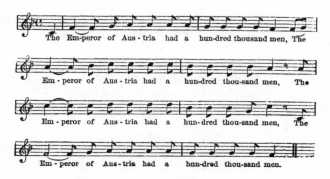

The second time the four lines are sung, the first word is omitted in the first three lines, the fourth line being given in full.

The third time, the first two words are omitted in three lines, still singing the whole of the fourth.

In this way the song proceeds, dropping word after word in the first three lines, but always singing the fourth line entirely, till the whole of the time for three lines is dead silence, the fourth line being sung in the proper time.

1ST TIME: The Emperor of Austria had a hundred thousand men;
The Emperor of Austria had a hundred thousand men;
The Emperor of Austria had a hundred thousand men;
The Emperor of Austria had a hundred thousand men.

2ND TIME: *The* Emperor of Austria had a hundred thousand men;
The Emperor of Austria had a hundred thousand men;
The Emperor of Austria had a hundred thousand men;
The Emperor of Austria had a hundred thousand men.

3RD TIME: *The Emperor* of Austria had a hundred thousand men;
The Emperor of Austria had a hundred thousand men;
The Emperor of Austria had a hundred thousand men;
The Emperor of Austria had a hundred thousand men.

4TH TIME: *The Emperor of* Austria had a hundred thousand men;
The Emperor of Austria had a hundred thousand men;
The Emperor of Austria had a hundred thousand men;
The Emperor of Austria had a hundred thousand men.

etc.

Yankee Doodle

Father and I went down to camp,
Along with Captain Goodwin;
And there we saw the men and boys
As thick as hast pudding.

> Yankee doodle, doodle-doo,
> Yankee doodle dandy,
> Mind the music and the step,
> And with the girls be handy.

And there we saw a swamping gun,
Big as a log of maple,
On a little deucid cart,
A load for father's cattle.
> Yankee doodle, etc.

I Laugh I Sing

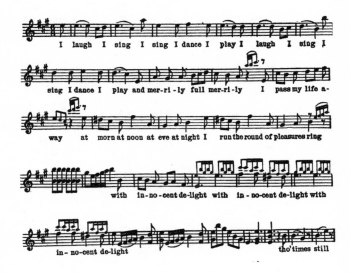

I laugh I sing I sing I dance I play I laugh I sing I

sing I dance I play and mer-ri -ly full mer-ri -ly I pass my life a-

way at morn at noon at eve at night I run the round of pleasures ring

with in-no-cent de-light with in-no-cent de-light with

in-no-cent de-light tho' times still

should strike nor his pur-pose re-lent his scythe his scythe is no ter-ror to me while in-no-cence war-bles the song of con-tent my bo-som from care shall be free my bo-som from care shall be free I laugh I sing I sing I dance I play I laugh I sing I sing I dance I play and mer-ri-ly full mer-ri-ly I pass my life a-way at morn at noon at eve at night I run the round of pleasure ring with in-no-cent de-light I laugh I sing I dance I play and mer-ri-ly pass my life a-way I laugh I sing I dance I play and mer-ri-ly pass my life a-way and mer-ri-ly pass my life a-way and mer-ri-ly pass my life a-way and mer-ri-ly pass my life a-way I laugh I sing I dance I play and mer-ri-ly pass my life a way

The Baby's Hush-A-Bye

A ba-by wan-der'd from its home, when day was gently breaking, Long did the pretty infant roam Each sim-ple wild flow'r seeking; But night came o'er the dreary sky, The wind a-mong the leaves so dry, Sung the poor ba-by's hush-a-bye Sung the poor ba-by's hush-a-bye.

Cottage of the Moor

The for-tune I crave, and I sigh for no more, Is health and con-tent-ment ap-par-el and food, The smile of af-fect-ion from one I a-dore. And a neat lit-tle cot-tage that stands in the wood. a neat lit-tle cot-tage a neat lit-tle cot-tage a neat lit-tle cot-tage that stands in a wood.

While slaves of ambition sell comfort for fame
    Be mine the applause of the wise and the good,
A conscience that daily acquits me of blame,
    And a neat little cottage that stands near a wood.

Let others for grandeur and opulence toil,
    I'd share not their turbulent joys if I could,
The treasure I seek is affection's sweet smile,
    And a neat little cottage that stands near a wood.

'Tis Home Where'er the Heart Is

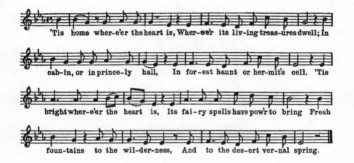

'Tis home wher-e'er the heart is, Wher-e'er its liv-ing treas-ures dwell; In cab-in, or in prince-ly hall, In for-est haunt or her-mit's cell. 'Tis bright wher-e'er the heart is, Its fai-ry spells have pow'r to bring Fresh foun-tains to the wil-der-ness, And to the des-ert ver-nal spring.

2

'Tis free where'er the heart is,
    Nor rankling chains, nor dungeon dim,
Can check the mind's aspirings,
    The bounding spirits pealing hymn.
The heart gives life its beauty,
    Its warmth, its radiance and its power,
Is sunlight to its rippling stream,
    And soft dew to its drooping flower.

COWBOY DANCING

Git yo' little sagehens ready;
Trot 'em out upon the floor-
Line up there, you critters! Steady!
Lively, now! One couple more.
Shortly, shed that ol' sombrero;
Broncho, douse that cigaret;
Stop yer cussin', Casimero,
'Fore the ladies. Now, all set:

S'lute yer ladies, all together;
Ladies opposite the same;
Hit the lumber with yer leather;
Balance all an' swing yer dame;
Bunch the heifers in the middle;
Circle stags an' do-ce-do;
Keep a-steppin' to the fiddle;
Swing 'em round an' off you go.

First four forward. Back to places.
Second foller. Shuffle back—
Now you've got it down to cases—
Swing 'em till their trotters crack.
Gents all right a-heel an' toein';
Swing 'em-kiss 'em if yo' kin-
On to next an' keep a-goin'
Till yo' hit yer pards again.

Gents to center. Ladies 'round 'em;
Form a basket; balance all;
Swing yer sweets to where yo' found 'em;
All p'mnade around the hall.
Balance to yer pards an' trot 'em
'Round the circle double quick;
Grab an' squeeze 'em while you've got 'em—
Hold 'em to it if they kick.

Ladies, left hand to yer sonnies;
Alaman; grand right an' left;
Balance all an' swing yer honies-
Pick 'em up an' feel their heft.
All p'mnade like skeery cattle;
Balance all an' swing yer sweets;
Shake yer spurs an'make 'em rattle-
Keno! Promenade to seats.
—JAMES BARTON ADAMS

Introduction

Very often at some dinner table or in some informal group, the discussion has turned to our strange enthusiasm for the old dances of the past, and we have found enough interest and curiosity developed to lead directly to the formation of a little group of friends who decided to join with us and to try a bit of the dancing for themselves.

It is the natural way to start—talk it over and then try a dance or two. One has to know what it is all about first. One naturally wonders where the dances came from, what their relationship may be to other forms of dancing. Are they still being done today? Just what do we mean by a square dance? Where is the sport?

So let's talk it over informally. Much that we say will have to be speculative. But guessing is good fun, and it often arouses more interest than a cold array of scientific and carefully classified facts.

When it comes to finding the origins of the Western square dance, for instance, one simply has to speculate. The dances and the calls, except in rare cases, were never written down, but were transmitted from caller to caller by the oral route. And all the footnotes and references and authorities are lost in the process.

One old caller said to us in answer to our question about a certain call, "Well, I reckon I don't know! My daddy always called it this away. But he said his daddy had a plumb different way, and I never felt sure about it. There's something the matter with that call, and I don't like it. I never use it unless I got to." A year later, in another place, we found what we suspect of being a variation of the old granddaddy's call. At least it was more complete and gave sense to the bobtailed lines he had used.

But where did the granddaddy get the original call? We can only guess. Back in the mist of the past, moving down from father to son, from community to community, the old calls spread without chronicler and without record. Usually something was lost at each step from the original call, until some semicreative natural genius, who liked to keep a continuous patter of words going all the time, filled in the omission with new words of his own, and a new variant was born.

But someone always protests that he had seen many an old call book—his aunt or his cousin still has a copy in the family trunk. We have patiently run down dozens of these old books, and so far they have always been call books of New England quadrilles. And that is a different fish. New England turned naturally to books. But these old Western square dances grew up without benefit of letters.

Had these Western dances been the dances of scholars, every variant would have been recorded and fully annotated. Chronologies and pedigrees and records would have been kept. But these were the dances of country folk, who kept all their essential knowledge written only on the uncertain pages of memory! They were the dances of laconic folk who didn't tell all they knew even under questioning! They were often the dances of secretive folk who were somewhat jealous of the special talent and special knowledge.

The First Dance

When a group of beginners are brought together for their first dance, doubts and embarrassments and reluctance are apt to be manifest. For this reason it is best to have no audience present to add to this embarrassment. There is always a group of the curious who like to sit on the side lines and watch others pioneer and who say that perhaps they will try it later. It is hard enough to go through what the psychologist calls the period of "initial diffuse movements" (and what the beginner calls "making a fool of himself") in learning a new set of reactions without having the curious smiles of the onlookers make the initial movements even more diffuse. So, for the best success, only those who are willing to try the dances themselves, should be invited to the party.

If one full set of experienced dancers can be present they will prove invaluable. They can first demonstrate the dance to be learned (and we learn most quickly by imitating what we have seen), and then the demonstrator set can split up first or head couple of each set of beginners and lead them through the figure with a great economy of time.

The Caller

The success of the first dance will depend upon the effectiveness of the "caller." The hostess, or the chairman, may make all arrangements and get the dancers and accoutrements together, but it is the "caller" who will have to put the dance over. Once started, the dance is in his hands. A committee of explainers and directors only outbabbles the tower of Babel itself. The call must give all the commands, all the explanations, all the directions. Of course, having explained a movement and asked the dancers to try it in a "time out" period, then and only then can the leading couples, and all the experienced dancers present, help and explain personally to all who do not know.

He, of course, must be thoroughly familiar with the calls before the dance begins. If it is all new to him it means only preliminary study, but he will probably have to get a few friends together beforehand and move them around and work it all out until everything is perfectly clear to him and practiced enough to be running smoothly. Our caller must have an infallible sense of rhythm, not only of the fiddle, but instinctively timing his phrases with the four- or eight-bar units that the music itself is built on. This must be instinctive, for with different groups on the floor, some fast and some slow, he never calls his dance twice alike. If he ever fails in the rhythm of his phrasing, the dancers find the dance no fun at all, even though they may not be able to analyze the source of the trouble.

Our caller must also possess an unerring geometric sense, that is a spatial sense of moving and interrelated pattern. We all recognize the presence or absence of a color sense or a sense of smell or a sense of taste. We would not expect a person without an "ear" or a sense of tone to participate in group singing, or a "color blind" person to execute a painting. And yet we are convinced that though psychologists have never recognized it, there are as many people who lack "spatial," a "gemetric" sense as there are those who lack a sense of color or of tone. And we find that they are never able to learn how to square dance. In spite of an otherwise high order of intelligence and in spite of endless instruction, the pattern means nothing to them and they are forever running off in the wrong direction. It goes without saying that an infallible spatial or geometric sense is essential to any good caller.

Always there will be distractions. Someone always wants to talk to the caller in the very middle of his call. And even though he does not listen he is severely distracted. Fast sets, slow sets, new arrivals, little accidents, all tend to distract him. But he must keep his eye on that unfolding pattern, and carry it on, and keep his place exactly timed in every call.

It is not an easy job. I have seen experts who regularly got their calls out of order, or left one couple completely out. And I have seen many experienced callers who could not keep two sets together in a dance. It is a special trick and not nearly as easy as it looks.

Yet there is always some simple-minded, rather loud-mouthed individual who keeps asking to be allowed to do the calling simply because he enjoys his own noise and loves to be at the center of things. Experienced dancers may carry on in spite of him. But beginners will fall in confusion before him, their enthusiasms all laid low.

The quick, intelligent, capable caller that we have described will find one more river yet to cross, and that is his own first embarrassment—and his finest qualities only make this river seem wider. He will feel everyone look at him most peculiarly on his least faltering or his tiniest mistake. But he must carry on clearly and smoothly and forcefully, in spite of the embarrassment. It comes mostly from the newness of his job. All good callers have had to swim this river. He may be tempted to carry cards in his hands to read from, but they are apt to make it worse. He had better put it all in his memory, and then plunge in. Soon he will find it going smoothly, and he will know the delight of controlling a great unfolding pattern of human beings through the contagious beauty of a dance.

Circle Two-Step

If the party is large it often pays to start with an "ice-breaker," such as the Circle Two-Step. This gets them all used to laughing and trying together, mixes them up thoroughly and breaks down all barriers and stiffness, and gives them all a chance to become familiar with a few fundamental elements of the old dances.

Have all the dancers stand holding hands in a great circle around the hall and all facing the center of the room. Men and women must alternate. Two or three extra women or a few extra men together in the circle will spoil the dance. The caller must see to it that they are evenly and alternately distributed.

He must then explain that the woman on each man's right is his partner, that each will constantly get new partners in this dance, but always the woman to the right is the man's partner. It is well to explain further that in all old-time dancing not only is the woman on the right the man's partner, but he must get the habit of always putting his partner on his right when he takes a position in the circle or in a square or when he promenades the hall. As soon as each man learns always to put his partner on his right side much of the confusion of learning is eliminated.

Now the caller briefly explains the few directions or "calls" that he will use during the dance, and has the group walk through them slowly before the music begins.

Circle right—Still holding hands, each dancer turns to the right and walks with a light gliding step around the circle in that direction until the call is changed.

Circle left—Each dancer, turning to the left and still holding hands, walks with the circle in the opposite direction, or to the left. The caller must explain that he will never call these circles in the same order and that they must get used to listening for the "call" and following the "call" on the instant, whatever it is.

Grand right and left—Each man, turning to the right, faces his partner and takes her right hand (she having turned to her left and faced him). Partners walk past each other holding right hands for a moment and then releasing them so that the man can take the next lady in the circle by the left hand, while the lady takes the next man by the left, and in this fashion they keep marching, each taking each new person they meet alternately with the right and then with the left hands. The men find themselves marching around the circle to the right, or counterclockwise, in a sort of serpentine through the oncoming line of ladies, taking the first by the right hand, the next by the left, and so on alternately until the call is changed. The ladies, in the meantime, are marching to the left, or clockwise, around the circle, passing to the right and then to the left of the individuals in the oncoming column of men.

(Note: This, of course, is only half of the regular call. But we have found it simpler to start beginners this way, and not to mention the "allemande left" with which this figure always begins until they have become thoroughly familiar with the simple right and left.)

Dance that pretty gal around or simply *Everybody dance*—Each man chooses the nearest girl to him, the one whose hand he has just reached, and swings her into an old-fashioned two-step, anywhere around the floor. Quite often the two lines are moving unevenly, and there will be a concentration or surplus of girls in one place, while in another part of the circle there will be a surplus of men left without partners. It must be explained that each man must run across the circle as quickly as possible and choose the first unengaged girl he meets as his partner. It often helps for some man who is dancing by her to call out *Here's an empty* so as to make it easier for the lone men to find these stray women, and incidentally this always puts more laughter into the party.

Form a grand circle, put your lady down on your right—All the dancers fall back to the wall and take hands again in a great circle. (Only for the first few times will it be necessary to call *Put your lady down on your right.* As soon as it becomes instinctive to put the lady on the right, we call only *Form a grand circle.* But until that time it is well to add this phrase and avoid the confusion that otherwise entails.)

Having explained the calls it is well to try it just once with the music, using the calls in the order in which they are given above. If the dancers get in trouble, it is necessary to stop and explain their difficulties. But usually they catch right on and you can go ahead.

As soon as the dancers are going nicely the call should be varied in order to get them used to following the call. The *Circle right, Circle left,* and *Forward and back* should never be given twice in the same order. But, of course, once the *Grand right and left* has been called, it must be followed by *Dance that pretty gal around,* and after a period of general dancing must be followed by *Form your grand circle.*

After the dancers have gone through the whole dance several times it may be necessary to advise them about the shuffling gliding step that is used, and about the carriage of the upper body.

The Steps

The Circle two-Step offers a good chance to practice the steps that are used in all square dancing. And though some of the variants are seldom used in this circle dance, it may be best to discuss them all at this time.

The step most frequently used is a light, gliding, shuffling walk with a promenade rhythm. The knees are loose, the step is light and somewhat shuffling and in complete swing with the music. The best dancers hold themselves quite erect or stiff from the waist up, shoulders back and elbows high, wide, and handsome, the dip and sway of the body being mostly produced from the loose-jointed hips and knees. There is a grace and beauty and swing to a good dancer that is very catching.

Some dancers take a little leap or jump on each step, springing up and down quite joyously. This is usually the mark of a beginner. The old-timers are always so smooth that if you saw them dancing beyond a low wall, you would think they were whirling and spinning and moving on casters or wheels, such is the action of the upper body. Watching their feet, however, one is fascinated with the flash and speed and loose-jointed abandon. Nearly all of them put in frequent "breaks" or "two-steps." (The same step that is used in marching to get in step with the platoon.) In step and out of step they continually interpolate this little "break." Now and then they "stamp" to accent the rhythm. And the best dancers throw in a little jig or "hoe-down" without ever missing their step, just a flashing little flourish to add fun and beauty to the figure. Once in a while, though very rarely, and always for some special call, the whole set may do a "hippety-hop," or skipping step. But this is very exhausting and is seldom seen. It is best to discourage it in the Circle Two-Step, though some beginners instinctively try to do it.

We once saw a very fine group of dancers in a state contest use a slow "cakewalk" step, with arms folded high on the chest, head well back, and knees lifted very high on each step. It was effective, but all the old-times around me insisted that it was not the real thing, that nobody ever danced like that in the good old days. We suspect, though, that even in the good old days special groups did whatever they pleased if it added fun to the dance, even as they still do today.

The most effective, the most fun, and the most fascinating step to watch is the good old gliding, shuffling, rhythmical walk, perfected until it has an uncouth grace all of its own.

When they choose their partners in the *Grand Right and Left* and dance freely over the floor they should use the old-fashioned two-step. This will prove a difficulty to some of them. Of course, the easiest solution is to let them one-step. But it creates more fun and gives the satisfaction of starting with a good old-time dance step if the two-step is more or less mastered. They came for an old-fashioned dance, and they are usually laughingly jubilant over their jerky two-step, no matter how badly they do it.

The Two-Step

The two-step is essentially a step-together-step or step-close-step, starting alternately to one side and then the other. Or it is analyzed more completely as follows, in which the directions are given for the man, the woman of course, using the opposite foot and the opposite direction from the man.

On the first beat of the music let the man slide his left foot out to the left, and before the second beat let him close his right foot to his left. Then on the second beat let him step backward in a short step with his left foot. On the first beat of the second bar of the music let him slide his right foot to the right and quickly close his left foot to his right, and on the second beat take a short step forward with his right foot.

If he repeats this through several bars of music, for practice, he will find that he is remaining almost in one spot, doing a sort of flattened square. But this will give him his rhythm and his steps most quickly, and when it is mastered he can step forward or back as he wishes and progress in any direction he may choose. To go forward, for instance, he will slide with his left, close together with his right and take a short step forward with his left—then on the next bar of music slide with his right, close together with his left and take a short step forward with his right. He will repeat this series as long as he wishes to continue forward.

Since on the first beat there is the "slide" and the "close" and on the second beat of the music only the "step," some beginners find it easier to count the music "one-and-two-and," "one-and-two-and," etc. In this case they "slide" on the "one," "close" on the "and," and "step" on the "two," holding through the final "and."

The real two-step should be smooth and beautiful to watch. But in a Western dance it is quite in kind to make it joyous and bouncy. In fact, the man will find that if he spins continuously to the right while he dances (that is, in the "right face" direction), it is good fun to lift the lady off the floor as he "slides" (or just before he "slides") with his right foot. As he leads with his left he does a regular two-step, but always as he leads with his right he lifts his partner as a high as he dares without spoiling her rhythm or her step, for she must come down exactly on the beat. And the faster the spin, the greater the centrifugal force, and the easier the lift. The ladies, bless 'em, seem to like it.

In fact if a group does not care to master a smooth two-step, it is wise for the caller to ask for a *Hippety-hop* and they will all fall into something sufficiently like the two-step to serve the purpose. And they will think they are having a very good time.

Allemande Left

After the dancers have the simple version given above so smoothly that the *Grand right and left* (where the trouble usually occurs) is faultless every time, the men all immediately starting to the right, or counterclockwise, and the ladies all going to the left, or clockwise, it is necessary for the caller to explain to them that a *Grand right and left* is almost universally preceded by a little introductory turn called *Allemande left*.

If they are a group who are interested in terminology and origins, he may want to discuss this familiar old word of the Western dance caller. It has been suggested that it comes from the French phrase "a-la-main" or "on-the-hand" and that "allemande left" is simply a corruption of "on-the-left-hand". But though it sounds reasonable enough, we doubt if there is a drop of French blood in the word. Nor do we think it is a corrupted form of the Swiss "allewander," their term for a "right and left" derived from the root "to wind". The spelling clearly indicates German. And we find that there was a famous old dance called the "Allemande" or "German", which was full of turns, the gentleman forever taking the lady's hand and turning around her. And I believe that "allemande left" simply means to do a left turn around your lady as they used to do in the old "allemande".

If your dancers are enjoying your explanatory talk while they catch their breath, it may interest some of them to know that the "right and left" which is part of this figure is a very ancient step indeed. Three or four hundred years ago it was known through Europe as the *chaine anglaise*, or the English chain. And even earlier in England it was called the "Hey"—the "shepherds' hey" that the earliest poets wrote about. This same interweaving chain survives in the "Grand right and left" of a Western cow camp. Shepherds' hey!

The caller will explain that the complete call is usually given in some such form as:

> *Allemande left with your left hand,*
> *Then right hand to your partner and right and left grand,*

But that until they get more used to the call and the idea he will use a simpler form which goes:

> *Swing your left hand lady with your left hand,*
> *Then right hand to partner and right and left grand.*

In this maneuver of the *allemande* each gentleman faces left, instead of turning right to face his partner, and each lady faces right, so that the gentlemen stand facing their left-hand ladies. They take left hands and walk once around each other and back to their own positions. This leaves them now facing their partners, whom they take with their right hands and march past them in the old familiar *Grand right and left* in the same direction and same manner as they first learned it. It is nothing but the *right and left* preceded by a little left hook, or complete turn, around the left-hand lady, holding her left hand as you circle each other.

It is so simple that it may seem labored to teach it in two parts in this way. But we have found, especially with a large crowd, that it saves a lot of confusion and innumerable collisions. Starting with the simple *Grand right and left* gets their directions established and the men get in the habit of always going right and the ladies always going left with a serpentine, touching alternate hands. Once this is established it is easy to add the preliminary left hook of the *Allemande*, and the trick is done. But try to teach the two maneuvers at the same time to a large crowd and you will have them all running off wildly in all directions, and the stampede will be hard to check.

When you start dancing again, after the explanation, it will be well for the first three or four times through the dance always to use the simpler call *Swing the left hand lady with your left hand.* It helps them get started. Once they are used to the figure, start calling *Allemande left with your left hand,* and use this more standard form always thereafter.

The Circle Two-Step is simple to learn and fun to do, and when you finally stop them (by simply having the music stop in one of the periods of the two-step) they will probably shout and clap and call for more. To keep their interest up you can then give them some other simple and popular variations.

Variations

After the two-step, instead of calling *form a grand circle* you may call:

> *Form a double circle—*
> *Ladies on the inside,*
> *Gents on the out!*
> *Ladies on the inside,*
> *Pretty side out!*

In this case there will be an outer circle of men only, holding each other by the hands and facing inward in the regular fashion. Inside them there will be an inner ring of only women, facing toward the men (pretty side out) and holding each other by the hands in a circle. When the two rings have formed, call:

Everybody circle right. Since the two rings are facing each other it makes each go opposite the other or past each other. When they have passed far enough to assure a new partner for everyone, call: *Everybody pick the prettiest gal and dance—* and they are off on the two-step again.

Since the two circles must always go in opposite directions a new caller often calls *Ladies go right and gents go left* hoping to make them do so. But since the two rings are facing each other this means that they will both go in the same direction or in a sort of double column. So, in order to send them past each other, be simple and call either *Everybody circle right* or *Everybody circle left,* and that will send the two rings past each other.

Once they are familiar with this variation the caller can either figure after the two-step and arrange all the parts in any way to suit his fancy.

Another pleasant variation after the two-step is to call *Promenade now two by two*. They should march side by side, lady on the right and holding both hands crossed over in front like a pair of skaters. And as soon as they are promenading smoothly (to the right of course, or counterclockwise), you can call *Gents go forward and the ladies turn back* (or *The ladies go forward and the gents turn back*, as your fancy dictates, and never twice alike). When they are well mixed you again call *Everybody choose the prettiest gal and dance*.

This variation is very helpful when the crowd is large and the hall is small, for the then *Grand circle* can hardly fit around the room without loops and scallops in the circle, and the allemande is very difficult to do with such crowding. When they *Promenade two by two* it makes the circumference of the circle just half as large and simplifies everything, in addition to being good fun.

A third variation can be enjoyed by calling *Promenade four by four* when two couples march four abreast with arms hooked in elbows. This often causes a little confusion by some couple being left stranded without another couple to fill out their four. But if they look around the circle and they can usually find another single couple who are stranded, and they can run across the circle and join with them to complete their four. When they are well arranged and marching smoothly four by four, you can call *Keep your four columns moving while the gents go forward and the ladies turn back*. This gets them milling even more amusingly until you call *Pick the prettiest girl and dance*.

Summary

To start the dance the caller often needs only to have the orchestra start a two-step and they are all out on the floor dancing he can call *Form a grand circle* and go on with the dance.

A typical form for the whole call might be something like this:

CIRCLE TWO-STEP

Form your grand circle;
Circle left (or Circle right)
Forward and back.
Now allemande left as you come down,
Grand right and left and so on around,
Right foot up and left foot down,
Make that big foot jar the ground,
Now dance that pretty gal around.
***

Form a grand circle—

And so on as long as desired, introducing whatever variation he wishes after the two-step period and stopping the dance by stopping the music during a two-step.

A Simple Square

The Circle Two-Step is so easy that your crowd will feel very confident and pleased with themselves as soon as they have done it a few times through. Now, laughing and friendly, with all their inhibitions stilled, they are ready for their first square dance.

While they are catching their breath from the Circle Two-Step is a good time to get them seated and give them a preliminary discussion on the theory of the square. It will help a good deal to put a set of dancers out on the floor in order to make your explanations clearer. If you have a demonstration set of experienced dancers it will make your task even easier. But lacking them, you can put any four couples out on the floor and make things clear enough by moving them around.

The Positions

A set of dancers or a square is composed of four couples, each standing on one of the sides of an imaginary square, or towards one of the four walls of the room and each couple facing the center of the square (or the opposite couple). Where space is crowded this imaginary square need only be eight or ten feet across. But it is better, especially with beginners, to allow ten or twelve feet across for each square.

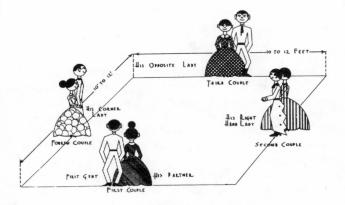

In each square and throughout the dance the lady's position is always to the right side of her partner. If this rule of always putting the lady on the right is carefully followed much confusion in learning can be avoided. In fact, the position of the lady gives her the name by which she is designated in the call. For each man the lady on his right is his "partner," the lady on his left is his "corner," the lady across from him is his "opposite," and the lady to the right beyond his partner is the "right hand lady," though she seldom figures in the calls. For each lady, likewise, the man on her left is her partner," the man on her right is her "corner," the man across from her is her "opposite," and the man on the left next beyond her partner is the "left hand gent".

Each couple is numbered according to the side of the square on which they are standing, and they always return to this same or "home" position after each promenade or special maneuver. The couple standing nearest to and with their backs to the head of the hall is called "first couple." The couple to their right is called is called "second couple," the couple opposite them is "third couple," and the couple standing on their left is called the "fourth couple." The head of the hall is usually that end of the hall nearest the orchestra. If the orchestra is located in the middle of one of the sides, the caller should announce before the first dance begins which end of the hall is considered the "head." Since the "first couple" stands nearest the head of the hall they are sometimes called "head couple." And, of course, the "third couple" is called the "foot couple." In this case the "second and fourth couples" are called "the sides," without differentiation between them.

Throughout any simple dance each couple is known as "first," "second," "third," etc., by the position they occupy at the beginning of the dance. And throughout this particular dance they always return to this same home position. For the second dance of the evening, however, they may each shift into a new set or square and take any position they happen to find open, keeping this position throughout any one dance. In a real old-fashioned square dance, where most of the evening is given to these old figures it is customary to call the sets out on the floor and to call two dances one after another. These two separate dances are called the first and second "tip" of the set. And when the first dance is finished everyone remains standing in his position on the floor, laughing and visiting until the music starts again, and then the set dances the second "tip," retaining through it their same positions or numbers.

The Introduction

It must be explained that a square dance usually opens with one of several possible introductory figures. The following is perhaps the commonest form:

Honors right and honors left—Each man bows first to the lady to his right, that is, his partner, and then to the lady on his left. The ladies all return the bow, which is executed quite quickly.

All join hands and circle to the left—The whole square with joined hands moves in a large circle to the left, walking around in a clockwise direction. They usually get more than halfway around when the next call comes.

Break and swing and promenade back—At the word "break" hands are dropped all around, and each man takes his partner in a modified dance position, her right hand extended in his left, her left hand on her shoulder, and his right arm around her waist. Where this differs from the standard dance position is that instead of standing face to face, the couples often stand right hip touching right hip, the man's right arm having to pass across the front of his lady and his wrist around her waist. The lady, with her hip braced against her partner, throws her shoulders back away from him in order to take advantage of the centrifugal force of the swing. With short steps the couple swings completely around twice in a "right about face" or clockwise direction.

Figure after figure in square dancing calls for this "swing" which is always done as above, and must be understood and mastered, if so easy a maneuver can be said to be "mastered," before one goes on with the dance. It is usually customary to make two complete revolutions when the "swing" is called for, but in some dizzy figures one revolution will be quite enough.

As soon as they have "swung," each couple promenades back "home," or back to the position they were originally standing in. They march two-by-two; that is, side by side, with the lady on the right side of the gentleman, and holding hands with arms crossed in front of them as in the customary pair skating position; that is, the man holds the lady's left in his left hand and her right hand in his right with his right arm across above or in front of her left. (In skating it is usually crossed under the lady's the better to support her, but in dancing it is always crossed above.)

The promenade is always to the right, or counterclockwise. It occurs again and again throughout the figure of the dance, an the right-hand direction must become a habit.

Other introductory figures are used, but these can be learned later. This *Honors right and honors left* is by far the commonest and is, therefore, the best to begin with.

After executing it the couples are back just where they started from, all facing the center as at the beginning, and ready for the dance proper to begin.

One of the easiest dances to start beginners with I have found to be:

Form a Star with the Right Hand Cross

This is in typical square formation with first couple visiting around to each of the others in turn, beginning with the second couple, going on to the third, and finishing with the fourth. Then the second couple visits around the square repeating the same figure in turn with each of the others, the third, the fourth, and lastly the first couple. Then the third and fourth couples each visit around the square in the same manner. While the first and second couples are doing the figure, the third and fourth couples merely stand and await their turn. In this type of square there are always two couples in action and two couples awaiting their turns. Of course, with experts the two odd couples may get in action too, just to make it more fun, but they have to scamper to be back in position in time to receive the visiting couple. And it is unwise for beginners to try this.

The simple figure used around the square in this dance is called:

> *First couple out to the couple on the right,*
> *Form a star with the right hand cross.*
> *Back with the left and don't get lost.*
> *Swing your opposite with your right,*
> *Now your partner with your left,*
> *And on to the next.*

The first couple simply walks over and faces the second couple. All four dancers grasp right hands at about the level of their heads, thus forming a star, and holding hands they march around to the left, or in a clockwise direction, until the next phrase of the call is given. They then let go their holds and each swings in toward the others (a right-face turn) and they grasp all four left hands at their head level and circle back to the right or in a counterclockwise direction.

On the last part of the call they let go each other's hands, and each man takes the opposite lady's right hand in his right and swings her completely around behind him. This brings them all into position so each man can then take his partner's left hand in his left and swing her around.

The second couple swings back into position and stands as they were at the beginning, while the first couple swings around and faces the third couple, with whom they repeat the whole figure, as the call is repeated for them.

The caller must be careful of his timing. It is best to allow just enough time in the *Right hand cross* for them all to take about four steps in this direction, then to reverse them with the *Left hand cross*, allowing time for only about four steps in this direction. Then let the opposites and the partners swing. In fact, it all times up with the music best if four or eight are allowed for each part of the figure.

As soon as the first couple reaches the third couple the caller must repeat the call again, and then again for the fourth couple. At the conclusion of this figure instead of calling *On to the next*, he usually says, *Balance home and everybody swing*.

At most dances and in most sets this *balance home* simply means *go home* or back to position. But with the more experienced dancers they not only *go home*, but separating from each other in a half curtsy they come together for the swing. At the same time the three other couples in the set *balance and swing*, that is, face each other and each takes four steps backward and then four steps forward to his partner and then they swing. It makes a graceful and finished maneuver in the set. For the *swing*, of course, all four couples take the modified dance position and swing around twice in place. He then calls:

> *Turn the left hand lady*
> *With your left hand*
> *Then right hand to partner*
> *And right and left grand.*

This is the same movement they learned in the Circle Two-Step. When they have all done the serpentine right and left and have again reached their partners he calls:

> *Take your partner*
> *And promenade home.*

Or, which means the same thing, he may call:

> *Promenade eight*
> *When you come straight.*

And each man taking the promenade position with his girl on his right walks counterclockwise around the square and back to his original place.

Before going on with the dance and sending the second couple around the square with the same figure, it is usually found necessary for the caller to straighten out some of the sets who have got badly mixed up. And it is best to take time out until the beginners get their difficulty cleared up.

In spite of the fact that they learned to do the *Allemande left* (or *Swing the left-hand lady with your left hand*) in the Circle Two-step, they often have difficulty executing it in a square with only four couples. And we often find it helpful to walk them through this figure slowly without music until they get the idea fixed. Then too, some couples find it difficult to promenade back to their own positions, keeping their place in their square while they do so. Some couples, lacking a strong geometric sense, loiter or wander off into other squares or out around the hall or simply stand bewildered, while other couples "cut-the-pie" and get the square all mixed up. A few minutes taken to walk them slowly through the whole *Allemande* and *Right and left* to the *Promenade* is well spent with beginners.

Another difficulty arises from the failure of the first gentleman to have his lady on his right when they present themselves to the third couple. If the lady is on the left side of him, it will put two ladies on one side of the right hand star and two gentlmen on the other side. This will make the swinging of the opposites with the right hands very difficult and confused. The two ladies should be opposite each other in the star. And this can be accomplished only if the lady is on her gentleman's right side as they approach the new couple.

As soon as all the difficulties are straightened out the music can begin again and the dance continue, going on where you left off and, of course, not repeating the introduction. The call continues:

> *Second couple out*
> *To the couple on the right,*
> *Form a star with the right hand cross, etc.*

With an *on to the next* and an *on to the next* and then a *balance and everybody swing* the dance continues. Again they all do an *Allemande left* and *Grand right and left* and a *Promenade to places.*

Then it is all repeated for the third couple around, and after another *Grand right and left* it is again repeated for the fourth couple all the way around. After the final promenade, the call is often given:

> *Promenade, you know where,*
> *And I don't care.*
> *Take your honey*
> *To a nice soft chair.*

And that set is over.

Since the call for the figure has to be repeated until it has been given twelve times, it is customary to alter it now and then for the sake of variety. Instead of *Form a star with the right hand cross* you may call:

> *Star by the right*
> *And how do you do?*
> *Back with the left*
> *And how are you?*

Or we have heard it called:

> *Right hands crossed*
> *And how do you do?*
> *Back with the left*
> *And how are you?*

All of which means exactly the same thing, and only adds variety to the calling. Another very easy square to execute with beginners is:

Forward Six and Fall Back Six

The same introduction can be used as in the previous dance, or you can call:

> *All jump up and never come down.*
> *Swing your honey around and around*
> *'Till the hollow of your foot*
> *Makes a hole in the ground.*
> *And promenade, boys, promenade!*

Which means only that each couple shall jump up into the air and then swing each other around and around until the call is finished and they are told to promenade, when with the regular promenade position they walk once around the square to the right, or counterclockwise, until they come back to their regular position, where they stand until the caller puts them in action.

In the first part of the call proper it must be explained that as always in square dancing the instructions are for the men, the women having always to do the complimentary or corresponding thing to the movement of the men.

The call starts with:

> *First couple out to the couple on the right* (a)
> *And circle four;*
> *Leave that girl, go on to the next* (b)
> *And circle three;*
> *Take that girl and go on to the next* (c)
> *And circle four;*
> *Leave that girl and go home alone* (d)

Though it sounds a little complicated, it is very simple to execute. (a) The first couple moves over to the right and faces the second couple. All four join hands and circle to the left, or clockwise. As they come around to the full circle (b) the first man lets go with both hands and moves on alone to the third couple. This leaves his lady standing with the second couple, still holding the second man's left hand with her right hand. The three stand in a straight row, with the second man in the middle between the two ladies.

The first man, having gone on to the third couple, joins hands with them, and the three circle once around to the left. (c) The first man and the third lady now break their hold with the third man and leave him standing alone, while they both go on to the fourth couple. As they advance to the fourth couple, and this is very important, the first man changes the lady from his left hand hand to his right hand, so she will be on his right side. (Remember that always when a couple approaches another, the ladies must stand on the right side of men.) All four (the fourth couple, the third lady, and the first man) join hands and circle to the left once around. (d) Then the first man lets go his hold, and returns to his first position - *goes home alone*. This leaves the third lady standing to the left of the fourth couple, the three of them in a row.

This is simply a maneuver to move the first lady over to stand in a row of three, while the third lady stands with the fourth couple in a row of three directly opposite them. The first and third men stand opposite each other and alone.

The call continues:

Forward six and fall back six;	(a)
Forward two and fall back two;	(b)
Forward six and pass right through;	(c)
Forward two and pass right through.	(d)

On the call *Forward six*, or (a) each row of three on either side takes four steps forward toward the other, then four steps back, still facing each other, into place. As they are falling back the call should be so timed that (b) the two lone men start forward four steps. Then as they fall back to place with four more steps, (c) the six (the two side threes) should be moving forward and pass through each other's formation to the opposite side. (d) The two lone men then pass each other and also trade places.

In dancing, it is always customary to pass to the left as they do in English traffic, instead of to the right as they do in modern American traffic. To get a group of beginners in the habit of always passing to the left it is well to advise them to take right hands with the opposite person as they pass. This will assure them of passing correctly to the left. If some pass left while others pass right, the collision and confusion ruins the dance. So take time to teach them always to pass left by touching right hands while passing.

Our figure is now just as it was, except that everyone has traded places with his opposite and is left standing on the wrong side. The last call, therefore, has to be repeated to put them right.

> *Forward six and fall back six;*
> *Forward two and fall back two;*
> *Forward six and pass right through;*
> *Forward two and pass right through.*

Then continue with:

> *Swing on the corner* (a)
> *Like swinging on the gate,*
> *And now your own* (b)
> *If you're not too late.*
> *Now allemande left* (c)
> *With your left hand*
> *And right to your partner*
> *And right and left grand.*
> *And promenade eight*
> *When you come straight.*

Remember that each man's corner, or his corner lady, is the lady on his left. So to come out of his figure of symmetrical three's and one's, each man (a) swings the girl on his left. Then (b) he swings his own partner, or the girl on his right.

Then (c) they go directly from this swing into the *Allemande left* and *Grand right and left*, as in previous dance. They then promenade back to their places.

The whole dance is repeated for the second couple, beginning the call with:

> *Second couple out*
> *To the couple on the right*
> *And circle four.*

And after a promenade it is all repeated for the third couple, and finally for the fourth.

After the fourth, or final promenade, you can again call:

> *You know where*
> *And I don't care.*
> *Take your honey*
> *To a nice soft chair.*

With this the dance is over, and they are all pleased because the dance is so simple and symmetrical and such good fun. If the caller times it right it keeps them moving back and forth through each other with a fascinating sort of routine.

Star by the Right

A very simple dance for beginners, in which only the last half of the docey-doe is used.

THE CALL:

1. *Honors right and honors left;*
   All join hands and circle to the left;
   Break and swing and promenade back.

2. a) *First couple out*
      To the couple on the right.
   b) *Form a star with the right hand cross*
   c) *Back with the left and don't get lost.*
   d) *Swing our opposite with your right:*
   e) *Now your partner with your left;*
   f) *And on to the next.*
      Repeat 2 as written beginning with (b).
      Repeat again, changing last line to:
   g) *Balance home.*

3. *And everybody swing*
   Now swing the left hand lady
   With your left hand.
   Right hand to partner
   And right and left grand
   Promenade eight when you come straight.
      Repeat 2 and 3 entire for second, third,
      fourth couples.

○	LADY
□	GENTLEMAN
ʃ	SWING

The squares represent the gentlemen and the circles represent the ladies. The letter *S* shows the position of the swing.

Where there is more than one swing, they are numbered with subscripts to show the order of the swings. Occasionally the tracks of action are also numbered to show the order in which hey are followed. Dotted and solid lines have no significance except to keep different track from being confused with each other.

The number in the circle or the square indicates whether it is first, second, third, of fourth lady or gentleman. By noting the crook or bend of the arm in some diagrams you can determine which direction a figure is facing.

THE EXPLANATION:

1. a) First couple join hands and walk to second couple.
   b) All four turn left face and join right hands held high and march around for four steps, still holding hands.
   c) Break holds, and each does a rightabout-face, and they all join left hands and march back.
   d) Break holds; first gentleman takes second lady the right hand and swings her around behind him and releases hold. Second gentleman does the same thing with the first lady.
   e) Each gentleman takes partner by left hand and swings her around behind him to place.
   f) First gentleman takes partner's left hand in his right and advances to the third couple, being sure his partner is on the right side when he faces the new couple with whom they repeat *b* through *f.* On the next repetition he advances to the fourth couple.
   g) After the last repetiion he walks back to place with his part ner, and all four couples do a balance by separating four steps then coming together again.

VARIATIONS:

The figures (b) and (c) are sometimes called as follows:

    1) *Star by the right*
       And how do you do?
       Back with the left,
       And how are you?

or 2) *Form a four hand*
       And how do you do?
       Now cross with your left,
       And how are you?

These variations can be alternated with the regular call in repetitions of the figure. Or sometimes a caller will make up a long string of variations such as:

    Star by the right; did you get a letter?
    Back with the left; yeh, the folks are better.

    * * *

    Star by the right; and how are you hittin'?
    Back with the left; let's do some sittin'.

    * * *

    Star by the right; its warmish weather.
    Back with the left; keep stompin' leather.

Forward Up Six

The Call:

1. *All eight balance, all eight swing,*
   A left allemande
   A right hand grand
   And promenande

2. a) *First couple out to the right*
      And circle four.
   b) *Leave that gal, go on to the next*
      And circle fthree.
   c) *Take that gal, go on the next*
      And circle four.
   d) *Leave that gal and go home alone.*
   e) *Forward up six and fall back six.*
   f) *Forward up two and fall back two.*
   g) *Forward up six and pass right through.*
   h) *Forward up two and pass right through.*
      Repeat (e) and (h).
   j) *Now swing on the corner*
      Like swingin' on the gate.
      Now your own if you're not too late.

3. *Now allemande ho, Right hands up*
   And here we go! And promenande.
      Repeat 2 and 3 entire for second, third, and fourth couples.

Sometimes this dance is ended by substituting for (j):
   Lone gents go right and circle four
   Now docey-doe with the gents you know,
   The ladies go si and gents go do.
   Now everybody swing.

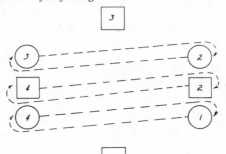

THE EXPLANATION:

1. a) First couple advances to the second couple. They join hands and circle left.

   b) The first gentleman leaves the first lady with the second couple (she reamins to the left of the second gentleman and the three join hands in a row). The first gentleman goes on alone to the third couple and joins hands with them while they all circle to the left.

   c) The first gentlman takes the third lady on with him (leaving the third gentleman standing along), and advances with her to the fourth couple. As he does so he changes her from his left hand to his right hand so that she is on his right side when they come to the fourth couple. They join hands with them and the four circle to the left.

   d) He now leaves the third lady with the fourth couple (standing in a line of three with hands joined and the third lady on the left of the fourth gentleman) and returns to his place where he stand along.

   e) The six dancers standing in the side positions (the second and fourth men each with a lady on either side of him) advance four steps and retire four steps.

   f) The two dancers standing alone (the first and third gentlemen) each advanc and retire four steps.

   g) The two threes now advance to each other and pass through so that each exchanges place with the other three. In passing through each gives his right hand to the opposite persons, thus passing to the left of him (in most dances the old English traffic rule of passing to the left survives).

   h) The two men advance to each other, touch right hands, and pass each other to the left. Each continues until he stands inthe other's place. In repeating (e) to (h) they all pass back and stand in own positions.

   j) Each gentleman now swings the girl on his left—that is, his corner girl on his left. He then returns to his partner and swings her back into home position.

* * *

If the second call is used the first and third gentlemen advance to and join hands with the three on their right. This makes two groups of four, who each circle to the left then do a *docey-doe*. After swinging to home position they are ready for any ending that may be called.